MILLENNIUM MANAGEMENT

better, faster, cheaper strategies

for managing 21st century

healthcare organizations

Russell C. Coile, Jr.

MILLENNIUM MANAGEMENT

better, faster, cheaper strategies

for managing 21st century

healthcare organizations

Health Administration Press

02   01   00   99   98   5   4   3   2   1

Library of Congress Cataloging-in-Publication Data

Coile, Russell C.
    Millennium Management : "better, faster, cheaper" strategies for managing 21st century healthcare organizations / by Russell C. Coile, Jr.
        p.   cm.
    Includes bibliographical references and index.
    ISBN 1-56793-084-0
        1. Health services administration. I. Title
RA971.C6847   1998
362.1'068—dc21

                                                        97-19872
                                                        CIP

Health Administration Press
A division of the Foundation
    of the American College of
    Healthcare Executives
One North Franklin Street, Suite 1700
Chicago, IL 60606-3491
312/424-2800

To my pathfinders in healthcare leadership and management

Donald B. Ardell, Ph.D., *Wellness Forum*
Michael Annison, *Westrends Group*
Karl Bartscht, CHE, *Chi Systems/Superior Consultant*
Warren Bennis, Ph.D., *University of Southern California*
Sue Cook, *Think Customer*
Thomas C. Dolan, Ph.D., FACHE, CAE, *American College of
    Healthcare Executives*
Paul Ellwood, M.D., HFACHE, *InterStudy/Jackson Hole Group*
Charles Ewell, Ph.D., FACHE, *Governance Institute*
Jeff Goldsmith, Ph.D., *Health Futures*
Kathryn Johnson, *The Healthcare Forum*
Leland Kaiser, Ph.D., *Kaiser Associates*
Charles Lauer, HFACHE, *Modern Healthcare*
Ian Morrison, Ph.D., *Institute for the Future*
Robert Myrtle, D.P.A., *University of Southern California*
Robin Orr, *The Orr Group*
Dennis Pointer, Ph.D., *University of San Diego*
Richard Rand, *Rand Healthcare Roundtables*
Stephen Shortell, Ph.D., FACHE, *University of California–Berkeley*

Contents

Introduction ix

1 Better, Faster, and Cheaper Strategies for Managing
Twenty-First Century Healthcare Organizations 1

2 Leaders of the Future: Seven Trends for Twenty-First
Century Healthcare Executives 17

3 Reassessing Reengineering 33

4 Making Integration Work: Implementing Vertical,
Horizontal, and Virtual Integration Strategies 49

5 Clinical Executives: Physicians and Nurses Create
Twenty-First Century Management Teams 65

6 Motivating "Work Force 2000": Management, Morale,
and Motivation in the Era of "Future Work" 79

7 Customer Service: Healthcare Organizations Turn on
to Customer Choice, Quality, and Service 95

8 Care by Design: "Hospitals Without Walls," Healing
Environments, and Buildings That Pay for Themselves 111

9 Strategic Planning: Building Stakeholder Commitment
by Setting Future Directions 127

10 Corporate Soul: Seven Pathways to Organizations 141

11 Excess Hospital Capacity: Recycling, Retrofitting,
or Closure! Alternatives for Surplus Inpatient Beds 161

12 Anticipating the Millennium: Healthcare Environment
Will Be Driven by Consumerism, Cyberhealth, and
Co-Opetition 179

Index 199

About the Author 215

INTRODUCTION

Bridging the "Leadership Gap" for Twenty-First Century Healthcare

When great intentions yield mediocre results, when the tried-and-true ceases to work, when every attempt to fix things is met with frustration and failure . . . then perhaps that design has reached its limits, and the paradigm is ready to shift. Opportunity is present, creative vision is called for, and bold action in new directions is the nature of things.

> —Robert Porter Lynch, "The Shift from Vertical to
> Networked Integration" (1996, 16)

Every healthcare executive knows these are changing times. Competitors are merging, even strong organizations have experienced layoffs, and public trust in physicians and hospitals has slipped. In many local markets, a game of "musical chairs" is now playing out, and every hospital and system must find a partner and scale up. Large healthcare organizations are often among the leading employers and businesses in their market. In American healthcare, like American business, "bigger" is often considered "better." But many healthcare executives are finding that the benefits of scale and integration are often elusive.

As American healthcare organizations face the twenty-first century, important questions are being asked by today's senior healthcare managers and their boards:

- Are large health systems becoming too big and unmanageable?
- Can physicians become true partners?
- Is vertical integration working?
- What management techniques and incentives will motivate tomorrow's diverse work force?
- Is healthcare's business orientation adversely affecting its community regard?
- How can hospitals become more "hospitable"?

This book's purpose is to provide a future-oriented perspective on achieving goals and providing superior service in the future healthcare market. As one of the healthcare industry's most active market observers, I see many examples of the "best and brightest" in healthcare who are setting new directions and providing benchmarks for industry adaptation. Leadership is the ultimate strategic weapon. Despite the challenges ahead from managed care or government regulation, this is an unparalleled time for healthcare organizations with vision, commitment, and a plan for the future.

THE "LEADERSHIP GAP" FOR MILLENNIUM MANAGEMENT

In the early 1990s, a national survey predicted there would be a "leadership gap" in needed skills and strategies for managing healthcare organizations in the twenty-first century. This pioneering study of healthcare leadership, known as the Leadership Gap study, was conducted by the Healthcare Forum, a national training and leadership organization headed by Kathryn Johnson, president and CEO. Partly funded by the Kodak Foundation, this study used a questionnaire to ask more than 500 healthcare executives, trustees, and physicians across the country to rate 36 leadership strategies and skills. Not many of today's best practices made the list of critical competencies for tomorrow's managers and executives.

The intersection between management and forecasting is critical for the future of healthcare. As an M.B.A. as well as a futurist, I had a natural interest in this study, and Clem Bezold, president of the Institute for Alternative Futures in Alexandria, Virginia, and I were its senior consultants. We were assisted by a number of healthcare's leading futurists, including Michael Annison, Jeff Goldsmith, and Leland Kaiser. Healthcare Forum's board of directors was our first focus group for a pilot version of the study.

Six critical leadership abilities for managing healthcare organizations in the twenty-first century were identified in the national survey:

- mastering change;
- shared vision;
- systems thinking;

- total quality management;
- redefining healthcare; and
- promoting the community's health.

Of those factors, only one—total quality management—was substantially in place in healthcare before the survey. Solid progress in implementing the other factors has since been made, although much remains to be done. It is clear that healthcare organizations have shifted from a reactive, defensive set of strategies—such as "filling beds"—to a proactive stance that recognizes fundamental market changes—such as provider-sponsored HMOs and managing populations' health.

It is less clear that healthcare executives are doing more "systems thinking," a rigorous intellectual process of analyzing and developing strategy, but they are vigorously *systems building*, on a regional and even statewide basis. In 1990, there were approximately 250 asset-merged health systems in the United States. Since that time, more than 500 integrated delivery networks and 3,000 physician-hospital organizations have been constructed for managed care contracting.

Progressive healthcare executives are "redefining healthcare" by adding new services to create comprehensive continuums of care. Some 1,500 hospitals have developed subacute units, freestanding outpatient surgery centers, and specialized rehabilitation programs. These activities help position healthcare systems and networks to provide comprehensive health services to enrolled populations as managed care and capitation become the dominant forms of healthcare payment.

The last of the Leadership Gap study's recommendations—promoting the community's health—is an emerging priority, although this strategy will take longer to implement. Since 1992, there has been notable progress. A growing number of hospitals and health systems are actively promoting the health of their communities through education and coalition-building efforts. The Healthcare Forum has dedicated its mission to assisting healthcare leaders and their organizations build healthy communities and has established a national awards program to recognize the most community-minded efforts. Hundreds of community hospitals and health systems have made community health a priority, establishing local coalitions and subsidizing outreach efforts to address health needs.

READING THIS BOOK

The goal of *Millennium Management* is to create a cadre of healthcare executives, physician leaders, and middle managers who have the core competencies to manage complex health organizations in the market environment of the twenty-first century. Each chapter addresses the latest trends in key management skill sets and predicts what state-of-the-practice changes lie ahead. For futuristic ideas and opinions, I have referenced many healthcare journals as well as the broad base of current management literature. Innovative examples from leading-edge healthcare organizations provide real-world examples of advanced practices. Sources for these examples and ideas are cited at the end of every chapter.

My best advice for readers is to pick up the book, open to any chapter you like, and start reading. Read the last chapter first, if you prefer. Few of us operate by the numbers. Design your own management outlook in whatever order appeals to you. You are welcome to be problem-driven, only delving into those chapters that match your immediate problems and priorities. Come back to the book at your convenience to read additional chapters. As an author, I will be very satisfied if healthcare executive readers are coming back to revisit chapters like "Corporate Soul" months from now.

Every author operates from a core of biases and assumptions. With 20 years of experience in California's competitive healthcare marketplace, I believe that managed care and capitation will be driving forces that will dominate healthcare economics. As an M.B.A., I believe that the underlying forces that will challenge healthcare organizations are strongly influenced by the underlying economic patterns. In external relations, I strongly favor partnerships and strategic business relationships, like "co-opetition." Internally, our large complex organizations need to be managed from a global perspective, but with a large margin of local control and decentralization. As a futurist, I believe that the future is a resource to be managed. Today's healthcare organizations will be even larger and more complicated in the future. We will need leadership, management skills, clinical expertise, and a fundamental humanism.

There are many examples of progressive health organizations that are creating tomorrow's health systems today. They may be as small as the Mid-Columbia Medical Center, a 50-bed hospital in The Dalles, Oregon, or as large as Catholic Health Initiatives of Denver, Colorado, with hundreds of hospitals across the nation. These organizations could not have become national models without leaders like Mark Scott of Mid-Columbia or Pat Mueller of Catholic Health Initiatives. The ultimate resources for managing the future in twenty-first century healthcare's rapidly evolving market are visionary leadership and millennium management.

REFERENCE

Lynch, R. P., and I. Somerville. 1996. "The Shift from Vertical to Networked Integration." *Physician Executive* 22 (5): 13–18.

1

Millennium Management: Strategies for Managing Better, Faster, and Cheaper Twenty-First Century Healthcare Organizations

When the consultants move on and the process map comes down from the wall, the painfully won gains will leak away unless the employees who have to live with the new work design had a hand in creating it and unless the human systems of the company—compensation, career paths, training—reinforce the changes.
— Warren Bennis and Michael Mische, *The 21st Century Organization* (1995, 105)

Healthcare organizations are scrambling to prepare for the new millennium. Hospitals, physician groups, and HMOs are not alone. In every sector of American enterprise, organizations are seeking fresh answers to issues like growth, quality, service, and profitability. To create the future, new alliances are being formed, competencies assembled, capital invested, and experiments created. As Tom Halloran, regional vice president for InterMountain Health Care of Salt Lake City, says: "There are so many 'pilots' going up or coming down in my organization that I feel like a member of the Iraqi Air Force."

America is standing on the edge—and for some it will be a cliff—of a revolution as profound as the one that gave birth to modern industry. In this race to the future, management consultants predict there will be "drivers, passengers, and road kill" (Hamel and Prahalad 1997). It will combine the digital revolution, the materials revolution, the information revolution, the genetic revolution, and the environmental revolution. All on a global basis, of course, this revolution will affect service industries such as healthcare, as well as manufacturing, agriculture, and government services.

Those who drive their industries' revolutions—companies that have a clear, well-developed strategy and the means to implement it—will be well rewarded. The future will be a riskier environment, without a "safety net" for excess hospitals, surplus physicians, or third-party payors or suppliers who do not add value to the purchasing chain. The future will belong not to those who possess a crystal ball but to those willing to challenge the dominant paradigm and "best conventional wisdom" of managing healthcare organizations.

COMPETING FOR THE FUTURE

Competition for the future will be a challenge. Nothing less than a global wave of change is washing over healthcare—just as with other businesses. Consider a healthcare marketplace of the twenty-first century, some 10 to 20 years from now, in which the following market assumptions are "givens":

- All hospitals belong to one of only two or three local delivery networks.
- Health plans and providers charge uniform prices with little regional variation.
- More than 20 to 25 percent of all enrollees are at high risk for continuous care.
- Most physicians practice on a salaried basis in large, well-managed medical groups.
- The entire population has continuous healthcare coverage—from an HMO.
- Fewer than six HMOs and insurers cover 80 percent of enrollees.
- Medicare and Medicaid have been converted to managed care plans.
- Expensive clinical technology is shared on a regional basis.
- Extensive clinical databases are used to "mass-customize" patient care plans.
- Clinical pathways and expert systems guide all physician and nursing care.
- More inpatient services are provided in continuum-of-care facilities than hospitals.

- Genetic testing identifies high-risk patients for prevention and risk management.
- Patients learn more about disease from the Internet than from their physicians.

Healthcare executives, think about it . . . . What would be the basis of sustainable strategic advantage in such a future marketplace? Not *price.* Intense price competition would have pushed that down below the 80th percentile, compared with today's prices. Not *technology.* All providers would have essentially the same clinical and information systems technology. Lowest *costs?* Efficiency is always a basis for differentiation, but most organizations would be using similar cost-management strategies. Better *physicians?* Profiling physician performance would weed out ineffective or inefficient doctors. Superior *outcomes?* Public report cards on outcomes would push all providers toward national benchmarks for quality. *Service?* Yes, but everyone will be competing to win high patient satisfaction ratings.

The ultimate sustainable advantage in such a post-integration environment will be *innovation,* the organizational capacity to improve all of these factors continuously and discover others that will become the new drivers of the marketplace. The choice is not between incremental "muddling through" or blockbuster "megadeals." The goal is to reinvent the market in ways that amaze customers and trounce competitors (Hamel and Prahalad 1997, xi). In modern times, healthcare has experienced several of these innovations: antibiotics, HMOs, and minimally-invasive surgery. More innovations are possible, and likely, as the healthcare economy evolves to provide comprehensive care to large—and aging—populations under a prepaid capitation budget. Chuck Lauer, publisher of *Modern Healthcare,* advises: "Get out and make 'the market' with an aggressive approach and the-customer-comes-first thinking. Risk is the precursor to success. But leadership and vision make it happen" (Lauer 1997, 1).

TEN NEW RULES: PROCESSES, PATHWAYS, AND STRATEGIES FOR MANAGING THE FUTURE

In modern times, the fundamental basis of competition has shifted three times. With each wave of rising customer demands and better competition, the bar was raised. The effects were cumulative, which means there is no such thing as "sustainable competitive advantage." Companies must innovate constantly to stay ahead. Services and products must meet the demands of the old marketplace, plus the imperatives of the new market:

Stage 1—Price and volume

Stage 2—Quality and speed

Stage 3—Mass customization (Kiernan 1996, 34)

The "new rules" of competition, performance, and customer satisfaction are emerging from experiments across a wide range of U.S. companies and economic sectors. Healthcare organizations must drive their own management strategies to meet the rapid growth of managed care and the resulting economic pressures that managed care is exerting on the core businesses of inpatient care, physician office practice, and health insurance.

Rule #1—Change the Rules

Be the first organization in your marketplace to play by new rules. This market advantage comes to those organizations that change the old rules—either by breaking them or by inventing new ones. Better yet, change the game. Innovators, mavericks, and tradition-breakers will be the managers—and companies—to break up the old paradigm and define the next one.

Healthcare organizations can break the rules by redefining their service scope, geographic domain, or core operating philosophy. Redefining the territory is one example of "breaking out of the box." In New England, Massachusetts HMO pioneer Harvard Pilgrim Healthcare merged with New Hampshire–based Matthew Thornton Health Plan, the state's oldest HMO (McGuire 1997, 1). For both plans, the deal represented an end to more than a decade of boundary warfare. Harvard coveted southern New Hampshire's growing urban population, while Matthew Thornton looked enviously at the northern Massachusetts market for expansion. Their merger will create the largest managed care plan in New England, with a multistate territory that recognizes the substantial cross-border migration between the two states.

Redefining the company is an even larger step for rule-breaking executives. In Birmingham, Alabama, HealthSouth was a regional provider of rehabilitation services that fundamentally shifted its market definition from local to national. HealthSouth adopted a modified "contrarian" strategy, buying heavily into sectors of the healthcare market perceived to have low growth and low profit potential. HealthSouth became a national company when it acquired Continental, the nation's largest chain of inpatient rehabilitation facilities, after the market shifted toward ambulatory rehabilitative care. With its recent acquisition of Horizon/CMS, HealthSouth now owns two-thirds of the market for inpatient rehabilitation services and 25 percent of outpatient rehabilitative facilities (Freudenheim 1997). With this move, HealthSouth acquired its largest competitor and the last major chain of inpatient rehabilitative facilities. HealthSouth has not only redefined rehabilitation, it now virtually owns the market in its region.

Rule #2—Strategic Foresight

To develop the most farsighted competitive strategy, start with the best assumptions about the future—the concept of "strategic foresight." Build the best possible assumption base and use that to form the strategic insights to identify the possibilities for future competitive advantage. Strategic foresight helps management answer three important questions:

1. What new types of customers and benefits should we seek to provide in five, ten, or fifteen years?
2. What new competencies will we need to build or acquire to provide those benefits to customers?
3. How will the organization need to reconfigure the customer interface over the next several years in the transition period? (Hamel and Prahalad 1997, 79)

Many organizations assume that the future will be pretty much like the past. They assume incremental change, overlooking the potential for revolutionary change that may be driven by the market—or the foresight of a competitor that opens a new window of opportunity. Other organizations assume that the future will continue to be uncertain, so they neglect any strategic planning, relying instead on short-term plans. Both of these viewpoints will substantially limit their organization's potential to create breakthrough strategies or become market leaders by any other strategy than buying competitors to acquire market share.

Industry foresight must be informed by insights into lifestyle, technological, demographic, and political trends. Most important, foresight must be focused on consumers. Consider that two-thirds of the gross domestic product consists of consumer spending. Some consumer trends are obvious to healthcare organizations today: the shift to managed care, aging of the population, and consumer fascination with technology. But what will be the strategic implications of other, lesser-noticed trends such as self-employment, ethnic diversity, widespread consumer use of alternative medicine, and the search for spiritual meaning? Healthcare organizations that read these tea leaves will develop an enlarged sense of future possibilities. Some HMOs are picking up the possibilities of alternative medicine. A recent study of HMOs in 13 states found that a growing number of managed care companies were planning to introduce chiropractic and acupuncture as covered benefits within the next one to two years (Pogue 1996, 13).

Rule #3—Innovation

Companies like 3M and Sony thrive on creating new products, even before their existing products have become commodities. These companies believe the price of industry leadership is the imperative to innovate continuously. To compete successfully for future, yet-to-be-discovered markets, an organization must be capable of enlarging its "opportunity horizon" (Hamel and Prahalad 1997, 90). This requires the organization to reconstruct itself as a portfolio of competencies rather than a portfolio of products or services.

The opportunities of the future are often found in the "white spaces" between products or business units. For example, Access Health, based in Sacramento, California, originated the "Ask-a-Nurse" call center concept to fill the gap that existed in the public's knowledge about how consumers could self-refer to doctors or hospitals.

Predicting market trends requires "thinking in the future tense." Organizational psychologist Jennifer James (1996) identifies six processes for predicting change and identifying new opportunities:

Extension. Imagine that the future has some relationship with the past. Historic patterns drive the future. Today's healthcare networks are the logical extension of the modern hospital, growing larger, connecting horizontally, and providing the management control for a hospital-built system.

Elaboration. This is the process of modifying, further developing, or perfecting an existing product or service. Each new generation of products or services is better than the last, or has been tailored to some specific need of the market. In-vitro fertilization is an example of elaboration. So is a hospice, a long-term care facility specializing in the terminally ill.

Recycling. When an old trend returns, recycling occurs. The current trend in service management is a recycling of the "guest relations" programs of the 1980s. Clinical pathways and reengineering are returns to time-and-motion studies and operations research of the 1950s and 1960s. Open-access HMO plans are a "retro" product that offer consumers direct access to specialists, a feature of indemnity products that HMOs have largely pushed out of the market.

Pattern reversals. When a trend turns on itself, innovation can result. As a reaction to sophisticated technology in the delivery room, family-centered LDRs were developed—labor-delivery-recovery rooms furnished like cozy bedrooms, with the technology hidden as much as possible.

Strange attractions. Sometimes trends emerge from unlikely sources. The new "open-access" plans offered by HMOs are remarkably similar to the indemnity health plans that managed care displaced over the past ten years.

Chaos. The theory of chaos cautions against assuming that the future is quite predictable. There is always room for breakthrough thinking, such as minimally invasive surgery, genetic engineering, or developing health information networks using the Internet.

Rule #4—Timing

Timing, of course, is everything. Whether the new direction is external growth or internal efficiency, the success of initiating change often depends on a well-developed sense of timing the move. Andrew Grove, chairman and CEO of Intel Corporation, says, "There is at least one point in the history of every company when you have to change dramatically to rise to the next performance level. Miss the moment, and you start to decline" (Kiernan 1996, 1). More than just timing is required, however. An organization—and its management team—must be willing and able to *commit* to the new direction (James 1996, 117).

Hit the market running, and the organization can leapfrog competitors. There are a number of dividends from the strategic use of timing:

- *Reduce business risk* by introducing new offerings at the time when the opportunities are first identified.
- *Stay on the leading edge of innovation* by incorporating technological advances in products and services faster than competitors.
- *Encourage employee acceptance of change* with innovative pilot projects and employee-led initiatives.
- *Reduce product development time* by responding more quickly to market shifts.
- *Set de facto industry standards* by being first to market.
- *Define customer expectations* by being the first to introduce a new concept.
- *Obtain premium prices* based on first-mover and technology leader advantages.
- *Lock up distribution channels* by contracting with the most attractive and strategically positioned distributing organizations.
- *Keep competitors off balance* and on the defensive by constant, quick-paced innovation. (Kiernan 1996, 71)

Rule #5—Speed

The organization that can think fast, respond quickly, and implement on a dime has a tremendous advantage. When an organization wishes to succeed in achieving a plan for the future, time becomes an important constraint to realizing the organization's objectives. The problem of organizational lag time is universal.

There is another dimension of time that goes beyond rapid action. Healthcare needs a new appreciation of time as a strategic resource. The industrial context of modern healthcare is curative medicine. Doctors—and the health system—focus on repair after disease has occurred. Healthcare focuses mostly on illness and spends little time on prevention. Defining medicine in terms of health improvement would overcome the lag time problem inherent in modern healthcare (Davis 1996, 48). If healthcare is restructured around capitation, providers will have a strong incentive to shift

from a reactive to a proactive stance, reducing costs by improving the health of their enrollees.

Rule #6—Mass Customization

The challenge of marketing products or services in the future is multiplied by the almost infinite variation in patient demands that will be placed upon the system. Healthcare customers have high expectations for personalized care, attention, and medical care. America is inventing technologies that will make it possible to provide essentially standardized products or services in a way that customizes it to each consumer (Davis 1996, 150). The concept of mass customization assumes that market and business relationships can be defined specifically and uniquely for each consumer. New technologies, information networks, the Internet, databases, and expert systems are putting new tools in the hands of marketers and managers. Managed care, information technology, and the Internet may come together in the exam room, where patient and physician sit down together to search for the latest information on disease (Engstrom 1997, 1). Doctors can obtain Internet printouts by accessing "Medical Matrix" at http://www.medmatrix.org, a collection of more than 2,400 specialty and disease-categorized sources from the American Medical Informatics Society.

Healthcare's adoption of mass customization is being accelerated by managed care. Managing an enrolled population is emerging as the central management challenge of the twenty-first century. Managing costs means applying standardized clinical pathways, fine-tuning care plans, and providing justifiable services on a patient-by-patient basis. Enrolled populations have predictable health risks. Care management programs are being developed that will identify high-risk enrollees; customized health improvement plans are also being created for the "worried well."

Rule #7—Reengineering

After almost a decade of experience in downsizing, rightsizing, and organizational flattening, a growing backlash is emerging against reengineering. This signals that the downsizing trend is winding down, as companies discover the limits of increasing profits through reducing the work force. Calls for increasing revenues and "growing the business" are coming next. Healthcare's experience with downsizing may not have been as severe as the widely publicized cuts at AT&T, IBM, Apple, and others, who cut their staff by 15 to 20 percent and more. Most hospital layoffs have been in the range of 5 to 6 percent in frontline workers, with a 10 to 15 percent reduction in middle management. Many of healthcare's layoffs have been managed through attrition rather than layoff or buyout.

Reengineering in healthcare is not dead. The ability to restructure the healthcare organization flexibly to accommodate market shifts is a *core competency* that will be essential in the twenty-first century (Boyett and Boyett 1995). In fact, healthcare restructuring has hardly started. The next five years will see a widespread effort to expand clinical pathways to all major inpatient and ambulatory care services. The standardization of medicine is gaining rapid headway, with thousands of practice guidelines and protocols. These programs now must be scaled up to a regional level, and corporate guidelines have to be hammered out. Managing patients will be centralized at a regional level by capitated provider networks and managed care plans. Nurses, not physicians, will be the integrators of care in consolidated care management programs.

Rule #8—Managing Diversity

The new work force is here. A major shift is occurring in labor force demographics that will affect every healthcare organization (Boyett and Boyett 1995). Tomorrow's work force will be predominantly female and ethnically diverse. In 1960, some 60 percent of U.S. workers were white males, but by 2005, white males will be a minority group, representing only 40 percent of all workers. Female participation in the work force has tripled since 1950, and women will close the gender gap to 47.5 percent of all workers by 2005, with almost two in three women (63 percent) participating in the work force. Most (74.5 percent) are working mothers. The 1950s stereotype family of an employed husband with a stay-at-home wife fit only 25 percent of all families in 1990.

America's hospitals and healthcare organizations are used to working women—and lots of them. Many healthcare settings have more than 75 percent female workers, from the executive suite to the service support jobs in dietary, housekeeping, and information systems. Issues of child care, family leave, flextime scheduling, part-time employment, and eldercare are widespread employee concerns in healthcare organizations. Charges of sexual harassment and racial discrimination have affected a number of Fortune 500 companies and are a continuing concern for health organizations with many female and minority employees.

The impact of increasing diversity in the workplace is a major challenge to American business. Issues of productivity, absenteeism, stress and burnout, turnover, and employee conflicts are part of the social fabric of work force changes. Healthcare employers are proactively responding with a number of programs, including employer-sponsored child care, emergency day care, direct financial assistance, counseling, employee assistance programs, stress reduction training, voluntary reduced part-time employment, flextime, telecommuting, and job sharing. Human resource consultants offer additional solutions, such as "de-coupling face-time" from performance evaluation, removing the stigma from nonlinear careers, and reengineering work with the family in mind (Boyett and Boyett 1995, 109–10).

Rule #9—Empowerment

Empowerment—the encouragement of intellectual energy and commitment broadly across an organization—is one of those appealingly simple concepts that is devilish to implement (Kiernan 1996, 129). The idea is to provide everyone in the organization with the authority and the resources to display real leadership within his or her sphere of competence. Despite a decade of management rhetoric about workplace democracy "no-boss" teams, relatively little has actually been accomplished in most organizations in terms of decentralizing power and responsibility to frontline workers.

Why hasn't empowerment gone further? One, it takes real energy, training, and dedication to make it work. Two, insecure managers may fear their subordinates could become competitors—probably a legitimate concern. For empowerment to work, employees need information that is often confidential, even within their own organization. Empowered workers need to have the right to rewrite their job descriptions, call on others widely across the company for support, and have access to the resources needed to do the job better, faster, or cheaper.

Three new trends will encourage empowerment in the workplace: flattening the bureaucratic pyramid will force authority and responsibility to lower levels; information networks will make important data available from practically anywhere in the organization; and performance-based compensation—"new pay" rewarding workers for meeting personal and work unit goals—will be implemented.

Rule #10—Learning Organizations

If healthcare organizations are to succeed in a complex, competitive future environment, they must strengthen the process of organizational adaptation. They must become "learning organizations" that combine systems thinking, team learning, and shared vision (Senge et al. 1994). When an organization thinks about the future, it organizes a mental model of expected future assumptions. An organization must be disciplined in developing its mental models but still remain open to new information that may challenge its assumptions. Scenarios and learning laboratories can simulate future conditions, providing an opportunity for a management team to test the models and extrapolate their future implications.

"Systems thinking" is a set of methods and intellectual tools, based on common principles. Much of systems thinking is inspired by the processes of biological science but is also informed by sociology and even physics. Systems thinking recognizes the interdependence of all systems and sub-systems. The application of systems thinking is particularly useful for identifying the vulnerabilities, limited understandings, and fallibilities of the past. One hospital's quality team focused on 300 potential solutions to speed up the time required to discharge patients without finding an effective intervention. Finally, a chance remark by a patient led to a systems thinking insight by the team—scheduling a ride in advance. The hospital had always assumed that it was the patient's responsibility to arrange post-discharge transportation.

The process of team learning is the institutionalization of systems thinking within an organization. Team members must learn how to align their efforts and skills (Senge et al. 1994, 352), which is different from developing consensus. Alignment means that the team uses its collective capabilities to build shared understanding. Conversations and dialogues among team members are skillful, thoughtful, and productive. Problem solving is faster. Implementation proceeds more smoothly. Think of a basketball team on a fast break, moving the ball downcourt with quick, sharp, and occasionally "no-look" passes. That is teamwork in action. Team learning assumes that the team has a collective mental model and a shared vision. The team builds shared aspirations, which drive performance. The team learns from its experience and continuously adapts its mental models and processes to adapt to changes in the environment. Becoming a learning organization is a rigorous process, but the results are worthwhile. The learning organization is prepared for the twenty-first century, by anticipation and shared vision.

DESIGNING A "REINVENTED" ORGANIZATION

The future of the twenty-first century healthcare organization began yesterday. Today is simply the bridge to the future. Healthcare's market revolution is already under way, and many future trends are already moving into place. But who will lead the change process? Frontline employees and middle managers often think of themselves as the victims of change, which is not true: They will have to be the change-makers, or the revolution will not succeed.

Top management may—or may not—recognize the need for change, but the revolution probably will not start in the executive suite. Those who will reinvent the organization are working somewhere in the middle of today's company, or in a small start-up enterprise that will become part of the future firm.

Even simple fundamentals are changing, such as the concept of "the job." When only half the working population of California is working full-time, this shows how far employment has destabilized. William Bridges, author of *Job Shift*, suggests that this trend is just coming to healthcare later and hitting harder (Flower 1996, 15). All kinds of organizations that are not part of healthcare systems are picking up work—housekeeping, outsourced lab work, specialized imaging. The system takes work out of the core institution and puts it with more entrepreneurial companies. People still work, but they are more likely to do so on cross-functional teams, and they do all kinds of different things, not just repetitive tasks.

IMPLEMENTATION—EXECUTING THE STRATEGY

None of this will come easily. It is important to remember that resistance to change is a natural instinct, but when left unchecked it can result in a complete reversion to former practices. Not surprisingly, a study of quality improvement in 1,000 companies found stiff resistance and outright sabotage in more than 35 percent of the cases (Bennis and Mische 1995, 79). A similar set of obstacles is rising over system integration efforts by hospitals and medical groups. Communities, employees, and patients are asking "What's in it for us?" (Scott 1997, 39). Their concerns range from antitrust issues and price-raising to layoffs and job security.

Turf battles and economic conflicts are inhibiting change in the healthcare field. Open-access HMO products are an example of a market trend that brings primary care and specialists into direct economic competition for patients (Droste 1997, 1). Insurers are bypassing primary care physicians to contract directly with specialty medical groups, with either fee-for-service or capitation.

The most stubborn barrier to organizational change may be the inability to implement the best-planned management strategies. Change must be driven through the heart of the organization—operations. The transformation of operations requires extensive reworking of practices, policies, and procedures at every level from the customer to the executive suite. Changes, once implemented, must be put in place swiftly and firmly. Management consultants have noted that once an organization makes a major change, a kind of "corporate vacuum" occurs while employees wait to see what happens. Management must fill that vacuum with positive ideas and accomplishments before change-resistors fill it with negative ones (Bennis and Mische 1995).

LOOKING FORWARD: THE ECOLOGY OF HEALTHCARE

It is time for healthcare executives to take a stand on the critical issue of business' relationship with society and the environment. Paul Hawken, author of *The Ecology of Commerce*, puts the case squarely for eco-social responsibility: Many organizations today no longer accept the maxim that "the business of business is business." Their new premise is simple: Corporations, because they are the dominant institutions on the planet, must squarely address the social and environmental problems that afflict humankind (Hawken 1993, xiii).

Corporations and executives are stepping forward to take stands on behalf of social issues and environmental concerns. Like Ben Cohen and Jerry Greenfield, founders of Ben & Jerry's Homemade Ice Cream. Everyone who has ever put a spoon into Ben & Jerry's Rain Forest Crunch ice cream knows that this small Vermont company is dedicating its heart, and some of its profits, to saving the environment (Lager 1996). There are other corporate examples, like Tom's of Maine, which makes toothpaste and cosmetics out of all-natural ingredients and donates a part of the profits to environmental repair projects. But which leading American healthcare companies have made a demonstrable commitment to the environment, either local or global? The answer? Only a handful.

This is not a criticism, only an observation. Hospitals, health industry suppliers, and managed care plans are part of a $1 trillion industry. Many are helping to provide the safety net for America's 40 million medically uninsured, and some are doing even more, with outreach healthcare programs for the homeless and other at-risk groups. These good efforts are commendable, but they are not enough. Charity care and community health initiatives only begin to scratch the surface of the real problem—creating a sustainable economy given limited environmental resources.

This kind of thinking may be an early signal of an emerging Fourth Wave in modern society, beyond Alvin Toffler's "Third Wave" postindustrial model (Maynard and Mehrtens 1996). In the Fourth Wave, a new consciousness about the connection between the individual and the environment is recognized. Economics and environmentalism become a common cause, with a proactive response from business. A new rank of business opportunities will arise in the "four R's"—repair, reuse, recycle, and recondition. These products and services will have unlimited applications in the postindustrial world, rebalancing the manmade environment with the natural one.

Economic changes in healthcare will drive such an ecologically balanced view. Capitation and managed care are reinforcing the necessity of recognizing environmental health problems. But healthcare's social responsibility goes beyond environmental health threats. There are many things that healthcare organizations could do to promote a sustainable environmental future:

1. Dedicate a share of profits to local social or environmental issues.
2. Encourage healthcare management and employees to volunteer service in community projects and organizations.
3. Recycle paper, plastic, glass, and other materials everywhere across the organization, and use recycled materials where possible.
4. Provide "transitional" comprehensive healthcare for those who have lost their insurance coverage.
5. Expand outreach programs to underserved in the community, such as homeless or high-risk populations.
6. Refocus the hospital's foundation to dedicate a share of its distributions to sponsor a range of community-based health improvement projects.
7. Take a proactive stance in addressing persistent social problems in the community, such as redeveloping low-income housing or sponsoring community schools.
8. Make the campus an environmental showcase/garden for patients, visitors, and employees.
9. Address social and environmental health issues in the community and public policy arenas.
10. Be a visible "corporate citizen" and leader in community projects and programs.

Ethicist Emily Friedman believes that healthcare's toughest patient-centered ethical issues—"Baby Doe" and Karen Ann Quinlan—must be linked to deeper-rooted social and environmental concerns, arguing, "The ethics net is cast wide enough to recognize 43 million uninsured Americans, inappropriate constraint on access created by some HMOs, and wild maldistribution of healthcare resources as true ethics problems" (Friedman 1996, xviii). America's healthcare organizations are among the largest and most successful social institutions created in the twentieth century. Much of the revenues of America's $1 trillion healthcare economy pour into the coffers of nonprofit institutions. They bear a social burden of care for the poor, and they bear it well. But it is time for America's hospitals, medical groups, suppliers, and managed care plans to stand up and be counted for the long-term problem of the future—creating a sustainable economy within its environmental limits.

REFERENCES

Bennis, W., and M. Mische. 1995. *The 21st Century Organization: Reinventing Through Reengineering.* San Diego, CA: Pfeiffer & Company.

Boyett, J. H., and J. T. Boyett. 1995. *Beyond Workplace 2000: Essential Strategies for New American Corporation.* New York: Dutton.

Bridges, W. 1994. *Job Shift.* Reading, MA: Addison-Wesley Publishing Company.

Davis, S. 1996. *Future Perfect.* Reading, MA: Addison-Wesley Publishing Company.

Droste, T. 1997. "Conflicting Models Put Specialists and Primary Care Physicians at Odds." *Medical Network Strategy Report* 6 (1): 1–3.

Engstrom, P. 1997. "Net-Linked Exam Rooms Open Up New Vistas for Both MDs and Patients." *Medicine on the Net* 3 (2): 1–2.

Flower, J. 1997. "Job Shift." *Healthcare Forum Journal* 40 (1):14–21.

Freudenheim, M. 1997. "Shares of Horizon/CMS Jump After Takeover Announcement." *New York Times* (February 19): C3.

Friedman, E. 1996. *The Right Thing: Ten Years of Ethics Columns from the Healthcare Forum Journal.* San Francisco: Jossey-Bass, Inc.

Hamel, G., and C. K. Prahalad. 1997. *Competing for the Future.* Boston, MA: Harvard University Business School Press.

Hawken, P. 1993. *The Ecology of Commerce: A Declaration of Sustainability.* New York: Harper Business.

James, J. 1996. *Thinking in the Future Tense: Leadership Skills for a New Age.* New York: Simon & Schuster.

Kiernan, M. J. 1996. *The Eleven Commandments of 21st Century Management.* Englewood Cliffs, NJ: Prentice-Hall.

Lager, F. 1996. *Ben & Jerry's: The Inside Scoop.* New York: Crown Publishers.

Lauer, C. S. 1997. "Publisher's Letter." *Modern Healthcare* 27 (1): 1.

Maynard, H. E., Jr., and S. E. Mehrtens. 1996. *The Fourth Wave: Business in the 21st Century.* San Francisco: Berrett-Kohler Publishers.

McGuire, D. 1997. "Harvard to Buy Matthew Thornton, Continue Northeast Expansion." *Managed Care Outlook* 10 (1): 1–2.

Pogue, J. 1996. "New Study Sheds Light on HMO's Opinions of Alternative Medicine." *Integrated Healthcare Report* 4 (10): 13–14.

Scott, L. 1997. "Communities Ask, 'What's in It for Us?'" *Modern Healthcare* 27 (1): 39.

Senge, P., C. Roberts, R. B. Ross, B. Smigh, and A. Kleiner. 1994. *The Fifth Discipline: Fieldbook.* New York: Doubleday.

2

Leaders of the Future:
Seven Trends for Twenty-First Century
Healthcare Executives

> *In the tenuous years that lie ahead, the familiar benchmarks, guide-*
> *posts and milestones will change as rapidly and explosively as*
> *the times, but the one constant at the center of the vortex will be*
> *the leader.*
>
> —Frances Hesselbein, "The 'How-to-Be' Leader"
> (1996, 122)

Twenty-first century healthcare executives will not be found in the executive suite, but will instead be found close to the customer, on the patient floor, perhaps, or in an ambulatory care center, or in a physician office with a home-bound patient linked by telemedicine. A new generation of healthcare executives is coming that will bring new attitudes and skills to America's hospitals, health systems, and physician organizations. The age of downsizing, decentralization, and computer networking means that the corporate office of the 1980s is obsolete.

In the future, many of the new healthcare executives will be clinicians with management training. There will be more lab coats and fewer blue suits in senior healthcare management positions (Coile 1996). These clinical executives know and can manage the core business of patient care. In ten years, holders of MBAs will be the support staff, as functions like finance and information systems are reshaped to support managed care and capitation.

Healthcare's leadership revolution is part of a broader trend shared by many sectors of American business. Many businesses are radically reshaping their corporate culture to become more agile and customer-driven. The new language of leadership shows how the field of management is adapting to a global, rapidly shifting economy:

- "How-to-be" leaders will teach beliefs and attitudes—not "how-to-do-it" standards.
- "Digging in the field" will mean staying very close to the customer.
- Fluid management systems will release people from the boxes of the old hierarchy.
- Reaching beyond the boundaries will develop new business relationships.
- Healthcare organizations will focus on building healthy communities as energetically as they build enterprises.
- Healthcare organizations will focus on their mission to create meaning in work. (Hesselbein 1996)

THE NEW LANGUAGE OF LEADERSHIP

Listen to how leaders of America's best corporations talk today. Language is a symbol, but it is also a signal of changing attitudes and styles in major companies that compete on a global basis. Leaders are communicators. They define the values and corporate culture. Many modern executives would agree that no one is smart enough to run a large corporation today. Leaders don't drive the business. Instead, they make it possible for managers at the operating level to set high goals—and then get the organizational support to achieve them.

One of the myths of American business management is the hard-driving executive like ITT's Harold Geneen, who once sawed a corporate board table in half out of anger when his managers could not keep up ITT's string of continuously rising profitable quarters in the 1980s. Today, America's most successful corporate executives talk a new game:

- Bank One's CEO defines his job as managing an "uncommon partnership" that fosters maximum local autonomy for its managers, combined with effective centrally provided services and common performance measures.
- ServiceMaster's chairman looked for a "servant's heart" in selecting his successor to serve as CEO.
- Girl Scouts' national executive described her job as ensuring that the organization was "mission-focused, values-based and demographics-driven."
- Southwest Airlines' CEO calls hiring managers his most important job and a "near-religious experience." (Heskett and Schlesinger 1996, 112–13)

Despite these high-level testimonies, some healthcare executives are skeptical of the latest management fads and buzzwords of the 1990s. A recent spoof in the *Wall Street Journal* ran under the headline, "Can a Fast-Tracker Vision His Career in a New Ecosystem?" (Lancaster 1996, B1). In the paradigm of the upwardly mobile, an executive on the rise must actively restructure the workplace into "cross-functional, cross-cultural and cross-species teams." Only those fully informed of such "proto-New Age" management currents could succeed in the "biosystem," a metaphor for the market environment. Our fast-tracking young executive was told to work on his "emotional intelligence" and to build better skills in "neurolinguistic programming," which meant learning how successful people think, speak, and act. Some of these ideas came from a conference entitled "A Values-Based Approach to Creating Alignment in Organizations," sponsored by the Human Resource Associates' Center for Enabling Leadership. Need the critics say more?

SEVEN TRENDS FOR TWENTY-FIRST CENTURY LEADERSHIP

Trend #1—Thinking in the Future Tense

The leader's first responsibility is to chart the path to the future. But which of the many possible future scenarios is the most likely? There are patterns beneath the current confusion of market events. The role of the leader is to recognize the arrival of new patterns and to interpret their significance to the organization. Sound market strategy depends on this process of "thinking in the future tense," argues Jennifer James, an anthropologist who works with major corporations.

There are six strategies leaders can bring to bear in the process of recognizing emerging patterns and trends:

1. *Extension* applies the logic of imagining how a condition, practice, or trend might continue to develop.
2. *Elaboration* is the process of further developing or perfecting a product or service.
3. *Recycling* is the familiar process whereby an old pattern or trend makes a comeback, rejuvenating an existing business.
4. *Pattern reversals* invite a leap of the imagination to look for the opposites in current trends, to identify a potential new direction.
5. *Strange attractions* are odd combination of patterns that seem unpredictable but may combine current trends in new ways that attract because of their novelty.

6. *Chaos* may not be without order, but patterns are not easily read; chaos is often a pretrend state, when new patterns are ready to emerge. (James 1996, 50)

The leader looks at the same trends and data as everyone else *and sees something different*. This capacity for thinking in the future does not require genius. The identification of emerging patterns can either be the outcome of leaps of intuition or the application of dogged analysis to identify underlying trends from mounds of data. The future-minded executive does not have to lead the process of discovery, but he or she must be the first one to act on the new information.

Trend #2—Loss of Control

The empowered, no-boss, team-member, computer-linked employee is not under much control today and will respond even less to traditional authority systems in the future. Some management experts question whether the concept of control—meaning power to direct others—has any utility when employees set their own goals, cooperate with peers, and get their work done just-in-time, like supplies arriving on a Japanese production line.

In the future, managers will find they influence performance less by control than by modeling the behavior they want from subordinates. Organizational psychologist Richard Farson, former head of the Esalen Institute, argues: "Many of us have the idea that as managers we can use our skills to shape our employees as if we were shaping clay . . . . It's more as if our employees are piles of clay into which we fall—leaving an impression, all right, but it may not be the impression we intended to leave" (Farson 1996, 41).

Trend #3—Mass Customizing

The concept of mass customizing is not an oxymoron, but rather one of the fundamental challenges of twenty-first century healthcare leadership. This paradox applies to products, services, and markets. The evolution of global markets has created billions of consumers who share a common set of values and customer expectations—and who even respond to the same advertisements. Speed, specificity, and economy of effort are the hallmarks of this leadership model. The solutions will require techno-savvy by leaders in tomorrow's markets.

In healthcare, every patient is unique, but to be efficient, every hospital and physician must standardize treatments for maximum efficiency. To do so will require adaptation of new technology, including computer networks and expert systems and artificial intelligence. Patient treatment plans must be standardized for efficiency, but customized for each patient. So must diagnostic modalities and therapies. "Shotgun" prescribing of antibiotics, for example, will be replaced by very specific applications of targeted antibiotics tailored to each patient's situation. The demands for mass customization will drive clinically trained managers into key leadership positions in healthcare organizations. Every hospital and health system will have a majority of clinician executives among its senior managers in the twenty-first century.

Trend # 4—Information-Based Networks

The technology that created a revolution in "data processing" is now driving a revolution in the organization and management of work. At the start of the industrial age, bureaucratic hierarchies were necessary to communicate orders from the top down and to produce goods and services from the bottom up. The future organization is virtually flat, with a minimum of intervening midlevel layers between executive management and the rank-and-file workers. Using information-based networks, workers in any division of the organization can communicate—and collaborate—with any other in a moment's time.

Not all organizations are rushing to adopt the network model, notes Stan Davis, whose book *Future Perfect*, published in 1987, was at least a decade ahead of its time. Authority-based organizations cannot make decisions or implement changes fast enough in a rapidly changing market. The concept of chain-of-command is outmoded and is a barrier to information-driven market adaptation. Davis argues that "the technology exists to make this possible [but] it is management's mindset that is mechanistic, lagging behind in a model from a world that no longer is" (Davis 1987, 206).

Trend #5—Servant Leadership

Are modern organizations too big and complex for one individual to lead? Richard Farson, a West Coast management consultant believes "there are no leaders—there is only leadership" (Farson 1996, 144). Leadership is distributed among members of the group, and each of the members has his or her own role, which may change by assignment and task. Farson argues that the strength of the leader is his or her ability to mobilize the strength of the group. In a modern organization, "everyone must learn both when and how to exercise the following part of leading and the leading part of following," argues Douglas Smith (1996, 204). Leaders must learn to follow the individual, team, or organization when the need for others to take leadership takes precedence over the leader's demonstration of power or competency.

Some management experts call this new model the servant leader—experts like C. William Pollard, chairman of the ServiceMaster Corporation, the biggest contract management company in the healthcare industry. As head of a company that has doubled in size every three to four years—and has done so for 20 years—Pollard believes that servant leaders listen and learn from those they lead (Pollard 1996, 245). Because leaders make things happen through others, they must be willing to delegate authority and responsibility generously. The servant leader will not track progress just by growth in revenues and earnings but in the way people in the organization think about themselves, their work, and their communities.

The servant leaders recognize the limits of individual knowledge, positional power, and personal charisma. In a team-based work environment, leaders are the ones who follow a vision, mission, and set of values. Their behavior is a role model for the organization. As leaders, they are servants of the organization's higher values. They are initiators, risk-takers, and change-makers, but they do so for the long-term benefit of the organization.

Trend #6—Knowledge-Based Work

The United States is moving from an industrial model of work to knowledge-based work. The difference is profound. Under the industrial model, work was subdivided into tasks performed by specialists. As work tasks became more complicated, the work was further subdivided. Like specialty medicine, under the industrial model each worker focuses more and more on less and less. Automation only speeded up the work flow and provided more specialized tools to enhance output. Productivity experts focused work analysis techniques of scientific management to find the one best way to perform every work task. This is the model of healthcare in the United States today.

Knowledge-based work is harder to divide than physical work. Future workers won't have "jobs" (Bridges 1996). They will instead face a continuously changing and highly complex set of workplace demands. Instead of being made up of repetitive actions, knowledge-based work requires a dialogue between individuals who will together diagnose complex situations and decide the best combination of solutions. That is why healthcare tasks are increasingly being done by cross-functional teams. This will be a challenge for physicians and nurses, whose domain ("turf") is now being crossed regularly by team-centered approaches. Traditional middle managers in healthcare organizations—department managers and supervisors—are undergoing rapid obsolescence. Position power is not important. Knowledge-power will drive the tasks of healthcare workers, within the framework of team-developed clinical pathways.

Trend #7—Changing the Corporate Culture

Enlightened leadership can change an established culture by changing the assumptions on which that culture is built. The challenge of changing an established culture is daunting. The leader must revise or replace values, attitudes, and behavioral norms that have been created over years. Think of this as a process lasting from three to five years. Leaders who cannot make this commitment to their organization for at least this period of time cannot hope to overcome the inertia of the status quo—even if the existing organizational culture is dysfunctional.

Leaders who seek to change the culture must first understand the underlying forces that drive the organization. Management consultant Jennifer James advises that leaders must pay attention to both the overt and covert behavior, asking such questions as:

- What are the basic assumptions of how people survive in the organization?
- Are managers expected to make decisions or wait for orders?
- Do managers tell the truth? Is straight talk the norm or exception?
- Who or what drives the group or organization? Profits? Customer satisfaction?
- How important is character in organizational behavior?
- Does the personal and professional behavior of the leaders match the articulated values of the organization? (James 1996, 143–44)

The process of culture begins with a redefinition of values and vision. Leaders of the organization must demonstrate both competency and compassion to begin to gain the trust of workers. Not all managers may feel a clear mandate for change. Demands—and rewards—for risk-taking help reinforce new behaviors. Leaders must make clear what new behaviors are expected and lead by example. Symbolic acts of leadership must be visible. There cannot be a difference between public and private behaviors by leaders, or hard-won trust can easily be lost. Skepticism will be widespread, sometimes persisting for years. Employees who are used to the management "slogan of the month" will be critical of new messages. Communicating new values or behaviors requires leaders to follow through on their message with an unswerving commitment.

"FUTURE WORK": THE NEW MILLENNIUM'S HEALTHCARE WORKPLACE

Some management experts believe that we are witnessing the end of the predominance of the large business organization in its present form. The only question that remains is how long will it take? (Birchall and Lyons 1995, 1) New leadership strategies, styles, and skills will be needed to manage the twenty-first century healthcare organization. This is a larger issue than the shift from inpatient to ambulatory and long-term care. Quite fundamentally, the best conventional wisdom about managing people in the workplace is being replaced with a new set of assumptions about how work tasks will be created and implemented.

But will these assumptions about "future work" also apply in healthcare, especially inpatient care, where government regulations rigidly prescribe treatment settings and staffing patterns? Will highly compartmentalized professions such as medicine and nursing accept a collegial "no-boss" team approach? Can healthcare organizations adopt a more decentralized approach to the tasks of patient care, when plaintiffs' attorneys are poised to exploit any failure to follow medical guidelines or nursing standards?

Future work entails several major characteristics (Birchall and Lyons 1995), which are described below.

Information Technology

With the information revolution comes a new portfolio of solutions to traditional work process systems that decentralize decision making in global enterprises. As the cost of information technology falls and computing power grows exponentially, some new challenges arise in managing both the technology itself as well as the newly liberated "knowledge workers."

This "atomized" model of the future organization could not exist without the proliferation of information/communications networks such as the Internet and local area networks (LANs). It allows numbers of workers to collaborate on work projects while working from home, mobile locations, or shared offices. In healthcare, the arrival of the information age is readily apparent from LANs in the executive suite, bedside computers, physician office linkages, and in-home diagnostic equipment that is networked to the health system. Financial and clinical data is available in real time from a variety of locations, improving the cost-management performance of care managers.

The transition costs of becoming fully networked with information technology are not insignificant. Healthcare organizations are doubling their information systems spending as a percentage of budget, from 1 to 2 percent to 3 to 4 percent. Medical work stations will be universal within five years in hospitals, medical offices, long-term care facilities, and other healthcare settings. Caregivers will rely on clinical decision-support systems that will compare individualized treatment plans with current diagnostic information. Care managers will also know whether patients' care costs are within budget and whether predicted outcomes are consistent with benchmarks for quality and customer satisfaction.

There is controversy associated with healthcare's information revolution that goes beyond the questions of capital investment and technology obsolescence. Will today's healthcare workers have sufficient computer literacy to operate such high-tech systems? Has downsizing and staff substitution resulted in a "dumbing-down" of healthcare caregivers? Critics complain that eliminating all-RN work forces means placing care responsibilities with lesser-skilled workers who will not have the educational background or training to function in this new world of computerized medicine.

People at Work

A new form of workplace democracy is occurring as individuals are able to detach themselves from traditional requirements of working at specific times and fixed locations. The promise of more personal freedom at work redefines "supervision." Semiautonomous workers set their own goals, define their own timetables, and increase individual and team outputs.

In healthcare, downsizing and reengineering has resulted in substantial reductions in middle management. These flattened healthcare hierarchies have reduced management levels from 7 to 9 to 3 to 4 between the CEO and the patient. The effects on quality and customer service are mixed. Better-designed processes through reengineering have reduced healthcare operating costs such as transportation, communication, record keeping, and down time spent waiting for patients or other caregivers to finish a process. At the same time, the drive for efficiency has made some patients anxious. As a result, caregivers such as Dr. Anne Billingsley are put in the awkward position of nudging elderly patients out of the hospital just a few days after she has operated on them: "Most of them are scared to go home after four days. You have to go around and get them out with a shoehorn" (Anders 1996, B1).

Virtual Organization

Tomorrow's organization exists in virtual reality. It is a project-focused, collaborative network not bounded by time or space. Organizational settings such as headquarters are obsolete. These virtual organizations have higher communication and coordination costs, but their increased productivity and lower facilities costs may more than compensate.

The rapid growth of the virtual organization will be driven by three factors:

1. rapid innovation of electronic technologies such as digital, wireless communications that can process video, audio, and text information in multimedia formats;
2. proliferation of computer networks on a local, national, and global basis—both "private" networks established by corporations and "public" networks open to a wide range of commercial users; and
3. growth of telecommuting that allows decentralized networks of workers to run complex processes and service customers from widely scattered workstations.

The virtual organization is results oriented rather than process driven. Can it work in healthcare, which has always been a process-driven culture like government or the insurance industry? In many ways, the nation's nearly 700 HMOs operate on the virtual model. Most modern HMOs are network or independent practice association (IPA) models, offering patient care across an HMO-credentialed network of hospitals, physicians, and other care settings. Coordination of care is often the patient's responsibility, unless the HMO is using primary care physician gatekeepers or nurse case managers to ensure continuity of care. In trend-setting California, large fully integrated systems like Kaiser are now considering switching to the lower cost, more flexible network model used by competitors like Health Net, PacifiCare, and FHP.

There are a growing number of examples of virtual organizations in healthcare:

- primary care networks;
- regional hospital networks;
- specialty medicine networks (such as back care or open heart);
- alternative care provider networks (such as chiropractic); and
- academic medical center hub-and-spoke networks.

The architectural skeleton of the virtual organization is an extensive computer linkage across healthcare settings. Real-time information management promises to end financial float and decision float by healthcare payors and professionals (Barner 1996). The concept of *float* comes from banking, where there has historically been a period between when a check was written and when the bank actually cashed it. With better, faster computer networks, physicians and case managers are given immediate financial information at the time the cost is incurred, not hours or days later when a bill is printed. Computer technology also eliminates decision float, providing real-time feedback from changes in patient therapy or condition. The result should be more precise diagnoses, less wasted effort in therapy, clinical interventions with pinpoint accuracy, shorter lengths of stay, lower cost per case, and better clinical outcomes.

Knowledge Workers

The American workplace is rapidly shifting from a work force that produces products to one that primarily manages information. Medical technology is one of the fields where technological innovation has put a premium on technical experts who can support the new technologies. High-tech medicine, computer-assisted diagnosis, and expert systems for care management demand healthcare workers with computer literacy and the ability to make rapid, complex decisions.

As healthcare downsizes, fewer hospitals and health systems will be able to afford the luxury of "paying managers just to manage." Robert Barner, a Florida-based consultant with Parry Consulting Services, predicts that "managers will be expected to roll up their sleeves and contribute technical expertise to their jobs" (Barner 1996, 16). Given the rapid emergence of new technology and clinical practice, managers will have to work hard to overcome the problem of technological obsolescence. Managers will have to make a commitment to lifelong learning or find themselves rapidly outdated.

Worker Diversity

In the next 5 to 10 years, the issue of diversity will have fully arrived in American workplaces. According to a prediction by the U.S. Department of Labor, by 2000, only 15 percent of incoming workers will be white males (Barner 1996, 17). New workers for tomorrow's organizations will be predominantly women or minorities. Today's Anglo majority of 76 percent will shrink to 52 percent by 2050, while the percentage of Hispanics will double to 22 percent and that of Asians triple to 10 percent, according to population forecasts by Towers Perrin, a national human resources and compensation consulting firm (Jones 1996).

Healthcare organizations must adapt to a marketplace of ethnic diversity and culturally conditioned consumer demands. Statistics like these make the case for accommodating a more diverse marketplace:

- Consumer spending by American minorities is greater than any single country that trades with the United States.
- Women spend 85 percent of the consumer dollar.
- Older Americans control more than 50 percent of all discretionary income.

Coordinating patient care in a multicultural workplace increases complexity in assigning work, task delegation, outcome monitoring, and communication. Managers and employees who can work successfully in ethnic and culturally diverse work teams will be at a premium. Healthcare organizations will be treating growing numbers of patients from diverse cultural backgrounds. Hospitals in melting-pot cities like Los Angeles, Miami, New York, and San Francisco are coping with rapidly growing ethnic populations and diverse languages. Sensitivity training will help managers understand the needs and perspectives of different members of work groups, including "white male managers who may feel disenfranchised from their traditional majority power base" (Barner 1996, 17).

New Pay

Performance-based compensation is rapidly supplementing conventional pay-for-time reward systems. The old compensation system of base pay schedules, cost-of-living increases, and merit pay is being replaced by schemes that harness the power of the paycheck for motivating higher levels of employee and managerial performance. The "new pay" revolution includes everyone from senior executives to hourly workers. According to Sandra O'Neal, a principal at Towers Perrin and author of *Compensation, Challenges and Changes*, "It's a change from paying people in fixed dollars to paying them in a portion of fixed dollars, plus a portion of variable dollars" (Neuborne 1996, 1B).

The adoption of more flexible, performance-oriented compensation plans is getting increasing support by major companies. A recent survey by Towers Perrin found that 58 percent of U.S. companies are reviewing their current pay structure (Neuborne 1996). There are a number of "new pay" options:

- *Fixed-base salary* plus year-end bonus is determined by performance; bonuses do not change base salary, which is updated periodically to reflect market conditions.

- *At-risk pay* puts a percentage of salary or hourly wages "at risk," depending upon goal achievement; hourly workers might find 5 to 6 percent of their pay in the at-risk category, while top executives might risk 25 percent or more of salary.

- *Gainsharing* expands the concept of performance-based compensation to many, or all, workers; companies set goals—profitability, for example—and share a percentage of dollars earned above the profit goal; gainsharing can be annual, quarterly, or even monthly.

- *Broadbanding* organizes employees into more segments within a job level, or band, allowing managers to advance employees without promoting them out of their jobs; the goal is to allow increased pay or responsibility without a traditional promotion.

- *Team-based pay* sets bonuses or incentives dependent upon the performance of the team; team incentives can be based on profitability, cost reduction, labor hour, productivity, or customer-service ratings.

- *Lump-sum merit increases* consolidate a merit-earned wage boost into one annual payout; employees can use the lump-sum payment for big-ticket purchases.

- *Competency-based pay* rewards employees for skills and expertise, not years-in-grade; raises are awarded only when new skills are acquired.

Promising results are emerging about new pay schemes, but most are still in the experimental stage. A study by the Employment Policy Foundation reported a 13 percent gain in productivity when pay-for-performance was combined with employee involvement and suggestions (Neuborne 1996).

Although interest is growing, only 20 percent of the companies surveyed have replaced merit and cost-of-living increases with alternative pay programs. Advocates of new pay concepts make the case that if employers manage wages as a variable, not fixed, cost, layoffs may be avoided. Labor-intensive healthcare organizations are looking closely at "new pay" schemes. Holding base wages constant, and only granting increases based on performance, can limit a healthcare organization's wage inflation and stimulate real productivity improvements.

LOOKING FORWARD: VISIONARY LEADERS

Phrases like *corporate soul* and *value-based management* are increasingly found in business management texts and on the covers of business magazines. The idea is that professional values and idealistic concerns about quality and community align very closely with healthcare's roots as a nonprofit social institution. The leader of the future, of the next millennium, will be one who creates a culture or a value system centered upon principles (Covey 1996, 149). At the same time, market observers are identifying companies like Columbia/HCA as the model of cost management discipline. The implication seems to be that healthcare executives are not aggressive managers because they are distracted by social goals like community service.

The reality is that healthcare leaders need both business discipline and a strong values platform to be effective in the future healthcare marketplace. Tomorrow's healthcare executive must lead with a balanced portfolio of styles and strategies. The demands of a twenty-first century workplace will pull healthcare executives in many directions:

- shifting the core business from acute inpatient to ambulatory and long-term care;
- becoming an at-risk comprehensive services provider for a large enrolled population;
- restructuring the hospital by downsizing and reengineering;
- creating physician organizations that can manage patients efficiently;
- building strategic business relationships with payors and purchasers;
- creating network alliances with hospitals and medical groups;
- inspiring staff concern for quality and customer service;
- reassuring anxious physicians, the board, and the public; and
- refocusing on improving the health of the community.

Healthcare executives must learn to balance the yin and yang of their roles. As *leaders*, they must inspire caregivers and support workers to be value-driven. As *managers*, these same health executives must achieve sustained profitability in a very unstable, low-margin business. Reengineering has challenged healthcare. Innovative management initiatives such as patient-focused care have reduced unproductive time and redundant management positions but have resulted in downsizing the very people who did the reengineering.

More than in the past, the challenge of healthcare leadership in the millennium will be substantial. In a downsized hospital or health system, employee paranoia is already widespread. There are fewer middle managers to defuse rumors, communicate with employees, and reinforce the message of change. Physicians are coping with declining net income and increased managed care controls. Tensions between primary care physicians and subspecialty physicians are a volcano of resentment in some healthcare organizations. Once compliant boards of trustees will set explicit performance goals for its senior executives for profitability, quality, and customer service.

Jeff Goldsmith (1994) used the analogy of "driving a nitroglycerin truck" to describe the volatility of creating a sustained business partnership between a hospital and physicians. In the twenty-first century, leadership may be likened to driving a spaceship through an asteroid field at light speed while trying to rely on outdated radar systems to avoid collisions and reach the destination. In the future, healthcare management decisions must be made at a high rate of speed, and teammates must function autonomously but with complete coordination—even though the navigation systems are primitive.

This is a high-risk assignment. Stephen R. Covey, author of *The Seven Habits of Highly Effective People* and *Principle-Centered Leadership*, states that the challenges of this new era "will only be achieved by leaders, be they emerging or seasoned, who have the vision, courage, and humility to constantly learn and grow" (Covey 1996, 149).

Today's healthcare leaders have a blind spot—they do not learn lessons from other industries. Most hospital and health system executives are graduates of specialized healthcare management programs who have never worked in any other field. Healthcare needs inspiration from many other economic sectors that have learned to cope with foreign competitors, price competition, and relentless demands from the market for better, faster, and cheaper products and services. Executives in many other industries have learned to adapt to market changes without losing their corporate values or customer-first priorities.

Healthcare should need no reminder to be a value-driven industry.

REFERENCES

Anders, G. 1996. "Who Pays the Cost of Cut-Rate Heart Care?" *Wall Street Journal* (October 15): B1, B12.

Barner, R. 1996. "The New Millenium Workplace: Seven Changes That Will Challenge Managers—and Workers." *The Futurist* (2): 14–18.

Birchall, D., and L. Lyons. 1995. *Creating Tomorrow's Organizations: Unlocking the Benefits of Future Work.* London: Pitman Publishing.

Bridges, W. 1996. "Leading the De-Jobbed Organization." In *The Leader of the Future,* edited by F. Hesselbein, M. Goldsmith, and R. Beckhard, 11–18. San Francisco: Jossey-Bass.

Coile, R. C., Jr. 1996. "The Twenty-First Century Management Team." *Healthcare Executive* 11 (1): 10–13.

Covey, S. R. 1996. "Three Roles of the Leader in the New Paradigm." In *The Leader of the Future,* edited by F. Hesselbein, M. Goldsmith, and R. Beckhard, 149–60. San Francisco: Jossey-Bass.

Davis, S. 1987. *Future Perfect.* New York: Addison-Wesley Publishing Co.

Farson, R. 1996. *Management of the Absurd: Paradoxes in Leadership.* New York: Simon & Schuster.

Goldsmith, J. 1994. "Driving the Nitroglyercin Truck." *Healthcare Forum Journal.*

Heskett, J. L., and L. A. Schlesinger. 1996. "Leaders Who Shape Performance-Oriented Culture." In *The Leader of the Future,* edited by F. Hesselbein, M. Goldsmith, and R. Beckhard, 112–19. San Francisco: Jossey-Bass.

Hesselbein, F. 1996. "The 'How-to-Be' Leader." In *The Leader of the Future,* edited by F. Hesselbein, M. Goldsmith, and R. Beckhard, 121–24. San Francisco: Jossey-Bass.

James, J. 1996. *Thinking in the Future Tense.* New York: Simon & Schuster.

Jones, D. 1996. "Setting Diversity's Foundation in the Bottom Line." *USA Today* (October 15): 4B.

Lancaster, H. 1996. "Can a Fast-Tracker Vision His Career in a New Ecosystem?" *Wall Street Journal* (October 8): B1.

Neuborne, E. 1996. "Meeting Goals Just Got More Rewarding." *USA Today* (October 15): 1B.

Pollard, C. W. 1996. *The Soul of the Firm.* Grand Rapids, MI: Zondervan Publishing Company.

Smith, D. K. 1996. "The Following Part of Leading." In *The Leader of the Future,* edited by F. Hesselbein, M. Goldsmith, and R. Beckhard, 199–208. San Francisco: Jossey-Bass.

3

Reassessing Reengineering

Here's what happened in reengineering . . . . Hospitals adopted the concept and implemented downsizing without changing their core processes. Quality problems soon surfaced, and many hospitals restaffed their reengineered units. These disappointments were inevitable unless the organizations were committed to fundamental change.

  —Steve Gray, Chi Systems, Ann Arbor, Michigan

C riticizing reengineering is almost as popular as actually applying this widely used management approach. Michael Hammer, one of America's top management experts responsible for the once-vaunted reengineering strategy, is now advising organizations how to move "beyond reengineering" (Hammer 1996). Hospitals, health systems, HMOs, and large medical groups have systematically applied reengineering to a variety of clinical and administrative functions. Many organizations have realized significant cost savings but have experienced a backlash of unanticipated "human costs" to morale, leadership, and innovation.

  In too many companies, reengineering has been not only a great success but also a great failure (Hall, Rosenthal, and Wade 1993). At the core of the criticism is the charge that reengineering has become just another management fad like zero-base budgeting or intraprenuership and has not produced lasting change. A national study of reengineering in 100 companies showed that projects could yield improvements of 15 to 20 percent in business processes, but the overall results often produced less than 5 percent in the overall business unit's net bottom-line performance.

Healthcare organizations have interpreted reengineering as downsizing, and layoffs have been widespread. According to Challenger, Gray & Christmas, a Chicago-based outplacement firm, some 23,910 workers and managers were laid off between 1993 to 1996 (Greene 1996). The average hospital shed 123 employees in this period. But layoffs are only the most visible outcome of the nationwide reengineering effort in America's hospitals and health systems. Promoters of reengineering argue that problems experienced in implementation are only part of the learning curve and that, in many cases, reengineering was not allowed to go far enough to make fundamental changes in the processes and culture of the organization.

A CONFUSION OF REENGINEERING TERMS

Reengineering has been blamed—not always fairly—for massive layoffs. There are a number of management methods now being applied to increase organizational efficiency. It is easy to get confused by the multiple management concepts swirling around reengineering. Here is a quick definition of terms:

- *Restructuring* is the process of modifying the formal organization and the relationships of its business units. Examples of restructuring include flattening the organization by removing excess layers of management structure or creating customer-focused units around categories of customers, such as hospitals, HMOs, or physician groups.
- *Business process reengineering* rethinks how work is done and radically reorders the functions and tasks performed by managers and workers. Examples of business process reengineering include multidisciplinary product development teams or just-in-time inventory systems.
- *Downsizing* is aimed at reducing labor costs. While downsizing can be a result of business process reengineering, it is more narrowly focused. Examples of downsizing include rightsizing a hospital or service unit to meet expected demand under managed care, or reducing the number of RNs by substituting other categories of lesser-trained caregivers.
- *TQM,* or *total quality management*, is the widely adopted set of quality improvement processes also known as *continuous quality improvement*.
- *Benchmarking* is an organizational improvement process that uses "best in breed" performance standards from a variety of sources to adopt new practices or improve existing processes. (Allcorn et al. 1996, 6)

Today, reengineering is being refocused on growth strategies, such as growing market share, developing new products, and improving customer satisfaction and repeat business. Companies are realizing that product performance and product consistence—satisfying customers—is becoming as important as, or more important than, cost (Moskal 1996, 24). Hospitals and health systems are now using the methods of reengineering clinical pathways to grow services in ambulatory care, home health, and the continuum of care (Greene 1996).

FROM PANACEA TO PARANOIA

At the start of the 1990s, excitement ran high among hospitals and health systems about the potential for reengineering to slash labor costs, shorten length of stay, and reduce support costs. The private sector experience had been very positive: Some companies had achieved cost reductions of 20 to 35 percent and improvements of 40 to 50 percent in process time (Hall, Rosenthal, and Wade 1993, 119). Michael Hammer's 1990 management bestseller, *Reengineering the Corporation*, was a primer for a business revolution (Hammer 1990). The targets for process reengineering were the bloated bureaucracies of underworked middle managers and high-paid vice presidents, while labor toiled away using tools and systems that often harkened back to Henry Ford's production lines of the 1920s.

Healthcare, with labor costs historically consuming more than 50 percent of the expense budget, was a prime target for reengineering. By 1995, some 56 percent of hospitals nationwide reported having implemented at least five cost reductions in the prior two years (Bebiak 1995). Many hospitals implemented job restructuring or work redesign, clinical pathways, nonclinical expense reductions, and layoffs. But the overall results were disappointing. A majority of hospitals achieved less than a 4 percent reduction in their costs to show for all the reengineering efforts. Employing a broader combination of work redesign and clinical pathways yielded somewhat better results—but with a cost reduction still under 10 percent. Worse yet, healthcare executives worried that reengineering could lead to reductions in quality.

Complicating reengineering's image problem is the popular link between downsizing and reengineering. Bring in the consultants and out go the workers, usually after the frontline troops and supervisors designed more efficient processes that contributed to their own layoffs. Fair or not, it is easy to understand the paranoia of nursing staff and department managers after dozens of healthcare reengineering programs have led to staffing reductions.

Perhaps hospitals were naive about introducing reengineering. Huge layoffs at Fortune 500 companies were a hint of what lay ahead for hospitals and health systems who took the path of reengineering and wound up mostly downsizing without much change in core processes. In fact, recent research suggests that American industry actually gained about 8 million new jobs in the 1990s, creating 40 million new positions as 32 million jobs were eliminated (Dentzer 1996). Reengineering is a much more comprehensive approach than downsizing. It involves a fundamental reassessment of every major production and support process in the organization and often generates radical prescriptions for change.

Introducing reengineering to healthcare has required some adaptation, as shown in Figure 3.1. Hospitals and health systems operate under a heavy blanket of state and federal regulation, where staffing ratios and the size of doorways are often prescribed by law. Physicians' independent status has meant that reengineers must coax cooperation from the doctors if significant changes were to be made in clinical or support processes such as materials management. Nursing initially cooperated enthusiastically with reengineering, often taking the lead in pilot projects. But nursing leadership turned to resistance when many reengineering projects resulted in substantial nursing layoffs.

REENGINEERING RECONSIDERED—THE SECOND WAVE

Today, reengineering is being reintroduced in a second wave of healthcare projects, but this time the goals are capitation-readiness, integrated care delivery, and business growth. Managed care and the assumption of risk are the driving forces compelling healthcare organizations to build regional care networks that can manage the comprehensive health needs of large enrolled populations. Successful systems will need more resources and will use them in different configurations. In the network model, there will be multiple hospitals, hundreds of physicians, and dozens of "alternate site" providers who must cooperate in a seamless care process that satisfies patients and holds costs within a capitated budget.

To survive and grow, integrated delivery systems must:

- structure a single enterprise with a clear strategic vision;
- involve a broad range of stakeholders in redesign and reengineering;
- reconfigure the service continuum to match a population-based model;
- significantly lower costs by reengineering patient care and business processes;
- redeploy capital, technical, and human resources on a regional-market basis;
- achieve clinical integration and reduce clinical utilization where appropriate; and
- win commitment from managers and caregivers to the new patterns and processes. (Gray 1996, 3)

When done right, reengineering healthcare organizations can achieve some results to shout about. In Birmingham, Alabama, the Brookwood Medical

Figure 3.1 Strategic Approach to Reengineering Processes

Assessment	Strategy	Design	Implementation	Evaluation
Clinical program and service inventory	Opportunities for improvement	Redesign clinical pathway	Implementation program rollout	Set benchmarks
Patient care/support program analysis	Priority matrix	Reengineer processes	Implementation work teams	Performance measurement
Clinical services utilization review	Resource allocation to reengineering effort	Options for substitution	Pilot projects	Feedback to teams
Information technology	Information systems plan	Redesign info	Install info	Quantitative results
Management structure	Management audit	Restructuring	Organizational rollout	Reward/incentives

Source: Gray, S. 1996. *Reengineering for Integrated Delivery Systems.* Ann Arbor, MI: Chi Systems, 3.

Center reduced its costs by $9 million in a six-year period (Herman 1995, 19). In the process, Brookwood brought together almost 100 work groups involving 700 employees and 100 members of the medical staff. From the beginning, Brookwood CEO Gregory Burfitt built confidence from employees and managers by guaranteeing no layoffs. With strong management support, a wide number of reengineering solutions were adopted. More than one-third of the hospital's 2,400-person work force—some 873 employees—changed their jobs as a result of reengineering.

FLAWED CONCEPT OR FLAWED EXECUTION?

In how many hospitals did the following meeting take place? After calling senior and middle managers together, the CEO said:

> "We are gathered here today to talk about reducing the budget of every department in this institution by 25 percent. I have no plan to present to you, no Ross Perot–style flip charts explaining what this means. That's because the plan hasn't been developed yet. You're the people who will do it." (Lumsdon 1994, 24).

Get a grip! The experience to date by healthcare organizations across the United States confirms both successes and failures from reengineering. There have been enough lessons learned to rewrite the book on reengineering, to improve the success rate, and to reduce backlash and adverse consequences. More fundamental issues about reengineering that have been raised include:

- projects too narrowly focused;
- lack of a long-term perspective;
- inadequate commitment or shifting priorities from top management;
- psychological and political disruptions; and
- failure to make extraordinary efforts to achieve potential gains.

Reengineering guru Michael Hammer, in his third book on this topic, *Beyond Reengineering*, originally believed that "Reengineering is the radical redesign of businesses for dramatic improvement—and the most important word is 'radical'" (Hammer 1996). Now Hammer believes the key is *process*, a perspective that turns an organization "sideways" to look at the core functions performed everywhere across the enterprise. A process perspective is holistic, as opposed to modern management's emphasis on tasks, which disintegrates the organization. This distinction between *part* and *whole* is fundamental to understanding how reengineering should work and why it has failed when managers focused on familiar tasks instead of harder-to-understand core processes.

An important problem—"turf"—was under-recognized in implementing reengineering. Organizational domains were structured around functional tasks, such as accounting, admitting, and food service, but nobody managed processes that cut across many organizational subunits. Frontline workers were often given new, broader responsibilities—but little training and no change in authority. Reengineering threw out the old organizational chart. But no one was in charge of implementation: It was not part of anyone's job description, and it was seldom rewarded by the organization's compensation system. In too many organizations, reengineering was an orphan.

One-shot improvements, says Michael Hammer, even if dramatic, are of little lasting value (Hammer 1996, 17). A number of hospitals and health systems that set performance benchmarks and downsized to meet them ran into a wall when asked to meet the next year's benchmarks. They had used their best ideas the first year, with little left to cut in the second one without seriously compromising quality or service. These limited-scope applications demonstrate the need for reengineering and benchmarking to focus on *best practices*, not just *best indicators* (Greeson and Lowenhaupt 1996). A process-centered organization must continuously experiment and achieve continuous performance improvement. It must seek and reward innovation not once a year but on an everyday basis.

Michael Hammer now believes that the single most important word in reengineering is *customer*. The customer does not see or care about the company's organizational chart or policy manual. To the customer, the company is defined by the way in which it delivers services or products. From a process perspective, the healthcare organization must start with the patient and work backwards to reengineer processes to meet consumer needs. Today's healthcare customers have choices, with 50 percent of hospital beds standing empty, 10 to 20 HMOs competing in most markets, and a nationwide surplus of more than 100,000 physicians.

Healthcare organizations that design their core processes around the customer may take many nontraditional approaches to patient services such as scheduling, admitting, food service, surgery, or nursing care. Hospitals, medical groups, and HMOs must "think customer" for reengineering to succeed in its ultimate goal—to attract and retain customers. All other market demands, such as cost efficiency, quality, and access, can be understood in terms of putting the patient first.

REENGINEERING THE CORPORATE CULTURE

Corporate culture—"the way things are done around here"—may be the most difficult barrier to successful reengineering. When a process changes, it threatens the status quo. More than jobs and skills change. Workers and managers must change their styles—the way in which they think and behave, and their attitudes—all that they think is important (Hammer 1995, 117). A new process needs new people. Reengineering business processes also requires reengineering people, and resistance can be expected. Workers feel threatened, as do managers, who fear loss of authority and responsibility. Their paranoia about reengineering is natural. In too many organizations, the term *reengineering* is a code word for downsizing and layoffs.

Top management has the ability to change the corporate culture, with sustained support and incentives to reinforce the new direction. But lack of management commitment can be fatal to reengineering's acceptance by the organization. A "Dilbert" cartoon on corporate life showed the boss telling Dilbert, the middle manager, "I just read this great book about how to 'reengineer' our business process. Everybody's doing it. We'd better jump under the bandwagon before the train leaves the station. I'm putting you in charge." The boss adds, "If you need any management support, you know where to go" (Hammer 1995, xii).

Reengineering work processes cannot ultimately succeed unless the core values and vision are also reengineered. Many healthcare organizations have followed the practice of summarizing their corporate values on small plastic-coated pocket cards. But by themselves, the cards cannot really effect new attitudes or behaviors. Changing the corporate culture requires such actions as:

- putting top priority on the desired changes;
- communicating new values in a fresh, distinctive way;
- reconstructing the budget to support new processes;
- openly monitoring performance;
- creating a new performance reward system aligned with reengineering goals;
- stressing that top managers "walk the talk" in personal dedicated commitment;
- continuously improving process and never being satisfied with performance; and
- aiming for sustained long-term commitment to the new behaviors and processes.

TEN STRATEGIES TO REENGINEER REENGINEERING

"No pain, no gain" has been the slogan of many reengineering programs. But in too many healthcare organizations, the process of reengineering was painful and the results yielded no sustained benefit. It is clear that downsizing, driven by restructuring and business process reengineering, can lead to little process improvement and unintended declines in organizational performance (Allcorn et al. 1996). With almost ten years of experience in the private sector and healthcare industry, reengineering has been tried often enough to know what works and the likely problems that must be overcome.

To persuade hospitals and health systems to launch a fresh wave of reengineering initiatives, it will be necessary to change the processes and goals drastically. Set goals higher! In some hospitals, setting "stretch goals" has led to high-level performance improvements. In Connecticut, the Middlesex Hospital set a stretch goal of reducing costs by 25 percent and achieved 15 percent in the first year—a savings of more than $10 million. Defending his high goal, Middlesex CEO Robert Kiely says: "How many times can you freeze wages, leave positions unfilled or make draconian cuts?" (Lumsdon 1994, 26).

Here are ten important strategies for improving the scope, depth, and effect of reengineering healthcare processes:

Strategy #1—Be Vision-Driven

There must be a call to mission and vision—a set of higher purposes and priorities—to motivate managers and employees to reengineer. If the goal is simply to improve the bottom line, only those senior managers whose bonuses are tied to profitability are likely to embrace reengineering enthusiastically. Goals like quality, reinvestment in new facilities or equipment, patient-centered care, and expanded community services can be compelling arguments for making reengineering work.

Strategy #2—Set Stretch Goals

Setting high goals for reengineering will have a galvanizing, empowering effect on the organization. Michael Hammer cautions that "being timid in redesign" is one of the easiest ways to shortchange reengineering's potential (Hammer 1995, 24). Setting stretch goals—also known as "big, hairy, audacious goals" (BHAGs)—creates a climate for clean-slate innovative solutions in an uncritical idea-generating process.

Strategy #3—Focus on Clinical Costs

It is imperative that clinicians and financial managers cooperate in planning and implementing reengineering projects (Meyer and Feingold 1995). Developing clinical paths must include "costing" the resources if the projects are to be comprehensively evaluated. Many clinical pathways lack sufficient detail to complete a thorough financial analysis. Costs must be addressed explicitly, not implicitly, as is often done.

Strategy #4—Implement a Strategic Plan

In the face of many possible reengineering targets, several hospitals have been tempted to "let a thousand flowers bloom," as the Chinese saying goes. This approach misses the opportunity to align reengineering with organizational strategies, financial priorities, and critical market changes. Strategic plans for reengineering lay out the objectives, methods, implementation steps, staff responsibilities, and benchmark indicators for evaluation. One mid-Atlantic hospital, Jersey Shore Medical Center, developed 60 redesign plans that covered the hospital's many departments, satellite operations, and teaching activities—and achieved a cost reduction of 14 percent on the way toward a stretch goal of 25 percent (Lumsdon 1995).

Strategy #5—Implement Benchmarking

Reengineering in the health field is more complex than simply making comparisons with other service industries. Because approximately 75 to 85 percent of all in-hospital costs are related to patient care, the focus should be on clinical reengineering. Thousands of clinical pathways have been developed nationwide in the past ten years in hospitals and leading health systems, and a growing body of outcomes research is now available on the effect of clinical improvement programs. To assist this analysis, benchmarks of clinical performance can be identified from competitive markets and "best in breed" organizations.

Strategy #6—Invest in Information Technology

No one will ever know if reengineering works without detailed performance assessment. Substantial investments in information technology are needed before many hospitals and health systems can calculate whether reengineering is meeting its goals. The most difficult aspect of measuring reengineering's effect will be to link clinical events with cost data. The process used to develop clinical pathways must develop a financial model—a "charge/cost model"—that captures and integrates the data for performance analysis (Meyer and Feingold 1995, 36).

Strategy #7—Establish Trust

There must be trust between management and rank-and-file for reengineering to gain acceptance and whole-hearted cooperation. This means candid communication with no surprises and an "open books" policy about results (Bebiak 1995, 9). Trust can be established and maintained when middle management and frontline workers are part of the planning and decision-making process from the beginning. Trust can be won when rewards are shared with all participants, not just senior management. And trust can be believed when top management demonstrates its priority to patient care, not just financial results.

Strategy #8—Promise No Layoffs

Assuming trust to be a critical success factor, then a strong "no layoffs" human resources policy must be clear from the outset of the reengineering program. This dramatically reduces paranoia and resistance and shifts the incentive structure to reward process innovation. With a management guarantee of retraining and alternative employment for any displaced workers, middle management and frontline employees can apply themselves freely to radical redesign concepts.

Strategy #9—Use Incentives

To achieve and sustain performance improvement, it is essential to support the change initiatives with "new pay" programs that are aligned with the business strategies and work process improvements. A national compensation survey by the Hay Group found that one-third of hospitals are restructuring their pay systems to incent performance and teamwork (Farrell and Pagoaga 1995). Incentives can include merit pay, noncash recognition, spot cash awards, and predetermined incentives. Although merit pay programs still cover some 60 percent of hospitals, more than 40 percent of healthcare institutions are rewarding workers and managers with recognition and bonuses.

Strategy #10—Share Values

Reengineering is a process of building consensus around new organizational goals and the best methods to achieve them. Commitment can result in a shared belief that the organization must change to survive—not just to add 3 percent to the bottom line. All key stakeholders—board, medical staff, administration, and employees—must accept the need for change and share a belief they are doing the right thing for patients and the community.

THE "VISION" THING: LINKING REENGINEERING TO MISSION AND VALUES

Reengineering the organization begins with renewing the vision, values, and mission. One large health system recently replaced their old mission statement with a new one: "To improve the health of the community." Despite some staff skepticism, this new direction has been widely supported by physicians and board members. But it will never be fully accepted if top management does not maintain a continuously high priority for this bold redirection of the organization.

Companies that are built to last have achieved continuing success despite many changes and trends in their industries. These companies have enduring values that infuse the corporate culture and can be sustained despite changes in top management over time. Healthcare organizations, with their origins as social institutions, have special reason to be value driven. Numerous healthcare organizations have found the concept of distinguishing their core values from their practices and strategies to be critical to maintaining their sense of social mission while adapting to the dramatic changes and increasing competitiveness of the world around them (Collins and Porras 1994, xviii).

"Patient-centered care" has been a popular reengineering concept for almost a decade, invented in 1989 by Chicago-based Booz, Allen and implemented by hundreds of U.S. hospitals. Over half of the healthcare executives in a national poll used the term to describe their reengineering efforts (Lumsdon and Hagland 1993). Some healthcare executives have launched multimillion-dollar patient-focused projects, such as the Genesys Health System of Flint, Michigan, which is building a 439-bed facility that will replace four existing hospitals. The project will "shift the paradigm" with a 500-acre master-planned facility, including a huge community sports and fitness complex.

A number of hospitals and systems share such an interest in patient-focused care, although few are making such large capital investments. Some 160 of them have banded together to share information through the Patient-Focused Care Association, based in Atlanta, Georgia. Although many patient-centered experiments have achieved goals such as reduced length of stay, few have resulted in more fundamental organizational transformations. "At least we haven't killed anybody," says Booz, Allen consultant Phil Lathrop, who worked with many of the pioneers in patient-centered care (Weber and Weber 1994, 48). But the projects have made satisfying gains in patient perceptions and staff/physician support.

Remember "guest relations"? A decade ago, this management strategy was widely adopted by U.S. hospitals, and at the height of its popularity in the mid- to late-1980s, some 4,000 hospitals trained their managers and front-line staff in the methods and techniques of customer satisfaction. But where is that emphasis on customers and service today? Many hospitals have quietly shelved their training efforts to improve hospitality management. As a result of widespread layoffs across the hospital industry, morale is low and resentment is smoldering among the rank-and-file. It should be no surprise that postdownsizing healthcare staffers would resent any attempt by management to add to their workload with new demands for service improvement.

Service management consultant Kristine Peterson of K.E. Peterson, Inc, in Chicago reminds us that the word *patient* is derived from the Latin word *patic*, meaning "to suffer or endure" (Peterson 1988, 8). Peterson argues that patients are customers and healthcare organizations are in the service business. Customer service is a business strategy—indeed, a new business vision—that will be essential for success in the next five years. Patients are demanding more choices, and they are getting their way. HMOs are broadening their provider networks, reducing the hassle factors and gatekeepers, and making it easier for patients to see specialists. Employers are demanding report-card data from HMOs on enrollee satisfaction. This is reviving a customer-first orientation. But a new guest-relations effort will not succeed unless top management demonstrates a long-term commitment and rebudgets its priorities to support patient-centered care.

LOOKING FORWARD: THIS NOISY PROCESS IS FAR FROM OVER

Reengineering healthcare has been a noisy process that has often pitted nurse and physician caregivers against managers and financial officers. At issue are fundamental priorities. Should the organization put patients first and spend whatever it takes to meet their needs? Or should it recognize the realities of managed care controls and government discounts and cut costs to the bone? These extreme positions have often framed the debate over the suitability of reengineering to improve the efficiency of healthcare services.

Love it or hate it, there is no question that reengineering is necessary. Everyone needs to understand that today's healthcare organization is a "burning platform" whose structural costs are being systematically reduced by government healthcare cuts, managed care, and capitation (Greeson and Lowenhaupt 1996, 10). Steve Gray, senior vice president of Chi Systems, Inc., a national healthcare consulting firm based in Ann Arbor, Michigan, believes that healthcare organizations have just scratched the surface in process reengineering. Chi Systems has worked with 25 healthcare clients in reengineering projects totaling $400 million in savings (Gray 1996). He believes the concept of reengineering is sound and the application in healthcare is needed. But how can healthcare organizations avoid past mistakes and use the tools of reengineering to build sustainable organizations?

Reengineering is not a fad. It is the process of continuous improvement that is essential in vision-driven healthcare organizations that seek to last well into the twenty-first century. Reengineering is much more than downsizing. Healthcare executives should prepare to use reengineering to respond to the next management trend from the Fortune 500—"upsizing" to grow the company, raise revenues, and boost profits. It will not be easy. Consultants report that only one in five American companies experienced real growth last year (*The Economist* 1996, 61). Think about it—reengineering for growth!

Where do efforts like reengineering and patient-centered care go from here? The answer is: Back to work! These concepts are not merely trendy. They are fundamental change processes that have not had enough time to mature. Already, reengineering and patient-centered care are evolving toward a greater focus on quality and patient satisfaction, with less emphasis on pure cost cutting. A clear management priority on quality resonates with the values of physicians, caregiving staffers, and middle management. Reengineering clinical care and support processes for quality will also yield significant cost-savings through improved coordination, faster through-put, and less rework to repair mistakes.

In the short term, in the next one to three years, reengineering should be targeted to improve patient satisfaction radically. The report-card movement will reward healthcare providers and health plans that can show high-level customer ratings. A midrange strategy for the next three to five years is to raise quality levels for the top 20 diagnoses to compare favorably with "best in breed" benchmarks, which will be added to report cards in the future. In the long term, over the next five to ten years, reengineering will become a transformational strategy when it is applied to the management of enrolled populations covered by capitation. Concepts like disease management and clinical pathways can be linked with risk management, community health education, continuum of care substitution, and population-based planning to create a very different health delivery system for the twenty-first century.

STRATEGIES FOR IMPLEMENTATION

Here are some preliminary answers and new directions:

Strategy #1—Reduce Variation

For too long, healthcare has resisted standardization. Physicians and nurses have argued that patient care must be customized to every patient. But reengineering is demonstrating that, through clinical pathways and standardized care plans, it can be. A reduction of 10 percent in variation of length of stay, for example, may yield cost savings of 20 to 25 percent by eliminating costly outliers.

Strategy #2—Benchmark with the "Best in Breed"

Prepare for a managed care world by using indicators from advanced markets and successful healthcare organizations. Benchmark standards are now available from consulting firms, actuaries, professional associations, and group purchasing organizations such as VHA and Premier.

Strategy #3—Innovate Continuously

The road to organizational improvement begins with creating a comfort zone for experimentation. Senior management must encourage innovations in service delivery and support processes. A truly innovative organization supports a culture of risk-taking, industry-setting practices, and testing of new models.

Strategy #4—Use Incentives

Performance rewards must be substantial and symbolic to change behavior. Incentives must equal at least 15 percent of compensation to achieve real changes in behavior. Rewards can be symbolic (non-cash) as well as financial to send a message that the organization appreciates its "pioneers" and "early adopters."

Strategy #5—Leave Money on the Table

Too often, change in healthcare organizations is delayed while management waits for the market to shift. That is not the way to become an industry or market leader. Many hospitals and health systems are beginning to organize for capitation but hesitate to treat every patient as if they were capitated. Once a market reaches HMO penetration of 15 percent, the future is clear. When it reaches 25 percent penetration, the war is over. Starting now may mean leaving money on the table, but the organization will be fully prepared for capitation and the new market when it arrives. Don't wait for the future. It's here.

REFERENCES

Allcorn, S., H. S. Baum, M. A. Diamond, and H. Stein. 1996. *The Human Cost of a Management Failure: Organizational Downsizing at General Hospital.* Westport, CN: Quorum Books.

Bebiak, J. 1995. "Process Design and Discipline Are Critical to Cost-Reduction Success." *Strategies for Healthcare Excellence* 8 (7): 8–11.

Collins, J. C., and J. I. Porras. 1994. *Built to Last: Successful Habits of Visionary Companies.* New York: HarperBusiness.

Dentzer, S. 1996. "The Fallout from Dumping Workers." *U.S. News & World Report* (March 11): 58.

The Economist. 1996. "Upsizing." (February 10): 61.

Farrell, J. P., and J. A. Pagoaga. 1995. "Making Change Pay." *Hospitals & Health Networks* 69 (17): 26–33.

Gray, S. 1996. "Reengineering for Integrated Delivery Systems." Ann Arbor, MI: Chi Systems, Inc., 1–6.

Greene, J. 1996. "Retooling Without Layoffs." *Modern Healthcare* 26 (9): 76–82.

Greeson, D., and M. Lowenhaupt. 1996. "A Benchmark Strategy." *Physician Executive* 22 (10): 10–15.

Hall, G., J. Rosenthal, and J. Wade. 1993. "How to Make Reengineering Really Work." Harvard Business Review. (November/December): 119–31.

Hammer, M. 1990. *Reengineering the Corporation.* New York: HarperBusiness.

———. 1995. *The Reengineering Revolution.* New York: HarperBusiness.

———. 1996. *Beyond Reengineering: How the Process-Centered Organization Is Changing Our Work and Our Lives.* New York: HarperBusiness.

Herman, J. 1995. "Restructuring the Health Care Delivery System." *Health Systems Review* 28 (2): 18–29.

Lumsdon, K. 1994. "Want to Save Millions?" *Hospitals & Healthcare Networks* 68 (21): 24–32.

———. 1995. "Mean Streets: Five Lessons from the Front Lines of Reengineering." *Hospitals & Health Networks* 69 (19): 44–52.

Lumsdon, K., and M. Hagland. 1993. "Mapping Care." *Hospitals & Health Networks* 67 (21): 24–40.

Meyer, J., and M. Feingold. 1995. "Integrating Financial Modeling and Patient Care Reengineering." *Healthcare Financial Management* 49 (2): 33–40.

Moskal, B. S. 1996. "Reengineering Without Downsizing." *Business Week* (February 16): 23–24, 28.

Peterson, K. 1988. *The Strategic Approach to Quality Service in Health Care.* Rockville, MD: Aspen Publishers, Inc.

Weber, D., and A. Weber. 1994. "Reshaping the American Hospital." *Healthcare Forum Journal* 37 (5): 47–57.

4

Making Integration Work: Implementing Vertical, Horizontal, and Virtual Integration Strategies

Is vertical integration a rapidly fading rose?
—Dean Coddington, "Vertical Integration:
Is the Bloom Off the Rose?" (1996, 42)

Vertical integration is not dead, but the concept of a "one-stop shopping center" for healthcare is coming under heavy fire. Critics charge that vertical integration is just a costly strategy to fill beds and bail out unneeded hospitals (Coddington 1996). Hospitals and health systems are aggressively purchasing physician practices, but many are losing money on their doctors, some as much as $1 million per month per 100 primary care physicians (Beckham 1996). Although integration has the potential to control costs, Steve Shortell's landmark study of healthcare systems integration, *Remaking Health Care in America*, shows that few healthcare systems can actually demonstrate cost savings (Shortell et al. 1996).

In trend-setting California, the Kaiser health system is abandoning its vertically integrated model to reduce overhead and better compete with network-model HMOs like Foundation/HSI and PacifiCare/FHP. Kaiser is closing its flagship hospitals in Oakland and Los Angeles and contracting out for beds. Last year, FHP divested its hospitals and spun off its staff-model medical group. Foundation Health, a Sacramento-based HMO, is also divesting its primary care physician network. Burbank-based Unihealth is selling hospitals and acquiring medical groups outside of its core market in Southern California. Unihealth sees a high-growth future as a management services organization (MSO) for physician networks.

Are vertical healthcare integration strategies a failed concept? Not yet, but symptoms of distress are widespread:

- More than 3,000 physician-hospital organizations (PHOs) have been organized, but few have capitated HMO contracts.
- Some 60 percent of U.S. hospitals have purchased physician practices averaging annual subsidies of $20,000 to $50,000, and more.
- Some hospitals are divesting HMOs, citing financial losses and retaliation from competing plans.
- Most of the large integrated delivery systems (IDSs) in the nation do not have a fully integrated information system.
- Vertically integrated delivery systems cannot demonstrate better clinical outcomes.

Today, there are about 270 asset-merged IDSs and more than 500 affiliated integrated delivery networks (IDNs). To make the picture more confusing, many IDSs have system-owned hospitals involved in local or regional IDNs. The traditional focus of integrated systems is achieving cost economies of scale, such as group purchasing. But that strategy has limitations. Increasing revenues is predominantly a local activity, and as the locus of control shifts to the local or regional market level, networks will take a leading role in contracting (revenue strategies) and a greater role in reducing costs and rationalizing services (expense strategies).

FIVE STAGES OF INTEGRATION

The process of becoming a fully integrated delivery system is evolutionary, not revolutionary. Many IDSs and IDNs are not sufficiently mature to have gained the financial and clinical benefits of integration. Some new systems find that the additional costs of creating a corporate hierarchy, and the system's constraints on local decision making, actually increase their costs. Vertically integrated systems have the potential to control costs but often lack the tools and management discipline necessary to succeed.

Research conducted by PCFA, an Atlanta-based consulting firm, suggests that true integration proceeds through five stages (Leander and Ewing 1996). The PCFA study is another overlay on the concept of the five stages of market evolution.

Stage 1—Stabilization

In this early phase, the goal of integration is to gain control over individual system components through a cohesive vision and leadership structure. Hospitals, physician practices, and other health systems are acquired, sometimes in a reactive process with little strategic foresight. Managed care relationships are fragmented and even competitive between facilities. Operational performance can actually decrease during this period, as costs rise to cover corporate overhead, legal and consulting services, and acquisition of additional system components.

Stage 2—Consolidation

A system gradually emerges in this phase, with consistency gained over key components such as management staffing, finance, human resources, and strategic planning. Physician practices are still semiautonomous but are linked into a common information network, while a regional MSO is created to manage the practices. Market share strategies are pursued by consolidating all contracting decisions at corporate headquarters. A strategic plan for information systems lays the groundwork for future consolidation around vendors, hardware, and software. Some cost savings are achieved as management levels are collapsed, and performance gains are acquired from other "low-hanging fruit" strategies such as standardization of purchasing and eliminating variations in staffing levels.

Stage 3—Rationalization

This is a more difficult phase for a system, as changes are pushed deeper into the organization and political issues arise. More substantial discounts from HMOs and insurers drive the system to reduce its costs radically. The system rethinks bringing services closer to the bedside, optimizing performance, and reducing unneeded capacity. Information system spending grows, and consolidation is guided by a senior chief information officer. Physician practices are placed under capitation or other performance incentives, with a common information system. Some acquired physicians who are disgruntled with system intrusion into their practices may exit. This phase includes clinical standardization, improved customer access, and enhanced quality across all system components.

Stage 4—Regionalization

The next step is to rationalize clinical services across the system, using systemwide clinical pathways and protocols to define levels of care and system resources. Additional continuum of care settings and services may need to be acquired in this phase. Physician practices are fully merged and region-alized into multispecialty or primary care groups or both. Spending on infor-mation systems continues to increase. Business relationships with HMOs and insurers begin to improve, with multiyear contracts and capitation. Product lines are resized, consolidated, or eliminated.

Stage 5—Integration

During this final stage, true financial and clinical integration occurs. The facilities capacity of the system has been "sized" to meet the clinical needs of the enrolled or affiliated population. The core business of the system is inte-grated healthcare. Physician executives and other clinical managers focus on care management initiatives to achieve system-defined benchmarks of clini-cal outcomes and costs. Integration works to increase patient satisfaction. Consumers perceive their care as coordinated and responsive to patient expectations. The system and its HMO partners shift their strategies from market share and cost reduction to capitation and prevention and wellness. Resources are commingled across the system, as the emphasis shifts to man-aging large enrolled populations with "seamless" care and high patient satis-faction.

Stage 6—Health Integration

In addition to the five stages of integration currently seen among U.S. healthcare organizations, a sixth stage describes a vision of integration not yet achieved. This stage should be reached by 2000 in at least a few mar-kets—Sacramento, Portland, Minneapolis–St. Paul. In this stage, 75 percent or more of the population is enrolled in an HMO. Stage 6 may include further integration of providers and payors, including mergers and long-term (five-to ten-year) exclusive business relationships. Capitation is at the system level. Physician organizations are at risk to control costs and utilization, with in-centives for health promotion, patient satisfaction, reenrollment, and clinical benchmarks of quality. Enrollee health promotion and wellness strategies are the most important cost-control strategies. Enrollees are given incentives to maintain continuity in plan and provider affiliation, as well as to reduce per-sonal health risks. High-risk enrollees are under continuous care manage-ment. Early detection and prevention efforts are continuous and universal. The system is involved in a number of community-based health improvement initiatives.

NATIONAL STUDY OF HEALTHCARE INTEGRATION

A landmark national study of healthcare integration has been released by Dr. Steve Shortell and a team of researchers from Northwestern University and

KPMG–Peat Marwick. The study, published as *Remaking Health Care in America* (Shortell et al. 1996), highlights the problems and progress of achieving integration by 11 of America's best-known healthcare systems, including Baylor (Dallas), Advocate (Chicago), Fairview (Minneapolis–St. Paul), Franciscan (Pennsylvania), Henry Ford (Detroit), Mercy (Farmington Hills), Sentara (Norfolk), Sharp (San Diego), Sisters of Providence (Seattle), Sutter (Sacramento), and UniHealth (Burbank).

Even these national systems ranked well down the scale of full integration. When the four-year study began, the systems scored only 4.25 on a 7-point scale (7 = high integration). The study is a snapshot of a moving target, as all systems are moving forward in their own markets toward integration. Shortell describes an ideal "community healthcare organization" as one that provides comprehensive care to large enrolled populations and takes accountability for their health. None of the study systems yet meets the full definition of integrated.

The largest problem confounding integration that the Shortell team found in every system was fragmentation, which arose because of the value placed on autonomy, individuality, self-determination, and diversity (Bader 1996). Fragmentation raises costs and leads to "mass suboptimization." The solutions include greater stress on primary care, prevention, and best practices. The research shows the 11 systems are moving forward on various dimensions of integration but are still behind the curve on physician integration and clinical coordination. None of the study systems has an ideal information system, either. Governance and control are confounding issues. Systems must decide whether they will be centralized or decentralized, and must define the roles of subunits and subsidiaries. Boards must be constructed more explicitly to obtain the needed skill-set to lead these very large, complex systems. Shortage of the "right" talent is another barrier.

The concept of an integrated system is still experimental and evolving. Successful systems will continuously modify their structures and processes to meet market and customer needs. There is no model for governance or control. Future systems will have greater accountability for the populations and communities they serve. Data on clinical performance, enrollee health status, and customer satisfaction will be public. Providers seeking integration must take a "holographic" view of the system and its components. Some processes clearly must be consolidated, such as finance and information systems. Other processes, such as clinical coordination and physician affiliation, must be developed on the concept of "mass customization," meaning standardized for efficiency but personalized for individual needs.

Integration is a journey, not a destination. Systems will evolve according to the stage of their market's managed care development. Ultimately, Shortell and the research team are hopeful about the prospects for successful healthcare integration. The message of *Remaking Health Care in America* is that organizations with the depth of leadership to learn from each other will succeed.

SEVEN ESSENTIAL STRATEGIES FOR INTEGRATION

After half a decade of dealmaking and restructuring, integrated healthcare organizations are still just emerging. The virtually integrated systems now becoming regional or national companies go beyond contractual vendor relationships by aligning the economic and philosophical relationships of their various partners. The result is an organization that operates and looks, to the customer and the buyer, like a seamless integrated organization.

More mature, sophisticated patterns of integration are evolving as managed care penetration rises in local markets. Kurt Miller, a partner at Andersen Consulting in Pittsburgh, states: "There's more pressure to bring competencies together at a competitive price" (Droste 1996, 1). In Stage 3 markets with more than 15 percent HMO penetration, the arrival of capitation and price competition is driving integration strategies that will meet buyer demands for large, decentralized provider networks capable of assuming risk and delivering comprehensive health services to large enrolled populations.

Strategy #1—Market Growth/Dominance

Integration is not just a cost strategy. It's a revenue enhancer. The successful integrated network should be *the* preferred provider in its market, so that no HMO or insurance company can sell its product without these essential providers. Aligning the leading hospitals and medical groups into a regional network should result in:

- provider-friendly contracts;
- increased revenues;
- market share gains over competitors;
- managed care contracting leverage;
- capitation with provider performance incentives;
- "brand-name" consumer recognition;
- physician affiliation preference; and
- regional consumer access.

The most important market gains may come from "growing the business." Market share gains at the expense of competitors are one way to increase volumes and revenues, but there are other strategies with which integration can facilitate market growth:

1. *Licensed products.* Successful services and specialty programs can be licensed and exported, elsewhere around the region with the net-

work or outside the local market with other providers who pay a license fee (such as specialty rehabilitation or geropsych).

2. *Bundled prices.* Package prices can be offered for services that may be provided at one or more facilities within the network (such as obstetrics).

3. *Specialty carveouts.* The network may offer specialty care services on a capitated basis at one or more facilities, such as open-heart or oncology.

4. *Fee-for-service.* Discretionary consumer spending may be attracted for health and related services (such as fitness, cosmetic surgery, or health foods).

5. *Continuum of care.* Network investments in continuum of care services can be consolidated and marketed on a regional basis (such as home health care).

6. *Direct contracting.* Local employers, business coalitions, and state governments (Medicaid) may be potential purchasers on a direct-contracting basis (such as workers' compensation or company health plan).

Strategy #2—Cost Competitiveness

The imperative for hospital cost integration is obvious—expenses are rising faster than revenues. The most recent financial performance data from the American Hospital Association's National Panel Survey shows expenses climbed 4.1 percent in the first six months of 1996 while revenues slipped from a gain of 6.2 percent in 1995 to an average of only 3.6 percent in 1996 (AHA 1996). A general slowdown is evident, driven by managed care and the growing effect of Medicare HMOs. Admissions for seniors were down by 0.6 percent, the first time in ten years that over-65 admissions have slipped. Under-65 admissions also fell, bringing overall admissions down by 0.8 percent. Inpatient days plummeted by 4.2 percent. Outpatient revenues are keeping hospitals profitable, but there are danger signs. Outpatient growth fell to 8.7 percent for the first half of 1996. As a result, hospital profits dipped from 6.0 percent in 1995 to 5.5 percent in 1996.

Academic medical centers (AMCs) have a special problem with achieving cost competitiveness. A recent study of AMCs found their costs averaging 15 to 35 percent higher than community competitors (Scott 1996). If teaching hospitals are to be successful, they must reduce their marginal costs. But cost-slashing alone won't do it. The academic centers need community allies, including consumers, community-based providers, and payors. AMCs must identify the cost of subsidizing "mission" activities such as teaching, research, and care of the poor and must enlist the aid of the market, charitable foundations, elected officials, and government.

Catholic healthcare providers will be challenged to meet the changes driven by managed care and government budget cuts. The recent round of New Covenant regional meetings sponsored by the Catholic Health Association promised Catholic providers that healthcare would be "rocked to the core" (Farren 1996). Predictions were tough, to galvanize Catholic healthcare organizations to respond to market changes before expected budget cuts from Medicare and Medicaid are enacted by Congress. Integration strategies are encouraged to make Catholic health providers cost-competitive on a local and regional basis. Some Catholic systems are consolidating to reduce the costs of corporate overhead. Kentucky-based Sisters of Charity of Nazareth is the latest system to announce affiliation discussions with Catholic Health Initiatives (CHI) of Denver (Gilfillan 1996). CHI was created through the consolidation of three major health systems with Catholic Health Corporation. It now has annual revenues of $4 billion and operates 60 hospitals and more than 50 long-term care facilities.

Strategy #3—Clinical Rationalization

The process of clinical standardization is the central management challenge of integration. Emphasis is shifting from facility-based quality improvement to systemwide or networkwide disease management of enrolled populations. Although most integrated systems and networks continue to focus on high-cost inpatient procedures, the process is already being broadened to incorporate outpatient and preventive care. As regional integrated networks take on capitation contracts for large population groups, the IDNs will confront the issue of excess capacity and uneven clinical performance. Development of clinical protocols must be on a networkwide basis, including all facilities, physicians, and levels of care.

Clinical reengineering is not easy. Peter Boland's *Redesigning Healthcare Delivery* notes that more than 70 percent of reengineering efforts in healthcare suffer from poor leadership, shortsighted downsizing, and piecemeal implementation (Boland 1996). Providers must cut costs by focusing on standardizing and improving the process of clinical care. The next generation of healthcare must shift the focus from filling hospital beds and physician waiting rooms to customer and purchaser satisfaction.

The development of disease management programs is driven by managed care. At Cedars-Sinai in Los Angeles, internist Scott Weingarten, M.D., states: "Today, commitment to quality improvement is no longer sufficient. It only gets you part of the way there" (Weber 1996, 1). After more than five years in developing clinical pathways, Cedars is committed to evidence-based guidelines. Weingarten is not discouraged that only 20 to 40 percent of medical practice today may be evidence-based. The hospital updates all of its guidelines every year with the latest medical literature.

Disease management is rapidly becoming computerized for regional and national dissemination. Cedars-Sinai is currently testing the Clinical Cost-Reduction System, a computer software program developed by VHA, a national 1,300-member healthcare association. After pilot-testing, the software has evolved into a generic pathway builder called the Clinical Pathway Constructor, which can be used to develop a wide array of clinical algorithms.

Strategy #4—Management Services Organizations

An effective MSO may be the most important building block of healthcare integration. It also may be the most difficult to organize and manage effectively. MSOs provide the infrastructure to coordinate and manage provider networks and physician groups and will provide the "single signature" authority to commit a distributed physician hospital network to a contract.

An MSO is a service company created to manage physician organizations; it may be either nonprofit or for-profit. If nonprofit, it will almost always be categorized as taxable. The MSO may own physician practices and medical office buildings and provide practice management services, staffing, billing, and information systems. The MSO is a highly flexible structure. It may manage some physician practices, while only providing management services to others. The MSO may also manage IPAs, including contracting, credentialing, medical quality review, and utilization management. The market for physician MSOs is growing dramatically. In the past five years, the number of multispecialty medical groups grew from 16,576 to 19,787, according to 1991–1995 data from the American Medical Association (Smith 1996).

There are at least four options for structuring an MSO:

1. *Hospital-owned MSO.* Many of the estimated 3,000 PHOs are managed by an MSO, which may be hospital-owned or joint-ventured with local physicians. The hospital-owned MSO may operate as a division of the hospital or health system or as an independent subsidiary. Hospital-sponsored MSOs have been criticized for lack of physician management expertise, undercapitalized MSO startups, and inadequate physician-specific information systems.

2. *Physician-owned MSO.* MSOs controlled by physician groups are expanding rapidly. The Carle Clinic in Illinois is creating a regional MSO that is providing managed care and practice management services to physician groups in neighboring Indiana, Iowa, and Wisconsin. Physician-led entities can be the most knowledgeable of any MSO model. Practice management services are constructed directly from the physicians' experience in managing their own successful group or IPA. Information systems are physician-tested and distributed to their physician members. Contracting, finance, human resources, and other

support services are designed specifically to meet the needs of physician practices. Despite these advantages, physician-owned MSOs can suffer from problems of lack of capital and the inability to grow rapidly when the MSO is expanding.

3. *Hospital-physician joint venture MSO.* Many MSOs are joint ventures, at least on paper. Physicians may share up to 50 percent of MSO governance, often without putting up a corresponding percentage of capital investment. The concept of physician-hospital joint venture should encourage an economic partnership model that aligns incentives. Shared governance may slow decision making unless the partners share a vision of the market and a compelling rationale for integration, such as capitation.

4. *Physician management company.* Investor-owned physician management companies (PMCs) offer practice management services, contracting, and a variety of support services to physician groups and IPAs. This is a national trend backed by $5 to $7 billion in Wall Street capital. Companies such as PhyCor, MedPartners/Mullikin, and FPA have acquired and managed thousands of physicians. PMCs are operating independently of hospitals in some markets, and joint venturing or providing contract management services in others.

Strategy #5—Information Systems

Information systems are the critical infrastructure for achieving clinical and economic integration. But few healthcare systems or regional networks have a fully functioning information system yet, according to a recent study by the Healthcare Financial Management Association in Chicago (HFMA 1996). The emphasis is shifting from financial to clinical data systems, and IDS managers are tackling ambulatory care before inpatient care, if possible, by aggressively implementing physician workstations with clinical systems that fit smoothly into the work flow of doctors, nurses, and other clinicians. Comprehensive order-entry systems are another high priority, to integrate the capture of financial charges and costs through the clinical data system. IDS information system managers believe that the IDS must spend 4 to 6 percent of its budget on information technology to be competitive.

The challenge of integrating competing hardware and software may be met by new solutions on the Internet. Sun Microsystems of Mountain View, California, has developed the Java operating system that creates both Internet and intranet solutions to integrate healthcare systems. The Java approach relies on low-cost computer terminals sharing computing power through Internet and proprietary electronic linkages, rather than investments in high-cost, high-powered PC-based computing.

Community health information networks (CHINs) may overcome startup problems of hardware and software incompatibility by moving to the Internet (Bazzoli 1996). The connectivity among providers will become more crucial as competition grows and information rises in importance. Internet applications by healthcare organizations are developing rapidly. Some 850 nominees have entered a competition sponsored by the National Information Infrastructure to encourage innovative use of the World Wide Web (Morrisey 1996). Physician "electronic house calls," nurse advice, and care management may all be conducted on the Net, as IDNs seek cost-effective processes for managing the "worried well" and chronically ill capitated populations (Engstrom and Brown 1996).

Strategy #6—Realign Capacity

Few integrated systems or regional networks have yet addressed their excess capacity. The cost of carrying unneeded beds and programs holds down profits and limits growth. It is also holding down HMO profits, which may lead to increased pressure from the plans on providers to close unused beds. Even in advanced Stage 5 managed care markets like Sacramento, California, there may be as many as one-third too many hospital beds still available (McGuire 1996a).

Excess capacity is a shadow over managed care contracting strategies. It forces providers to accept deeper discounts from HMOs and payors and to provide marginal revenues to subsidize the underutilized capacity. If providers had the discipline to bring capacity into balance with supply, and lessen bed availability, it would strongly increase suppliers' clout in contracting with HMOs and insurers.

Hospital closures are slowly rising for the first time since 1988. According to the American Hospital Association, the number of hospitals that stopped providing acute care services rose from 17 in 1994 to 30 in 1995 (Burda and Weissenstein 1996). Eleven of the facilities were in Texas, by far the largest affected region. Thirteen specialty hospitals, including seven psychiatric facilities, also closed. Even with the increase, this was still the second-lowest annual closure rate in more than a decade. Nearly all of the excess facilities had fewer than 200 beds. Many of these facilities are being recycled. Almost one-half have been converted to urgent care clinics, long-term care, or home health care.

For-profit hospital management companies may take the lead in eliminating excess capacity, where it strengthens regional market position or eliminates a cost center that cannot be turned around. Columbia/HCA, the nation's largest hospital chain, has plans to close seven hospitals in markets where the company operates at least one other facility (Burda and Weissenstein 1996).

In Houston, Texas, the Paracelsus Healthcare Corporation is evaluating the closure, conversion, or sale of as many as one-third of its 31 hospitals (Japsen 1996). Tight finances are driving the move. Paracelsus is trying to close an $80 million loss position. The company's eight hospitals in Los Angeles are under the knife, as are two more in Louisiana and Missouri.

Strategy #7—Managed Care Component

IDSs and IDNs need a managed care component. Nothing will accelerate the clinical and economic integration of a health system or network faster than capitation. Sharing per member per month revenues provides a compelling mandate for integration. With their combined capital and market reputation, network providers can sponsor their own managed care products or bring in a managed care partner, such as small-employer product or Medicare-risk.

Providers now sponsor more than 130 HMOs and participate in dozens of other managed care joint ventures with Blue Cross, HMOs, and insurers. According to data from SMG Marketing in Chicago, some 13.9 percent of the more than 500 IDNs in the United States have an HMO component (Henderson 1996). In North Carolina, two local health systems, North Carolina Baptist and the Carolinas HealthCare System, have teamed to buy MedCost, Inc. from Coastal Physician Group (McGuire 1996b). MedCost operates preferred provider organizations throughout the Carolinas as well as offering utilization management services to 5,000 employers across the nation representing nearly 900,000 lives.

Under new legislation, provider-sponsored networks will need their own managed care component to compete on a direct-contracting basis, without an HMO license. Physician and hospital-sponsored networks could sign up Medicare eligibles to compete with HMOs. Providers are seeking legislative access to direct contracting. HMO-provider relations have turned hostile in some advanced managed care markets. The California Public Employees Retirement System (CalPERS) has told its health plans to get along better with providers (Shinkman 1996). At issue are ten health plans that terminated providers, triggering 400 requests from CalPERS enrollees to switch plans to maintain relationships with primary care physicians.

LOOKING FORWARD: CRITICAL SUCCESS FACTORS FOR INTEGRATED SYSTEMS

Does integration actually reduce costs? Market observers believe that the savings that could potentially be realized in the system have not yet been achieved. The best conventional wisdom of integration is being tested in advanced markets like California, Oregon, and Minnesota, although there is no one successful model, even among the best-known health systems. There may never be a definitive model because dynamic competition continues to change the underlying market assumptions that guide system development (Beckham 1996). CHI, the largest of the national Catholic systems, is tailoring its local strategies to the characteristics of each subregional market.

From these advanced markets, a number of questions are being raised that suggest a new set of critical success factors for integrated healthcare systems will emerge. Key issues include:

- *Role of facilities.* Are hospitals the high-visibility "billboards" of the system or simply underutilized capital-intensive overhead?
- *Physician acquisition.* Is the high cost of physician acquisition the symptom of a flawed concept or a failure of implementation?
- *Primary care network.* Will the system still need a widely distributed network of primary care gatekeepers if consumers don't like controls on access to specialists?
- *Capitation.* Will HMOs really shift risk to providers and potentially lose control of their enrollees?
- *Specialty care.* As consumers demand access to specialists, is the answer subspecialty capitation carveouts?
- *Make or buy capacity.* "Renting" provider networks is cheaper than owning them, but will they deliver the same level of customer service and systematic cost control as system-owned components?
- *Clinical standardization.* Will physicians allow systems to dictate clinical standards and resource levels, including ambulatory and in-office care"
- *Excess capacity.* Is provider over-capacity distorting regional healthcare economics and propping up prices at higher levels?

There are no easy answers, but a pattern of "new rules" for successful integration is emerging. Critical success factors for the future include:

1. *Market dominance.* One rule of thumb for establishing market dominance is to strive for market share that is at least two times that of the nearest competitor. Large networks can offer the best regional access to the broadest enrolled population, making it attractive to the largest corporations in the market and overcoming union resistance to contracting with a single network.
2. *Customer focus.* As HMO prices stabilize, purchasers and consumers will shift their health plan choices motivated by service and satisfaction. Providers will need to look beyond their efforts to improve intraorganizational operations; they will need to focus on how their services are actually delivered to patients and the public.
3. *Physicians as full partners.* The integration imperative begins with physicians. Given the need to control clinical costs under capitation,

physician cooperation is essential. Put physicians on the system or network board, share governance fully, and make no decisions without their full participation. Healthcare integration cannot be done without them.

4. *Open-book management.* Make open communication a hallmark of the system or network, including free access to sensitive financial information. There will be few secrets anyway. Physicians, employees, and the community need to understand the integration strategy and budget and support the priority for integration.

5. *Cut when successful.* Make the tough decisions about excess capacity and clinical consolidation while profitable, then phase them in with a reasonable transition plan. Downsizing has given reengineering a bad reputation. Integration decisions made while the organization is in a "crash-dive" mode will be resented by employees and physicians. Do it now, while the organization is still able to chart its own future.

REFERENCES

American Hospital Association. 1996. "Key Trends for First-Half 1996." *Emerging Trends* 12 (3): 1–11.

Bader, B. S. 1996. "Book Review: Remaking Health Care in America." *Health System Leader* 3 (9): 26–27.

Beckham, J. D. 1996. "The IDS as Moving Target." *Healthcare Forum Journal* 39 (5): 48–54.

Bazzoli, F. 1996. "Restoring the Image of Networks." *Health Data Management* 4 (11): 39–47.

Boland, P. 1996. *Redesigning Healthcare Delivery: A Practical Guide to Re-engineering, Restructuring and Renewal.* Berkeley, CA: Boland Healthcare Inc.

Burda, D., and E. Weissenstein. 1996. "Hospital Closings Up for First Time Since 1988." *Modern Healthcare* 26 (48): 2–3.

Coddington, D. 1996. "Vertical Integration: Is the Bloom Off the Rose?" *Healthcare Forum Journal* 39 (5): 42–47.

Droste, T. M. 1996. "Virtual Organizations Emerge in Many Different Forms." *Medical Strategy Network Report* 5 (12): 1–3.

Engstrom, P., and M. S. Brown. 1996. "Electronic House Calls: New Rules, New Roles as Healers Swarm the Net." *Medicine on the Net* 2 (12): 1–8.

Farren, S. 1996. "The Ministry Can Survive Despite the Coming Cuts." *Catholic Health World* 12 (21): 1, 4–5.

Gilfillan, S. 1996. "SCNHS, CHI Talking." *Catholic Health World* 12 (21): 1–7.

Healthcare Financial Management Association. 1996. "Study Finds IDSs Successful with Data Integration Are Similiar." *Report on Healthcare Information Management* 3 (9): 1–3.

Henderson, J. 1996. "Aligned Missions of MCOs and IHNs Spark Alliances." *SMG Marketing Group Market Letter* 10 (6): 1.

Japsen, B. 1996. "Paracelsus Posts Big Loss; Sales, Closures Considered." *Modern Healthcare* 26 (48): 11, 16.

Leander, W. J., and C. S. Ewing. 1996. "An Operating Strategy for True Integration." *PFCA Review* (Summer): 2–10.

McGuire, D. 1996a. "Provider Over-Capacity Remains High Despite Managed Care." *Managed Care Outlook* 9 (24): 1–2.

———. 1996b. "Two Carolina Hospital Companies to Buy MedCost Inc. from Coastal." *Managed Care Outlook.* 9 (24): 8.

Morrisey, J. 1996. "Med Center, School Finalists for Award." *Modern Healthcare* 26 (49): 62.

Scott, K. 1996. "The New Reality: Academic Medical Centers Partner with the Community." *Health System Leader* 3 (9): 4–13.

Shinkman, R. 1996. "CalPERS Tells Plans, Providers: Get Along." *Modern Healthcare* 26 (49): 6.

Shortell, S. M., R. R. Gillies, D. A. Anderson, K. M. Erickson, and J. B. Mitchell. 1996. *Remaking Health Care in America: Building Organized Delivery Systems.* San Francisco: Jossey-Bass.

Smith, M. 1996. "Multispeciality Groups, Post-Managed Care Style." *Medical Network Strategy Report* 5 (12): 8–10.

Weber, D. O. 1996. "Cedars-Sinai, Los Angeles, Makes Progress Toward Disease State Management as the Ideal of Managed Care." *Strategies for Healthcare Excellence* 9 (12): 1–9.

5

Clinical Executives: Physicians and Nurses Create Twenty-First Century Management Teams

In a marketplace dominated by capitation and prepayment, health organizations will rediscover that the core business is patient care.
—Russell C. Coile, Jr. (1996, 1)

T he management group of twenty-first century healthcare organizations will devote at least 80 percent of its collective efforts to *managing care*. The dominance of finance and the MBA perspective in health organizations' decision making will change. Doctors and nurses will retake control of their hospitals and medical groups. Finance, strategic planning, marketing, human resources, information systems—those are all support tasks to clinical cost management and quality assurance.

In a managed care future, the core business is managing risk of enrolled populations under capitated or prepaid reimbursement arrangements. Much of the financing will be front-ended, paid in advance on per member per month rates or bundled service fees. Managing risk is different than managing a budget. In advanced Stage 4 and Stage 5 marketplaces with 25 to 40 percent HMO penetration, and more, here are multiple types of capitation/risk challenges for management teams of physician and nurse executives:

- enrollee health risk;
- inappropriate utilization patterns;

- inefficient services delivery;
- inadequate cost management;
- incomplete database or information linkages;
- insufficient care and undertreatment;
- inattentive customer service;
- inadequately credentialed provider network;
- competing economic objectives of providers;
- customer expectations of "zero defects" and state-of-the-art technology; and
- malpractice risk. (Coile 1995a)

MANAGED CARE IS DRIVING CLINICAL CARE MANAGEMENT

In the twenty-first century, the majority of physicians, nurses, and hospitals will provide services to HMO enrollees. HMOs are becoming the nation's most popular health plans (see Table 5.1). On a national basis, HMOs now enroll 63 million Americans, nearly 25 percent of the population, and HMO enrollment grew 18.7 percent in 1996, according to InterStudy, a managed care market research organization based in St. Paul, Minnesota (Hamer 1997). To maintain their revenue streams, providers have little choice but to maintain relationships with HMOs. Physicians and nurses know what happens next: Because labor costs constitute 50 percent of hospitals' operating costs, bedside caregivers—mostly nurses—will be targeted for cost reductions,

Table 5.1   Managed Care Enrollment: 1990–2000 (in millions)

Payor Type	1990	1992	1995	2000
HMO (traditional)	36	39	47	80
HMO (point-of-service)	2	5	8	20
PPO	19	26	33	18
Indemnity (managed)	80	70	59	40
Indemnity (traditional)	22	17	6	2
Medicare (non-HMO)	32	33	33	17
Medicare (HMO)	1	3	7	18
Medicaid (fee-for-service)	21	22	20	10
Medicaid (HMO)	—	—	5	20
Medical Uninsured	34	37	40	35
National Health Reform?	0	0	0	10
Totals	247	252	258	270

Source: SMG Marketing Group, SMG Market Letter, August 1993, 4; Estimates for 2000 by Health Forecasting Group, January 1995, cited in Coile, R. C., Jr. 1995. "Managed Care Outlook." *Health Trends* 7 (5): 6.

reengineering of tasks and roles, substitution of lesser-paid "nursing extenders," reduced nursing positions, and layoffs.

Peter Buerhaus of the Harvard Nursing Research Institute, identifies key consequences of the managed care squeeze on hospitals and nurses (Buerhaus 1994):

1. *Hospital resizing.* Following the pattern of private industry, hospitals will consolidate services, close underused facilities, and eliminate unprofitable services such as trauma care or definitive observation units), resulting in fewer caregiver positions and more layoffs.

2. *Substitution by lesser-trained, lower-skilled workers.* Hospitals will expand use of "nursing extenders," changing 20 years of increased reliance on professional nurses and returning to a staffing pattern with substantial use of non-RN substitutes.

3. *Constraint of the rate of wage growth.* To slash labor costs, raises for healthcare workers will be reduced to the rate of consumer inflation, and hospitals will make increasing use of part-time, casual employees who will get few or no fringe benefits.

4. *Elimination or narrowing of wage differentials.* Unless RNs with a baccalaureate degree in nursing can demonstrate added value, expect hospitals to reduce or eliminate any wage differential between four-year and lesser-trained nursing staff.

5. *Employee buyouts, early retirements, and layoffs.* Early retirement, buyout programs, and layoffs will reduce the number of higher-paid workers on the payroll, opening the door for substitution of newly graduated nurses and nonprofessionals with less experience and lower salary levels.

6. *Ethical dilemmas.* Increased economic pressures to cut costs and discharge patients early will place the RN in the middle of ethical dilemmas as the patients' advocate, which may conflict with nurses in the role of resource controllers, care supervisors, and case managers.

Managed care's most immediate result may be downsizing of hospital facilities and bedside nursing. Former Colorado governor Richard Lamm looks at the expansion of managed care and its downward spiral of demand and asks: "Where will all the nurses go?" (Lamm 1995, 60). With one nurse for every 145 Americans, the United States has the highest nurse-to-population ratio in the world. More than 60 percent of the nation's 1.6 million active nurses work in acute care settings. Some 40 percent of these hospital-based nurses are concentrated in critical care units.

On a national basis, America has 3.8 hospital beds per 1,000 people, but managed care plans and staff-model HMOs use only 1.2–1.5 beds per 1,000 enrollees. Some aggressive capitated physician groups in California use only

0.6–0.8 beds per 1,000 enrollees (Cowden and Stepnick 1994). One hospital administrator quips: "By the year 2000, the average hospital occupancy will be what it was last year on Christmas Eve" (Lamm 1995, 61).

In a landmark study of future health work force requirements in the twenty-first century, the Pew Health Professions Commission recently recommended reducing the number of nursing education programs—now at 1,470—by 20 to 25 percent, with the majority of these reductions coming in associate degree and diploma programs (Pew Health Professions Commission 1995). A similar study of physician education recommended that the number of medical students and residents likewise be slashed by 25 percent. At the same time, the Pew Commission also saw a need to double the number of advanced nurse practitioners (ANPs), currently about 25,000. At the primary care level, ANPs can satisfy the routine medical needs of 50 to 60 percent of the ambulatory patient population.

HEALTHCARE TEAMS MUST MANAGE HEALTHCARE

Managing the cost, content, and outcomes of care are the critical challenges of the managed care era. Surprisingly, few healthcare organizations are well organized to do so. Northwestern University–based Steve Shortell's research on IDSs, based on a four-year study of nine large healthcare systems, clearly identifies the critical success factors for managing integrated health systems (Shortell et al. 1996). Superior financial IDS performance is directly related to three key strategies: physician integration, clinical integration, and information system integration. Not surprisingly, these are the same three areas that were ranked lowest in terms of current integration—and needed the most development and resource investment for the study's nine systems to reach their performance goals.

Managing risk means managing the content, cost, and outcomes of patient care. A set of IDS-wide care standards and clinical pathways will provide a framework for more efficient care delivery. Continuous monitoring and care management will extend the breadth of the continuum of care. These are the most important management functions of an IDN in a capitated, prepaid market environment. Most are clinically focused:

- utilization management;
- clinical protocols and pathways;
- continuous improvement of quality and service;
- performance reporting (to payors);
- physician group practice management;
- ambulatory or primary care network management;
- provider evaluation and credentialing;

- continuum of care network management;
- customer service;
- health risk appraisal (of capitated enrollees);
- management of chronically ill populations; and
- access management/triage.

To facilitate the process of managing clinical care, there will be a number of administrative and support functions. Most important of these will be the community health information network (CHIN). The information architecture will provide the "glue" and communications media for continuous care management across a decentralized communitywide network. Data must be available at all points in the system in real time. The time-value of information will be critical in managing patients along clinical pathways. Optimum efficiency will come from rapid but sure-footed diagnostic work and delivery of the most appropriate treatment in the least-cost (but safe) setting.

"FREE-RANGE" MOBILE EXECUTIVES

To meet the challenges of managed care, traditional healthcare management must be radically revised. Start by downsizing the executive suite! That's not where tomorrow's "free-ranging" executives will be spending time. Much of their clinical management activity will occur in close proximity to patients— at bedsides, in physician group offices, in satellite clinics, and in continuum-of-care settings. Senior and middle managers will be located close to functional activities, widely dispersed across a regional network of facilities and service settings. Busy clinical and business unit executives will be encouraged to be mobile managers, moving to solve problems and fine-tune implementation strategies very close to the customer. The management team may not even work for the same company but may instead represent a network of collaborating providers and support companies, linked by capitation contracts and economic joint ventures.

Conveniently located conference facilities and scheduled-by-the-hour meeting rooms located in care sites will be the substitutes for today's well-paneled executive suites. Tomorrow's healthcare management team members will be much too busy communicating and collaborating with their colleagues from diverse, decentralized locations, using intranets, e-mail, fax, and phone to connect across IDNs.

In composition and appearance, the future management team will bear little resemblance to the business-suited MHAs and MBAs who currently inhabit the administrative offices of U.S. hospitals and health systems. Many will be women. Even more important, many senior healthcare managers will have clinical backgrounds as well as management training. Casual Friday wear will prevail for many key positions, as health executives and middle managers spend most of their time working with ad hoc work groups on projects and problem solving. Cellular telephones, laptop computers, and message-bearing pagers will free health managers to work wherever healthcare is being delivered, from the doctor's office to the critical care unit.

BUILDING A TWENTY-FIRST CENTURY MANAGEMENT TEAM

Tomorrow's management pyramid may be flatter but broader than today's lean, mean executive group. The style will still be nonhierarchical, with few layers of reporting relationships.

Managing a decentralized continuum of care network will require a broader range of skills and expertise. Today's health organizations have consolidated the top management positions to a handful of key executives. Management consolidation and position elimination isn't over. Some of these jobs will be shifted to the IDN level for corporate management. Other positions will be new, reflecting the expanded emphasis on managing clinical care for a large enrolled population. Physicians and nurses will hold key assignments in at least half of the IDN management team functions. Compare the job titles and management responsibilities of today's senior executive ranks with those of an IDN in a capitated marketplace (see Table 5.2).

At least half of the members of the expanded IDN management team will be physician and nurse executives whose functions require strong clinical backgrounds. Key positions that will require clinical executives include COO/ patient care executives, medical group/physician division, quality and customer service, continuum of care services, and continuing care management. Clinical executives will hold advanced degrees in management/healthcare administration, making them more versatile than nonclinician MBA/MHA administrators.

Tomorrow's IDN executives will know a great deal about their core business, and a majority of senior healthcare managers will be recruited from clinical ranks. Their knowledge of the core process of medical and nursing care will be essential for cost-effective management of the biggest variable cost—the patient. Drawing from clinical ranks will call on the leadership skills of lay managers and clinicians. Trust must be developed in a collegial management partnership between clinical leaders and management support staff.

A shared vision that puts the patient first must be articulated. In a capitated, at-risk environment, it will not be enough to have low costs and utilization rates. Every surviving health organization must be competitively efficient or it will be consolidated or eliminated. Enrolling and holding the loyalty of covered lives will be the critical secret of success. The manage-

Table 5.2 Executive Job Titles

Today's Health System	*Future Integrated Delivery Network*
• Chief Executive Officer	• Regional Network Executive (hospital CEO eliminated)
• Chief Operating Officer	• COO/Patient Care Executive (consolidates positions of CEO, COO, and Patient Care Executive at the local level)
• Chief Financial Officer	• Director of Financial Services (Finance is managed at IDN level)
• Chief Information Officer	• Director of Information Services (Information is managed at IDN level)
• Vice President, Planning and Marketing	• (Local vice presidents eliminated— Business Development Directors will operate at the business-unit level)
	• System Planning and Marketing managed at IDN level
• Vice President, Medical Affairs	• (Eliminated—Medical Affairs is managed at IDN level)
	• CEO of Medical Group/Physician Division (new position)
	• Director of Quality/Customer Service (new position for quality management)
	• Director for Managed Care Relations (new position servicing HMOs and employers)
	• Vice President for Continuum of Care Services (new position coordinating nonacute care)
	• Vice President for Continuing Care Management (new position managing high-risk enrollees)

ment team of the twenty-first century must be dedicated to a vision of healthy enrollees functioning to their maximum potential in a healthy community.

NURSING TAKES CHARGE OF ITS FUTURE

Cyber-nurse, telecommunicator, access manager, resource allocator, quality monitor, care coordinator, and *hands-on therapist*—these are a few of the roles that future nurses will play in the twenty-first century. American healthcare is being radically reshaped by managed care, systems reengineering, competitive health policy, and cost-sensitive employers. Nursing is responding to the challenges of the market, reshaping bedside care and clinical management. There is no alternative for nursing but to face the future, predicts Richard Lamm: "Given the expected closure of many hospitals and the downsizing of others, a modest estimate would be that 350,000 nurses presently employed by hospitals will be looking for work in non-hospital settings" (Lamm 1995, 61).

Nursing is at the vortex of competing pressures for cost containment and quality improvement. Many healthcare organizations have experimented with task redistribution, downsizing, and "de-skilling," but most have come back to reemphasize the registered nurse as the core unit of healthcare delivery and care management. Leah Curtin, editor of *Nursing Management*, forecasts: "A number of experiments in health service delivery will be tried, but the only really successful ones will be those in which nurses remain at the heart of patient care delivery" (Curtin 1994a).

Across settings, services, and even time zones, nurses will play a central role in the leadership and provision of all future healthcare services. They are:

- managers of the gateways to the health system;
- centrally positioned as system controllers and care managers;
- the caregivers and health team leaders closest to the patient;
- clinical informatics specialists interpreting data;
- risk-managers for those with genetic and lifestyle health risks;
- behavioral modifiers who promote healthy habits;
- continuous care coordinators for frail and chronically ill patients; and
- community-based intervenors who mitigate health threats.

But the transformation process in the next five years will not be easy. Powerful economic forces are at work to bring under control the nation's $1 billion annual health expenditures. A domino effect of managed competition is under way (Buerhaus 1994). Cost-conscious employers are forcing price-based competition between HMOs and insurers, and as health plan premiums decline, reimbursement to providers falls and controls over utilization tighten.

The result of economic competition will be lower volumes of services, shrinking payments to providers, and reduced demand for healthcare. On the provider side, layoffs, reengineering, and continuous budget pressures will be the inevitable result. Competition will have an upside potential as well: Demanding purchasers in the future will select health plans and provider networks based on clinical outcomes, quality of care, and patient satisfaction.

Nursing is being launched into the twenty-first century without a chart or compass. As the major staffing component of the nation's health system,

2.1 million nurses face the future with a mixture of dread and anticipation. Will the new century bring expanded opportunities and rewards or reduced expectations and dismal career paths? Will nurses become "invisible," as their care roles are supplanted by lesser-trained extenders (Stannard 1993)? Or will the rise of managed care create unprecedented opportunities in a wide array of roles and settings, from entry level to executive level (Ballard 1993)?

EXPANDING ROLES AND DOMAIN

Whatever happens next, there will be nurses at the heart of the health team as well as the management team. As the caregivers who are most consistently at the patient's bedside, nurses should and will take the lead in care delivery and care management. According to a national survey by Premier Hospitals Alliance in Westchester, Illinois, nurses as case managers can reduce patient length of stay, improve the quality of care, and reduce the use of resources (Sherer 1993). Within five years, surveyed healthcare executives predict that virtually 50 percent of all patients would be under case management systems and critical pathways. Nursing will consolidate its authority as the resource controller of the system. Many more hospital departments will report to nursing in the future (see Table 5.3).

A view of nursing's future is increasingly a nonhospital one. Nursing opportunities in tomorrow's market will be found in ambulatory settings,

Table 5.3   More Departments May Report to Nursing in the Future

Departments	*Percentage Who Agree*
Ambulatory care	63.8%
Emergency department	63.3
Home care	62.1
Operating rooms	59.3
Infection control	55.9
Utilization review/management	54.2
Social services	52.0
Respiratory therapy	48.6
Housekeeping	46.3
Physical/occupational therapy	39.5
Dietary	37.9
Quality assurance	37.3
Pharmacy	33.3
Radiology	24.9
Laboratory	24.9

Source: Reprinted from *Hospitals & Health Networks*, Vol. 67, No. 16, by permission, August 20, 1993, Copyright 1993, American Hospital Publishing, Inc.

physician offices, home care, and long-term care. The supply of RNs has increased at a substantial rate over the past 30 years, averaging 50,000 additional RNs graduated each year (Aiken and Salmon 1994). Today, two-thirds of nurses are employed by hospitals, but nursing employment in nonhospital sectors is growing rapidly. Outpatient departments hired 66 percent more nurses in the five years between 1988 and 1992, while public health and community nurses increased by 30 percent.

SEVEN NEW ROLES FOR NURSE MANAGERS

The growth of HMOs, ambulatory care, and IDSs is likely to support expanded roles and responsibilities for nurse managers and advanced practice nurses. Demands for more independent decision making and clinical management will especially reward nurses with higher education, such as BSN or MS degrees (Coile 1995). Legal challenges and malpractice have not been a problem in the advanced practice nursing experience. Nurses may play key roles in the integrated delivery networks of managed care.

Role #1—Access ("Demand") Management

The real gatekeepers to the system will be access management nurses who channel demand for primary or urgent care to the most appropriate service or setting in the IDN. Access managers are working for HMOs, capitated physician groups, and IDNs. The concept merges the roles of patient advocacy, customer service, information and referral, and triage into a new function that will be essential under managed care and capitation.

Role #2—Primary Care Extenders

Nurses can help alleviate the shortage of primary care physicians, expected to last well into the twenty-first century. The supply of primary care–trained nurses could be increased quickly and cheaply, as suggested under a study by the Office of Technology, which demonstrated that nurses could provide patient care at a lower cost than physicians in a selected range of patient care activities—with equal or superior quality (Office of Technology 1986). By using more nurses as substitutes for primary care physicians, an HMO could lower its per-enrollee costs and be more price competitive. Kaiser-Permanente in California is experimenting with "pods"—teams composed of six physicians and six nurses—that will manage 20,000 enrollees.

Role #3—Cost Management/Clinical Efficiency

Nurse managers will apply clinical expertise to a variety of cost management activities. A national wave of reengineering projects under nursing leadership demonstrates new approaches to more cost-effective care. Clinical pathways developed by joint nurse-physician teams are reducing costs per case and per patient, in both inpatient and ambulatory settings.

Role #4—Managing the Chronically Ill

In the future, nurses may be the preferred patient choice for primary care and management of chronically ill patients (Mezey and McGivern 1993). Obstetrics, diabetes, arthritis, and pediatrics are likely services for nurse-coordinated care.

Role #5—Managing High-Risk Patients

Nurses can take the lead responsibility in providing case management for high-risk patients. Working in staff-model HMOs and IDNs, nurses will use sophisticated patient management tools and information systems to coordinate and control the care of high-cost patients.

Role #6—Case Management/Care Management

Nurses as case managers can be a major asset in HMO efforts to reduce costs and integrate clinical care. Peter Buerhaus predicts: "As HMOs seek to lower costs, the monitoring and controlling of enrollees' consumption of resources will become an increasingly important management responsibility for which nurses are uniquely well qualified" (Buerhaus 1994, 78).

Role #7—Health Promotion/Prevention

Under capitation, the incentive of the IDN is to keep patients as healthy as possible, treat them early, and use as few resources as necessary (Madden and Ponte 1994). As HMOs put more emphasis on reducing costs through health promotion, nurses can take leadership in wellness, health education, and disease prevention efforts.

TAKING THE LONG VIEW REQUIRES CLINICAL PERSPECTIVE

A long-term view of American healthcare recognizes that managing an aging population is the major challenge of the future. Aging baby boomers will require new approaches to managing the content as well as the cost of care. A dynamic health industry will use nurses and physicians in a broad array of services, settings, and roles. The fundamental economics favor nurses: They outnumber doctors 3 to 1, can be employed at a cost of only 30 to 40 percent of an average physician and can be trained at 25 to 35 percent of the annual cost of medical education for specialized roles in one- to two-year educational programs.

The economic pressures of managed care and government health reform will reset the level of supply and demand on a short-term basis. But a longer-range outlook should anticipate the future effects of aging, population growth, and new technology, all of which will intensify demand for health services. America's hospitals could be hale and hardy in the future, despite the concerns about managed care and government health reforms (Curtin 1994b).

Despite the difficulties of transition, all providers can anticipate a significant increase in volume in the coming years. Increased demands on the future health system will require an integrated network that includes:

- offsite emergency services at several locations;
- ambulatory surgery facilities on and off hospitals' campuses;
- integrated subacute services;
- access to alternative and nontraditional therapies;
- case management services;
- benchmarking based on outcomes; and
- telecommunications linkages to physician offices, patients' homes, payors, and regulatory bodies. (Coile 1995d)

This expanding view of the demand for physicians, nurses, and the wide range of healthcare professionals has a future rationale. Population growth and the "age wave" will contribute to increased demand for health services. Changes in work patterns to fewer hours and more flexible staffing will mean that more caregivers will be needed to treat the same number of patients. And, of course, the population is growing and will reach 300 million by 2020.

Increased health insurance coverage will also drive up demand. Within 15 to 20 years, all of the nation's 40 million uninsured may come under some federal, state, or employer sponsorship. State-level health reforms in Oregon and Tennessee have already expanded insurance coverage or Medicaid benefits to some of the uninsured. Proposals to expand Medicaid to cover 5 to 10 million children are under way and could be implemented before 2000. New technology and advanced clinical practices may induce demand for new services and provide new treatment options for patients.

Taking the long view should reveal the beneficial effect that managed care will have on the population's health. The shift to managed care is not purely an exercise in reducing costs and utilization. Instead, managed care plans and HMOs will expand efforts to prevent high-cost disease, increasing their focus on health promotion and wellness services. HMO risk management programs will identify patients for education and treatment to offset their unhealthy habits, poor family health histories, and high-cost utilization patterns. The mix of inpatient, ambulatory, noninstitutional, home-based, and alternative therapies will continue to change and grow. Whatever the model, *clinicians* will be the primary component of caregiving and care management at all levels and service settings.

LOOKING FORWARD: DEVELOPING CLINICIAN EXECUTIVES

Building a twenty-first century management team must start now. Here are ten important steps that can be taken to position a healthcare organization's management team for effective decision making in a capitated market:

1. *Promote clinical managers* to higher-level management positions by combining clinical departments and collapsing service lines.
2. *Bring more physicians* into senior management in the areas of medical affairs, managed care medical director, medical group management, or quality assurance.
3. *Subsidize management training* for clinical managers.
4. *Promote team and culture building*, beginning with awareness of perspectives and professional biases.
5. *Assign collaborative teams* to manage all major projects and problems.
6. *Monitor clinical performance* as well as financial indicators.
7. *Increase clinical participation* in governance and at the board level, with at least fifty/fifty clinical participation in all committees.
8. *Base management incentives* on clinical as well as financial objectives.
9. *Devote substantial management* time to solving clinical issues.
10. *Select a clinician* as either chief executive officer or chief operating officer—or both.

REFERENCES

Aiken, L. H., and M. E. Salmon. 1994. "Health Care Workforce Priorities: What Nursing Should Do Now." *Inquiry* 31 (3): 318–29.

Ballard, M. 1993. "Opportunities in the Managed Care Industry." *American Nurse* 25 (6): 20.

Buerhaus, P. I. 1994. "Economics of Managed Competition and Consequences to Nurses: Part II." *Nursing Economics* 12 (2): 75–80, 106.

Coile, R. C., Jr. 1995a. "The Five Stages of Managed Care." *Health Trends* 7: 1–8.

———. 1995b. "Managed Care Outlook." *Health Trends* 7 (5): 6.

———. 1995c. "Integration, Capitation and Managed Care: Transformation of Nursing for 21st Century Health Care." *Advanced Practice Nursing Quarterly* 1 (2): 11–18.

————. 1995d. "Nursing Trends 1995–2000: Advanced Practice Nurses, Case Management and Patient-Centered Care." *Health Trends* 7 (7): 1–8.

————. 1996. "Management Teams for the 21st Century." *Healthcare Executive* 11 (1): 10–13.

Cowden, S. L., and L. Stepnick. 1994. *Capitation I: The New American Medicine.* Washington, DC: The Governance Committee, Advisory Board.

Curtin, L. L. 1994a. "The Heart of Patient Care." *Nursing Management* 25 (5): 7–8.

————1994b. "Learning from the Future." *Nursing Management* 25 (1): 7–9.

Hamer, R. L. 1997. *HMO Facts and Trends.* St. Paul, MN: InterStudy.

Lamm, R. D. 1995. "The Coming Dislocation in the Health Professions." *Healthcare Forum Journal* 39 (1): 58–62.

Madden, M. J., and P. R. Ponte. 1994. "Advanced Practice Roles in the Managed Care Environment." *Journal of Nursing Administration* 24 (1): 56–62.

Mezey, M. D., and D. D. McGivern. 1993. *Nurses, Nurse Practioners and Evolution to Advanced Practice.* New York: Springer Publishing Company.

Office of Technology. 1986. "Nurse Practitioners, Physician Assistants and Certified Nurse-Midwives." *Health Technology Case Study 37.* Washington, DC: Congress of the United States.

Pew Health Professions Commission. 1995. "Critical Challenges: Revitalizing the Health Professions for the 21st Century." San Francisco: UCSF Center for the Health Professions.

Sherer, J. L. 1993. "Next Steps for Nursing." *Hospitals & Health Networks* 67 (30): 26–28.

Shortell, S. M., R. R. Gillies, D. A. Anderson, K. M. Erickson, and J. B. Mitchell. 1996. *Remaking Health Care in America: Building Organized Delivery Systems.* San Francisco: Jossey-Bass.

Stannard, D. 1993. "A Dangerous New Trend—the Invisible Nurse." *Cricical Care Nurse* 13 (5): 140.

6

Motivating "Work Force 2000": Management, Morale, and Motivation in the Era of "Future Work"

We can quibble over the fine points, but the trend is crystal clear. A massive change in the numbers, types and skills of health professionals is underway.
        —Richard Lamm (1996, 58)

The new world of work will provide one of the greatest managerial challenges of twenty-first century healthcare. Few enterprises are more labor-intensive than healthcare, with 80¢ of every healthcare dollar spent on personal services. Labor strategies must be linked to business strategies. Human resources planning is needed to complement financial and market plans (Jones 1996, 22). Market pressures, demographic shifts, and rising patient acuity must all be accommodated.

In the past five years, healthcare organizations have cut much of the labor "fat" out of the system, and the "low-hanging fruit" of obvious labor-cost solutions have already been implemented—downsizing, layoffs, and reductions in non-nursing personnel. Healthcare executives will need fresh approaches to employee motivation, performance and productivity, service level improvement, and corporate culture issues if they are to succeed in the next century's intensely competitive market.

Downsizing and cutbacks have taken their toll in healthcare. America's hospitals resemble a battleground, with jittery workers shell-shocked by loss of job security at all levels in healthcare organizations. Morale is falling and nurses are actively criticizing management for compromising patient safety with staff reductions (Aiken, Sochalski, and Anderson 1996). Union organization is on the rise in healthcare, and some nursing unions are taking an aggressive stance. In Sacramento, California, nursing unions introduced statewide ballot propositions that would protect healthcare workers from layoffs and make it more difficult for tax-exempt hospitals to convert to for-profit status. Some proprietary healthcare companies have been targeted by unions because of their profits, which unions blame on labor reductions.

Hospital rank-and-file workers resent highly paid administrators, griping that hospital CEO salaries rose 7.7 percent in 1995, to an average of $178,200, while the typical American worker got only a 2.7 percent pay raise (Moore 1996, 33). The average nurse made only 53.3 percent of a hospital administrator's salary, while food service and housekeepers made less than one-third of the CEO's annual pay. One compensation consultant describes executive compensation practices as "berserk" given current market conditions: "It takes a $100,000 bonus to get a CEO out of bed in the morning" (Moore 1996, 34).

The postmillennium future of American healthcare may be seen today in California, one of the most affected managed care markets in the nation. More than 40 percent of Californians are enrolled in an HMO today, the highest level of any state (Hamer 1997), and in the past decade, the number of full-time-equivalent workers rose only 3 percent and (non-RN) patient support personnel fell by 10 percent. California hospitals actually increased staffing from the early 1980s through the early 1990s, but many of the new workers were not caregivers. Nonclinical personnel increased 28 percent. The ratio of four caregivers per one administrative staffer fell to two to one in the 12-year period, as California hospitals boosted their administrative capability in response to the demands of the West Coast's highly managed care market.

DOOMSDAY FORECAST OF MAJOR DISLOCATION FOR THE HEALTH PROFESSIONS

Books like Jeremy Rifkin's *The End of Work* (1996) present strikingly unattractive images of the future, based on assumptions that technology displacement will make millions of workers redundant. These projections about the postautomation work world would have sweeping consequences, totaling perhaps 850 million surplus workers worldwide—a number that could rise in the future (Snyder 1996, 8). The outcome could be a permanent underclass with massive unemployment and attendant social ills. Could these "doomsday" predictions be right?

Healthcare executives should not discount Rifkin's outlook just because they do not like the implications. Looking back at futurists' predictions in the 1960s and 1970s, some of the forecasts were strikingly accurate. Anticipating the trend toward virtual organizations, leadership guru Warren Bennis of the University of Southern California coined the term *adhocracy* in his book with Philip Slater, *The Temporary Society* (1968), to describe how giant industrial bureaucracies were going to become smaller, much more adaptive organizations. Futurists like Alvin Toffler, author of *The Third Wave*, were absolutely correct about the effect of computers and the information age. The United States has substantially shifted from labor-intensive to information-intensive production and management. Downsizing, reengineering, and layoffs have all come as predicted. The American ideal of a comfortable salaried position for life no longer exists for many workers.

The future of U.S. healthcare is clouded by signals of a major surplus of today's workers, and there are predictions that a watershed change in the numbers, types, and skills of health professionals is under way. Colorado's former governor, Richard Lamm, cites forecasts from the Pew Foundation's Health Professions Committee that there will be a "dramatic alteration in who delivers care to whom, when and where" in the twenty-first century. Among causes for alarm, Lamm cites:

- Without substantial cuts, Medicare's trust fund will be bankrupt by 2002.
- There is a current oversupply of 100,000 to 150,000 physicians out of a total medical community of almost 700,000.
- Some 120,000 of these excess physicians are specialists.
- Each year, another 17,000 new physicians graduate from the nation's 125 medical schools.
- Managed care could reduce the need for hospital beds and facilities by one-third.
- An estimated 350,000 hospital-employed nurses will be looking for work in nonhospital settings.
- As many as 20 to 25 percent of medical and nursing schools may close.
- The current supply of advanced practice nurses and physicians is only 50 percent of what is needed.
- Under managed care, 30 to 40 percent of pharmacists may be redundant. (Lamm 1996)

Healthcare market observers like former governor Lamm believe that the healthcare market is out of control as a result of decades of health spending at rates two to three times higher than the consumer price index. Lamm predicts that the American hospital will no longer be the center of the healthcare universe, and no longer the centerpiece of a healthcare career. Under his scenario of widespread hospital closures and job cutbacks, massive displacement is in store for healthcare. More and more people will be looking for jobs in the health field because the market is a "ruthless reorganizer" in the face of this level of surplus capacity. If he is right, healthcare is overdue for a major shakeout that could far exceed the downsizings and layoffs of the past five years.

DOWNSIZING IS SLOWING, GROWTH IS RISING

On the other hand, Governor Lamm may be wrong. Healthcare's job reductions could be largely behind us, which is the emerging pattern in other industries. Across all economic sectors, today's labor force indicators show that the crest of downsizing in American industry occurred before 1993 (Risher 1996, 8). According to annual surveys by the American Management Association, job cuts are slowing from an annual rate of 8 to 10 percent over the past ten years, to below 5 percent in the recent three-year period 1993 to 1995. Despite widespread publicity focused on layoffs at Fortune 500 firms like AT&T, job reduction is now below average. In 1996, barely one percent of U.S. workers suffered layoffs. Today, unemployment is below 4 to 5 percent in most markets, at rates among the lowest figures for joblessness in the past 20 years. The economy is producing some 2 million new jobs each year.

Although very visible, corporate downsizings have resulted in only 12 percent of the recent job losses, according to recent data from the Bureau of Labor Statistics for firms with more than 50 employees (Risher 1996, 9). Most of the layoffs that occurred—more than 50 percent—were caused by seasonal employment or occurred in firms where work was slack and projects were completed. But laid-off workers are less likely to be rehired than in the past or to be offered job-sharing. Those employers shedding workers are holding labor costs down by outsourcing or using of temporary workers, whose pay levels and benefits are below full-time displaced workers.

To be successful in the twenty-first century, organizations should emphasize *growth*, not downsizing. An emerging theme in recent thinking about corporations, work, and markets is a renewed focus on expansion. "No company ever shrank to greatness," argue business strategists Dwight Gertz and Joao Baptista, senior consultants with Mercer Management Consulting in New York (Gertz and Baptista 1995, 37). The emphasis on growth is not just market share expansion through acquisition and consolidation. Successful growth companies achieve expanded revenues from "customer franchise management" strategies, superior product development, and "channel management" to expand into new customer and distribution outlets. Growth-minded companies have superior value, as defined by customers, and superior economics through the value chain. Their products and services are more attractive to customers, and they bring higher profits.

Despite the perception that healthcare is slumping, many sectors of the health industry are growing. Healthcare companies are moving to cash in on the trend toward consumer access and choice. In New York, Oxford Health Plan, with 1.7 million members, has become one of the region's fastest-growing, and profitable, HMOs by emphasizing quality (access to specialist physicians), service (by nurse "access managers"), and value-added (alternative medicine) services (Oxford Health Plan 1997, A16–17). Under Oxford's new model, specialty care will be handled on a case-based approach in nine specialty areas, ranging from obstetrics to oncology. More than 200 specialty care teams have already been formed, and the company anticipates that another 700 care teams will be developed in the year ahead (Cochrane 1997, 3).

Today, a renewed emphasis on growth is replacing downsizing to drive the expansion of many sectors of the U.S. economy. Overall, more companies (68 percent) reported creating jobs than those firms (49 percent) that eliminated them, according to the American Management Association's 1996 survey. In the healthcare industry, jobs grew from 7.1 million in 1988 to 9.5 million in 1996, a 34.6 percent increase. The computer field grew by 77.3 percent in the same period, while personnel supply companies expanded by 96.1 percent. Hospitals are among the growing number of firms using outside arrangements to obtain labor skills. Independent contractors represent 6.7 percent of the work force, while contingent workers in temporary assignments have risen to almost 5 million, or 4 percent of all American workers today.

TRENDS IN WORK: HEALTHCARE'S MILLENNIUM WORKPLACE

In only a few years, the millennium workplace will be here. All the changes that experts predicted will now be tested by reality. Many of these predictions will be tested against reality. Some trends are already very evident (Barner 1996).

"Virtual" Organizations

A highly mobile, distributed healthcare work force will use electronic technology to coordinate care and manage costs from a variety of scattered sites along the continuum of care. The universal patient record will consist of digital wireless transfer of data, video, audio, and text information. Many "back-room" employees will be telecommuters whose jobs can be performed from home—or anywhere—because of information technology.

Customer-Centered Focus

Note that the patient—not the organization—will become the hub of this information technology universe. Processes such as utilization management or quality control can be managed from anywhere in the organization, and physical location of the care manager will not be a political or economic factor. Instead, all activities will be organized around the customer, and the information network will create a virtual care system that is "mass-customized" for each patient.

"Migrant" Workers

As many as one-third to one-half of tomorrow's healthcare work force will be casual or part-time employees. The trend is already widespread in the private sector, with the use of temporary workers soaring by 240 percent in the past ten years (Barner 1996, 16). Many hospitals are adopting flexible staffing plans that are adjusted daily, even hourly, to match fluctuations in census and workloads. Many healthcare workers prefer the flexibility of part-time work and the financial incentives for working 12-hour or unpopular shifts. Concerns about quality are rising as acuity and severity of patients rise. Casual healthcare employees may not have the clinical experience to manage sicker patients, especially on specialized units. Part-time workers will need more orientation and supervision until they learn jobs that are increasingly defined by clinical pathways.

Efficient Staffing

Downsizing, de-skilling, and task redistribution have changed the U.S. healthcare workplace. Labor costs are down, as is the percentage of budget allocated to staffing. The evidence suggests that healthcare—always a labor-intensive activity—is becoming more efficient. But can these labor gains be sustained? There are anecdotes that complain that perhaps nursing has been cut too hard. If correct, these concerns about quality of patient care could pose problems for cost-efficient healthcare. Even if patient care is not yet compromised, the situation could get worse in the future, as the aging and acuity of patients rises in the twenty-first century. A recent study confirms what nurses fear: There are fewer employees per patient, especially when acuity is factored into the equation (Aiken, Sochalski, and Anderson 1996, 90–91). Hospitals engaged in significant staffing cuts in 1995 and 1996, but most of the displaced workers were non-RN patient personnel. But there are more RNs now, almost 30 percent more than a decade ago. The perception by nurses of shortages despite a richer RN mix is likely to continue, especially in high-supply regions such as New England, where downsizing means there are few job opportunities for local RNs or new nursing graduates.

Electronic Monitoring

There will be a dramatic increase in the use of electronic monitoring to accelerate process improvement, standardize employee decision making, and evaluate performance. Computerized clinical pathways and electronic benchmarks are already widespread in hospitals and are now spreading quickly into physician organizations. At its best, electronic monitoring can provide instant feedback to flag potential problems and improve quality. But the downside is that healthcare workers may become paranoid and resentful when their performance is continuously monitored.

Knowledge Workers

In the future, more than 90 to 95 percent of healthcare workers may work on or near computers. Even the most mundane functions such as typing have now become data processing. Patient care is close to adopting universal electronic medical records, which will probably be a reality within five years. Clinical pathways, diagnostic data reporting, and online patient monitoring are already routine. Virtually every support function in healthcare is extensively computerized, from staffing schedules to just-in-time inventory. Given the shrinking shelf-life of many technical skills, staying current with technology will be a growing problem. If healthcare workers—and their managers—are to avoid falling behind the technology curve, training programs must be expanded with continuous learning opportunities.

Diversity

By 2000, some 85 percent of people entering the U.S. work force will be women or minorities, and just 15 percent will be white males, according to U.S. Labor Department projections (Barner 1996, 17). Multicultural work teams will be the standard in many U.S. hospitals and medical groups. In some hospitals, racial tensions have already flared in situations where ethnic workers have sought to speak their native languages on the job in front of patients. There is also a concern that healthcare workers who speak English as a second language may experience quality issues when complying with physician orders or care guidelines whose terminology they do not completely understand.

Aging

By the turn of the century, the median age of U.S. workers will be 45 years. By 2005, some 15 percent of employees will be over age 55. By 2015, more than half of the American population will be over age 55 (Rich 1996, 28). The trend of the 1980s toward early retirement is reversing itself. Economic pressures are keeping older workers on the job longer—even past the traditional age of retirement. Age bias is giving way to age preference for workers with old-fashioned work ethics. Experienced hands working with tightly staffed patient units is reassuring when many healthcare employees are casual or part-time.

Physician Surplus

There will probably be too many physicians in the twenty-first century, but not nearly as many extra physicians as once feared. The Pew Foundation's "doomsday" projections of 20 to 25 percent excess physicians may be overstated. A recent evaluation of future work force demand for physicians by Richard Cooper, M.D., of the Health Policy Institute at the Medical College of Wisconsin, predicts that the "doctor glut" may not be as deep as believed (Cooper 1995, 1534). In the next ten years, demand for physician services may expand by 18 percent, caused by service growth and reductions in physicians' work efforts. Supply of physicians is also growing, but the actual surplus may be a modest 31,000 physicians—5 percent of total supply—in 2000, increasing to only 62,000 excess physicians by 2010. These more modest predictions of physician surplus come as a reassessment of previous studies, which predicted that 73,000 to 165,000 doctors could be unnecessary by 2000. The surplus is predicted to fall to 13,000 physicians in the year 2020. Teamwork in clinical settings is an effective response to fragmentation in service delivery. Collaboration among physicians, nurses, and other health workers enhances the quality of care and boosts patient satisfaction. The process of total quality management/continuous quality improvement relies on teams to solve problems. Many barriers to quality are found at the interfaces between caregiver roles and responsibilities. Teams can create breakthrough strategies through multidisciplinary cooperation.

Health Teams

Will patients accept the phrase: "The health team will see you now"? A growing use of multiskilled teams is a major trend for the future, from the critical care unit to the physician office and home health. Healthcare is being provided with increasing interdependence (D'Aunno, Alexander, and Laughlin 1996), and patients need multidisciplinary care. Martin Hickey, M.D., chief medical officer at Lovelace Health System in Albuquerque, New Mexico, argues, "Without integrating the patient into some type of coordinated care process where you're sure that you are dealing with all of the conditions, you may save money on a particular disease—and we have lots of evidence that works, particularly for congestive heart failure—but who's managing the patient's psoriasis or depression?" (De Guzman 1997, 1)

Salaried Physicians

Physicians are more likely to be salaried team members in the future. More than 30 percent of all U.S. physicians are salaried today, exceeding the number of solo physicians, according to the American Medical Association. While hospitals have targeted primary care physicians (PCPs) for acquisition in the past the five years, recruiting and incentives are now shifting toward specialists. Wage increases for specialty physicians outpaced primary care practitioners last year, up by 2.7 percent for specialists versus 1.9 percent to PCPs, the first time since 1991 where specialty pay rose faster than primary care (Guglielmo 1996, 31). Doctors in high managed care markets, like California, are relocating to the Midwest and other markets where HMOs have not fully taken hold, a phenomenon that Donald W. Fisher, vice president of the American Group Practice Association, refers to as the "Oregon Trail in reverse" (Guglielmo 1996, 34). Salaried doctors may not be as productive as their fee-for-service counterparts. A recent forecast of physician demand in 2020 estimated that 241 doctors will be needed in 25 years to do the work of 205 doctors today (Cooper 1996, 1538).

Information Technology

Information technology is the "architecture" to support high-performance teams that are working in a distributed mode (Birchall and Lyons 1995). Wherever it may be located, tomorrow's patient care team will be linked by information technology. Bedside care may be directed by physician specialists across the street in a medical office building or thousands of miles away in an academic medical center linked by telemedicine. Remote robotic "telesurgery" is possible now and is being tested. If patients can be operated on using minimally invasive surgery with the surgeon located 12 to 18 inches away from the microincision, why not three thousand miles? The patient may be in a critical care unit or in his or her own bed at home. Each patient care team is selected by a care manager, based on the evolving needs of the patient. Information technology makes their collaboration possible, in real time or whenever team members are needed. Technology such as the electronic universal medical record, Internet and intranet networks, telecommunications, telephone, fax, and digital imaging will all be used in future medical care, supported by computerized clinical pathways, diagnostic software, and electronic monitoring.

NEW MODELS FOR WORK FORCE 2000: HIGH-PERFORMANCE TEAMS

Employees want to contribute when they work for high-performance organizations, which set high expectations but let workers define their own stretch goals and even set their own incentive pay targets. This new paradigm of work assumes that many of today's employees would like to use their full capacities at work, but many do not have the opportunity. When workers find their contributions are important and valued in the organization, they are willing to work harder. In some situations, performance improvements of 30 to 40 percent have been achieved where new work organizational structures, human resources policies, and technology are combined for productivity (Risher 1996b, 13).

In healthcare, the high-performance unit will be the team, which will share cooperative responsibility for patient care. As capitation covers larger patient populations, the challenge of twenty-first century healthcare is managing an aging population within a per-patient budget, the capitation payment. Concepts such as virtual integration, disease management, and mass customization are the processes by which individual consumers will have their comprehensive health needs met. Health promotion, diagnostic, and therapeutic services will be coordinated by in-charge care managers and implemented by teams whose members are hand-picked for each patient. Team members will come and go, depending on the needs of the patient over time, eventually on a lifelong basis.

"NEW PAY" FOR PRODUCTIVITY AND HIGH PERFORMANCE

Compensation, productivity, and motivation are being radically redesigned under various "new pay" strategies. Futuristic new financial and noneconomic incentive packages are being developed that recognize how work is changing in virtual organizations competing in a global market. Three levels of compensation and benefit programs will be applied to different employee and managerial situations (Rich 1996, 29):

- *Executive compensation* will reward strategic vision, change management, attraction and retention of talented associates, and success in achievement of the firm's long-term objectives. Senior executives will be paid only a modest salary, with benefits to enhance quality of life. Most economic incentives for executives will be based on a sliding scale of objectives to be rewarded over years with stock and options, which are deferred into the future. This compensation plan shifts the incentives from quarter-to-quarter profitability to long-term sustained growth and increased value to shareholders. While some companies have adopted variations on this compensation scheme, many organizations are still focused on short-term results.

- *Associate compensation* will reward those key individuals whose skills and experience contribute significantly to the firm's success. Pay opportunities for associates will be based not on their position or grade but on their value to the organization. A large part of their company's wealth is represented by these knowledge workers' experience and education. Their compensation will reflect in part the success of other workers—their affiliates—whose work they manage, or pay will be driven by their contributions to other key organizational goals, such as product development. Recognizing the long-term value of these key associates, the firm will place a significant share of the associate's annual incentive into a career investment trust—replacing pensions—which will be matched by the company to raise performance.

- *Affiliate compensation* is closer to today's pay-for-performance plans and is based on completion of work as jointly agreed upon by managing associates and the affiliates. In this model, affiliates may be independent contractors, part-time or casual workers, or even subcontracting firms. Individual affiliates would be allowed to defer a portion of their earnings into company stock or a broad-based mutual fund choice, similar to an IRA, but the company will make only modest contributions to their deferrals.

EMPLOYEES OF THE FUTURE WILL HAVE DIFFERENT EXPECTATIONS

One of the most striking differences between young workers of this generation and their parents are their career expectations. Job hopes of "Gen-Xers" between 18 and 30 are radically different from those of previous generations. One of the striking variances is the future outlook of young men in contrast with young women. When pollsters ask high school seniors what careers they intend to pursue, females list roles such as doctors, lawyers, engineers, accountants, and police and firefighters—all jobs once dominated by men. Their male counterparts have much lower expectations. Some young men dream of being sports stars or media personalities, while one-third have no real idea of what they will do as adults (Snyder 1996, 11–12). Nearly half of these soon-to-be-adult males express a nostalgic preference for the once-traditional male-headed, single-income nuclear family. It is not surprising that two-thirds of America's 18- to 24-year-old males are still living at home.

Members of Generation X have good reason to be concerned about their futures. Job insecurity is higher today than in the past, according to labor economists (Mishel, Bernstein, and Schmitt 1996, 33–34). While periodic joblessness has always been part of the boom-and-bust cycles of the U.S. economy, it was blue-collar workers who historically bore the brunt of downsizings. What is new is that job reduction has now spread to higher-wage men and middle-aged women. Insecurity has been compounded by a decline in net worth of middle-class workers and an erosion of employer-sponsored health benefits. Even working more hours has not been enough to offset declining wages experienced by American males from 1989 to 1994, and increased work force participation by women has not covered the lost wages, either.

Generation X is numerically smaller and demographically more diverse than previous generations of young American workers. Minority populations tend to be concentrated in the most populous cities and states, especially the Western states and largest metropolitan areas, according the Bureau of Labor Statistics' report Work Force 2000 (Cohen 1991). As the size of the 18- to 24-year-old demographic declines, there will be shortages of entry-level workers. Young workers are not well prepared for the challenge of knowledge work. Inadequate education systems are blamed for low literacy levels and lack of math or computer skills.

Quality-of-life issues important to Gen-Xers are getting attention from the corporation. Some innovative firms are combating worker stresses with a portfolio of employer-sponsored services and policies to address the real needs of modern employees. Jane Rastallis, a senior consultant with Watson Wyatt Worldwide, a human resources consulting firm, states: "As companies downsize and people have longer working hours, companies are going to offer a full menu of services, including banking, mail services, cafeteria, medical services, library and video rental" (Gilbert 1996, 1). In Cleveland, Ohio, the Kaiser Permanente healthcare organization surveyed its employees and discovered that flexible work schedules were the highest priority. As a result, Kaiser has accommodated the demand for flexibility, offering compressed work weeks, ten-hour days, and even the possibility of working at home.

CRITICAL SUCCESS FACTORS FOR LEADING WORK FORCE 2000

Despite healthcare's turbulent transition from fee-for-service medicine to managed care, some leaders and organizations are achieving high performance, according to a recent survey of 250 hospital and health systems by the national executive recruiting firm Witt/Kieffer, Ford, Hadelman & Lloyd. The national survey of CEOs found that, for every gloom-and-doom story, there are senior-level staff actually thriving in this chaos (Hadelman 1997, 1). The top five traits needed for success were vision, strategic thinking, personal integrity, ability to change, and ability to take risks (see Figure 6.1). Key leadership capabilities for future healthcare were good communications skills, ability to lead, ability to build coalitions, ability to build good physician relations, and ability to manage.

The management of cultural change may be the most difficult challenge for any leader. At a recent strategic retreat, one innovative hospital decided

Figure 6.1 Leadership Traits Needed for Success

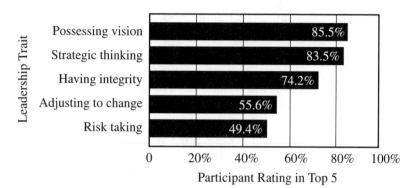

to do away with the traditional "administration-medical staff" model and create something entirely new (Losee 1997, 9). This kind of "out-of-the-box" thinking is essential to transform organizations in times of change. Healthcare's rapidly changing environment will create a whole new world of work for managers, physicians, nurses, and other healthcare staffers. But managers who are fearful, stressed, and unwilling to experiment will only be barriers to change.

Transforming attitudes begins at the top, but by the end of the process everyone throughout the organization must believe they did it themselves. In Charlotte, North Carolina, Presbyterian Hospital and the Nall Clinic have created an innovative partnership between a nonprofit hospital and a for-profit physician management company (Weber 1997). The Nall Clinic, a 110-physician multispecialty group practice, was acquired by PhyCor of Nashville, Tennessee. The two organizations joined to form a single managed care organization, a virtual partnership that could become a national model.

LOOKING FORWARD: MOTIVATING FUTURE WORKERS

Concepts of work and motivation are in flux in the modern era. Despite complaints about loss of their work ethic, most adult Americans are gainfully employed in a broad range of economic activities. U.S. unemployment today is at a record low, below 5 percent of the work force. Under these conditions, even young, unskilled, and marginal workers have found jobs. Future work will be an important source of social and psychological rewards, in addition to economic incentives and survival. Through work, many people will find self-expression, personal fulfillment, and social recognition. Healthcare, a healing profession, has a strong social role that will continue to make it a rewarding career.

Employee satisfaction and organizational success are closely linked. Social psychologist Michael Maccoby, author of *Why Work: Motivating and Leading the New Generation*, argues that future workers will be inspired to work for a new set of value drivers that expand on past emphases on economic rewards and psychological achievement. These value drivers and related characteristics include:

- *Survival.* Sustenance, nutrition, livable environment, relief of stress and maintenance of health, avoidance of danger, self-defense, and defense of one's group or family.
- *Relatedness.* Attachment, caring, protection, recognition, communication, sociability, and community.
- *Pleasure.* Comfort, sex, tasty food and drink, exercise and rest, novelty, fun, and beauty.
- *Information.* Sensory stimulation, directions, cues, signals, feedback, knowledge, and understanding.
- *Mastery.* Competence, control, ownership, autonomy, achievement, and power.
- *Play.* Exploration, fantasy, adventure, competition, experimentation, creativity, and innovation.
- *Dignity.* Respect, self-esteem, glory, and integrity.
- *Meaning.* Universal, cultural, and individual meaning. (Maccoby 1988, 58–59)

Leadership of a diverse work force will require a broader set of motivators and strategies than in the past. Managers must be able to apply varying approaches such as "administrator, entrepreneur, expert, protector, facilitator, and innovator" as appropriate to the situation and task (Maccoby 1988, 232). In dynamic, frequently changing environments, "protector-entrepreneurs" will gain organizational strength not only by sharing power but by creating it through empowerment to take risks and share rewards, in contrast to "expert-administrators" who manage in low-change environments that require task mastery and zero-defects outcomes.

There is definite evidence that the psychological state of healthcare workers affects their performance—and patient satisfaction. In Ohio, a study of consumer satisfaction at a 1,000-bed hospital found that the job satisfaction of nursing staff was a key determinant of patient ratings of their quality of care, whether they would recommend the hospital to others, and intent to return (Atkins 1997, 14). Satisfying employees as a strategy for improving consumer ratings may never be more important than in the near future. As HMOs, employers, and government agencies adopt report-card ratings for health plans and provider networks, one of the first factors to be rated will be customer satisfaction.

Healthcare's most effective future leaders will facilitate a strategic dialogue with physicians and nurses about customer needs and how to produce high-quality services in a competitive market. Powerful shared visions will infuse corporate cultures where the health organization's vision engages workers and managers in a sense of shared values to enhance organizational performance. In healthcare's rush to become competitive, something has been won—cost-effectiveness—but something may have been lost, too—a clear vision of always keeping patient priorities first. The healthcare industry has learned from the private sector how to reduce labor expenses and how to reward performance with pay. Now healthcare's leaders must demonstrate that the health field has aligned its values with those of the healing professionals who make up 80 percent of its cost structure. These noneconomic incentives may make all the difference in motivating work force 2000.

REFERENCES

Aiken, L. H., J. Sochalski, and G. F. Anderson. 1996. "Downsizing the Hospital Nursing Workforce." *Health Affairs* 15 (4): 88–92.

Atkins, P. M. 1997. "Happy Employees Lead to Loyal Patients." *Journal of Health Care Marketing* 16 (4): 14–23.

Barner, R. 1996. "Seven Changes That Will Challenge Managers—and Workers." *The Futurist* 30 (2): 14–19.

Bennis, W., and P. Slater. 1968. *The Temporary Society.* New York: Harper.

Birchall, D., and L. Lyons. 1995. *Creating Tomorrow's Organization: Unlocking the Benefits of Future Work.* London: Pitman Publishing.

Cochrane, J. D. 1997. "Year of the Consumer." *Integrated Healthcare Report* 5 (3): 1–10.

Cohen, J. 1991. "Managing Tomorrow's Workforce Today." *Management Review* 80 (1): 17–21.

Cooper, R. A. 1996. "Perspectives on the Physician Workforce to the Year 2020." *Journal of the American Medical Association* 274 (19): 1534–43.

D'Aunno, T., J. A. Alexander, and C. Laughlin. 1996. "Business as Usual? Changes in Health Care's Workforce and Organization of Work." *Hospital & Health Services Administration* 41 (1): 3–18.

De Guzman, M. M. 1997. "Are Specialists Staging a Comeback?" *Healthcare Leadership Review* 16 (6): 1.

Gertz, D. L., and J. P. A. Baptista. 1995. *Grow to Be Great: Breaking the Downsizing Cycle.* New York: Free Press.

Gilbert, E. 1996. "Employers Flex for New Workforce." *Employee Benefits Review* 21 (15): 3–4.

Guglielmo, W. J. 1996. "What You Can Earn in a Large Group." *Medical Economics* (March 25): 31–43.

Hadelman, J. 1997. "Envisioning the Future: Critical Factors for Future Success." *Spectrum* 1 (3): 1–3.

Hamer, R. L. 1997. *HMO Facts and Trends.* St. Paul, MN: InterStudy.

Jones, M. 1996. "HR Management: Four Trends to Reckon With." *HR Focus* 11 (7): 22–23.

Lamm, R. D. 1996. "The Coming Dislocation in the Health Professions." *Healthcare Forum Journal* 36 (1): 58–62.

Losee, R. H. 1997. "Revitalizing Hospital Culture by Questioning Assumptions About Employee/Management Relations." *Strategies for Healthcare Excellence* 10 (7): 9–12.

Maccoby, M. 1988. *Why Work: Motivating and Leading the New Generation.* New York: Simon & Schuster.

Mishel, L., J. Bernstein, J. Schmitt. 1997. *The State of Working in America 1996–97.* Washington, DC: Economic Policy Institute.

Moore, J. D., Jr. 1996. "Riding High: Hospital CEO Pay Has Surged as Bonus Plans Proliferate." *Modern Healthcare* 26 (27): 33–44.

Oxford Health Plan. 1997. "A Different Perspective." (Advertisement). *New York Times* (March 27): A16–17.

Rich, J. T. 1996. "Future Compensation Shock." *Compensation & Benefits Review* 28 (6): 27–33.

Rifkin, J., and R. L. Heilbroner. 1996. *The End of Work: The Decline of the Global Labor Force and the Dawn of the Post-Market Era.* Putnam Publishing Group.

Risher, H. 1996a. "Behind the Big Picture: Employment Trends in the 1990s." *Compensation & Benefits Review* 29 (1): 8–12.

———1996b. "The End of Jobs: Planning and Managing Rewards in the New Work Paradigm." *Compensation & Benefits Review* 29 (1): 13–17.

Snyder, D. P. 1996. "The Revolution in the Workplace: What's Happening to Our Jobs?" *The Futurist* 30 (2): 8–13.

Weber, D. 1997. "Virtual Integration, Less Costly Than Vertical Integration, Allows Organizations to Focus on Core Competencies." *Strategies for Healthcare Excellence* 10 (7): 1–9.

7

Customer Service:
Healthcare Organizations Turn On to
Customer Choice, Quality, and Service

> *"When was the last time you had freedom of choice in, of all places, a hospital? . . . One choice is no choice at all, and it only makes people feel frustrated and powerless. People have a fundamental need to choose for themselves—give your customers the power of choice."*
> —Roger Dow and Susan Cook (1996, 45–46)

H ealthcare has another megatrend—consumerism. U.S. hospitals, doctors, and HMOs are beginning to listen to the marketplace, and consumers are telling them they want choice, service, and healthy outcomes. The price revolution in healthcare is not over, but buyers are sending new signals that factors other than the "four P's" of marketing—price, price, price, and price—will be driving the market. Informed consumers want data on their plans and providers, and major employers and business coalitions are insisting that managed care plans use extensive HEDIS (Health Plan Employer Data and Information Set) data. These report cards will be public information, helping consumers select between competing HMO options.

Choice is in and gatekeepers are out. The Governance Institute in Washington, D.C., reports that narrow-gated medical panels and hospital networks are not being accepted by consumers, even some plans that are $15 to $35 cheaper per member per month (Governance Institute 1995). As a result, the widely regarded Institute is changing its forecast that low-cost, restricted-choice health plans would dominate the 1990s. Consumers simply were not buying the limited-choice options, even at lower prices.

NATIONAL POLLS SIGNAL CONSUMER DISCONTENT

Consumers are trying to send a message to health insurers, hospitals, and doctors. That message? They hate the current system. A recent consumer poll showed that more than half (55 percent) of all U.S. residents were dissatisfied with the current health system (Colonial Life & Accident Insurance and Employee Council on Flexible Compensation 1995). Women were especially unhappy: Almost 60 percent of female respondents to a national poll categorized themselves as "dissatisfied" with the way the healthcare system currently operates. Consumers want choice. Almost three in four (73 percent) said they could do a better job of keeping their health costs down if their employer would give them more flexibility in choosing their health benefits.

Consumers of all political persuasions are increasingly dissatisfied with the system. A strong majority (58 percent) of consumers reported they had little in common with their political leaders, according to a recent *U.S. News & World Report* survey (1995). The national poll identified seven distinct sociopolitical types (see Table 7.1). Futurist Roger Selbert, editor of *FutureScan*, asserts there is no longer any "center" in American politics (Selbert 1995). It is difficult to categorize these groups with terms like *liberal* or *conservative*, because they tend to align with other groups in shifting alliances, with little stability, on an issue-to-issue basis.

TOMORROW'S CONSUMERS

Social issues such as demographics, family structure, work force participation, spending patterns, consumer expectations, and values—not just economics—will drive healthcare markets. Futurist Michael Annison, president of Denver-based Westrend and author of *Managing the Whirlwind* (Annison 1993), which in 1995 won the American College of Healthcare Executives' James A. Hamilton Book of the Year award, predicts that eight key social trends will influence healthcare organizations:

- *Aging.* The population is getting older, led by an aging baby boom, a rising number of the oldest age groups, and a postboom reduction in population.
- *Changing work force.* Over the next decade, approximately 70 percent of those entering the work force will be women and minorities.
- *Two-income families.* The traditional family of one wage-earner with a stay-at-home mate is almost extinct; both adults work in over 45 percent of U.S. families.

Table 7.1   Consumers Split into Seven Groups

Sociopolitical Group	Percentage of Voters	Types/Description
Populist Traditionalists	15%	Male, under age 45, few college graduates, middle income, "working class"
Stewards	15%	Relatively affluent, college graduates, married but with no children at home, retired
Dowagers	7%	Elderly women, few college graduates
Liberal Activists	20%	Relatively young, single, often women, black males, higher education levels
Conservative Activists	15%	Mostly men (66%), high incomes, college graduates, married with children, "talk radio listeners"
Ethnic Conservatives	16%	Mostly women (61%), ethnically diverse, often older, lower income, few college graduates
Agnostics	12%	Older baby boomers, college and post-graduate study, above-average income, mostly middle class

Source: Adapted from *U.S. News & World Report* Survey, cited in R. Selbert. 1995. *FutureScan* (August 21): 3.

- *Population shifts.* The population center in the United States continues to shift southward and westward, with the majority attracted to fast-growing "megalopolis" regions.
- *Deinstitutionalization.* Americans are willing to do more for themselves and are trusting big institutions like government or business less.
- *Social activism.* A rising tide of social and political action groups are gaining influence, especially in local communities, sometimes confronting government and private-sector companies.
- *Litigation.* As the number of lawsuits grows, an unhappy populace is turning to arbitration, mediation, and collaborative mechanisms as well as to the courts to address grievances.
- *Values.* There is a growing interest in values, incorporating them into public policy, business activity, and private-sector organizations. (Annison 1993)

"RETRO" MANAGEMENT ADVICE REFOCUSES ON CUSTOMERS

Hospitals are returning to their roots—hospitality. The earliest concepts of "hospital" were deeply rooted in the traditions of hospitality and community responsibility, but in the 1980s and 1990s, intense competitive pressures forced today's healthcare organizations to focus more on the bottom line than on customer satisfaction. Two service management consultants, Roger Dow and Susan Cook, authors of *Turned On: Eight Vital Insights to Energize Your People, Customers and Profits*, are challenging the conventional wisdom of price-led competition. They call on today's companies—including hospitals and health plans—to renew their emphasis on customers, service, and quality: *"The future of business lies in the ability to use modern capabilities to recapture the personal relationships of times past"* (Dow and Cook 1996, xxiv). The authors know customers and service. Roger Dow has been a vice president with Marriott for 25 years, and Susan Cook founded Apple University before starting her own firm, Think Customer, based in Tiburon, California. Their insights are based on healthcare as well as private-sector companies. These Fortune 500 companies, and many smaller high-growth businesses, turn technology into a customer-service tool, measure their results, and make changes continuously. Healthcare organizations can learn customer-focused lessons from retail, service, and manufacturing firms.

Mid-Columbia Medical Center in The Dalles, Oregon, is a case example of a customer-centered institution that gives patients what they want—choice, a caring attitude, and individualized treatment. Patients have choices at Mid-Columbia, starting with the hospital gown. How about coral, blue, green, hot pink, or purple? And none of them are "shortie" or "moonie" style. Gowns provide old-fashioned privacy. At Mid-Columbia, patients select "care partners"—a spouse, relative, or friend—who will be trained about their condition and how to care for the patients after discharge. Patients eat when they are hungry, select pictures for their walls, and listen to personal stereos in surgery. Mid-Columbia even lets patients read their own medical charts. Medical staff and administration believe that trust and open communication promote a climate for healing and patient self-responsibility. Patient satisfaction is highest of any hospital in the region, and staff turnover is a remarkably low 3 percent (Dow and Cook 1996).

Harbor Hospital is an inner-city wonder of patient-first care and community service. No waiting in the admitting department at Harbor Hospital. Patients are checked in at bedside, where they are assigned a "care pair"—a registered nurse and a clinical assistant—who will be their primary caregivers. A case manager coordinates their stay through discharge and follow-up. High-tech communications eliminate noisy hallway paging. Employees wear badges that transmit an infrared signal, so each unit's communications center knows where every staff member is working. Patient information is uploaded from bedside computer terminals. ATM-like drug dispensers on the floors eliminate long trips to the pharmacy for medications. This type of technology allows caregivers more time to be where they are needed, at the bedside with patients (Dow and Cook 1996, 145).

LINKING THE CONSUMER AND INFORMATION REVOLUTIONS

Innovators and entrepreneurs are finding ways to link the consumer and the information revolution. Silicon Valley's Jim Clark, founder of Netscape Communications, the profitable Internet software firm, launched an online medical information company called Healtheon Corporation. Industry observers believe this could be a smart move: "There's a huge untapped opportunity out there to invest in healthcare information companies," states Sage Givens, managing partner of San Francisco–based Acacia Venture Partners (Olmos 1996, D8). Healthcare has lagged behind other industries in automation. Putting medical information online for consumers and providers could be the ultimate information architecture for health system integration.

The hardest part may be to convince those who hold the data—insurers, HMOs, and government agencies—to release them for use by publicly accessible networks. Information about practice guidelines is being made available online by some medical organizations. Consumer support groups have proliferated on the Internet and are sharing data on treatment outcomes and new pharmaceuticals. There is much sensitivity about patient data. Confidentiality and security issues must be overcome. Compiled data could be made accessible, but who will pay to pull it together for use by consumers or providers? Providers like Salick Health Care of Los Angeles are compiling oncology data, as is Value Oncology Services, a Santa Monica–based subsidiary of Value Health, which is compiling data on managed care guidelines and treatment effectiveness.

THE NATION'S BEST HOSPITALS

American health consumers want the best medical care available, but how can patients know which university medical center or community hospital is best for a particular disease or condition? Selecting top-quality hospitals and physicians is getting easier with publicly available rankings of some 1,000 hospitals across the nation, compiled by *U.S. News & World Report* (1996). The book-size reference guide is an expansion of *U.S. News'* annual listing of top U.S. hospitals in 16 specialties.

Ratings represent best scores on three dimensions of quality: *reputation* of a hospital's medical specialty in comparison with a national cross-section of other board-certified specialists; *mortality rate,* reflecting the rate of patient deaths when compared by specialty; and other *objective indicators* that vary by specialty, such as the ratio of cardiologists to beds. The reputational data is based on an annual survey of 2,400 physician specialists, some 150 doctors in 16 specialties, conducted by the National Opinion Research Center at the University of Chicago. Mortality data is based on review of the MEDPARS database maintained by the federal Health Care Financing Administration.

From their comparative assessment, editors of *U.S. News & World Report* select an "honor roll" of elite hospitals, which won high ratings in several specialties (see Table 7.2). The number-one institution, Johns Hopkins Hospital in Baltimore, Maryland, is a repeat winner in the *U.S. News'* rankings. Mayo Clinic, Massachusetts General, UCLA, and Duke University round out the top five medical centers. Elite hospitals were cited as superior in as many as 14 (of 16) top-rated specialty programs. To simplify patient use, the report ranks specialty programs for each state to guide consumers toward the best local specialty programs available. The *U.S. News* ratings are coveted. Medical centers such as UCLA use them widely in marketing and advertising.

REDESIGNING FACILITIES FOR "THE WHOLE PERSON"

Healthcare's consumer movement is well aligned with the New Age concept of holistic health—treating the whole person, not just the disease. Capitation and managed care are providing new incentives for providers to take a more comprehensive approach to anticipating and managing health. In Minneapolis, Minnesota, the Allina Health System is placing strategic priority on a new patient-centered clinical model. The goal of the model, according to John Kleinman, M.D., Allina's vice president for clinical care services, is to shift the focus from disease management to a more anticipatory approach (Scott 1996, 15). Allina, a unique merger of health system and HMO, will target five clinical areas for its new care model: cardiovascular, diabetes, asthma, pregnancy, and oncology. The integrated delivery system recognizes that these population groups may not be the most appealing from a marketing standpoint, or yield the greatest cost savings. Allina's goal is to demonstrate tangible evidence of clinical excellence, as measured against competitors, through their patient-focused model.

Healthcare facilities are being designed to foster a health promotion emphasis. In Tampa, Florida, the Adventist Health System/Sunbelt Healthcare Corporation recently completed a new $14 million health facility designed

Table 7.2 America's Top 10 Hospitals

Hospital	Location	Points	Number of Specialties
Johns Hopkins Hospital	Baltimore, Maryland	119	15
Mayo Clinic	Rochester, Minnesota	107	14
Massachusetts General Hospital	Boston, Massachusetts	75	10
UCLA Medical Center	Los Angeles, California	65	12
Duke University Medical Center	Durham, North Carolina	42	9
Cleveland Clinic	Cleveland, Ohio	40	8
University of California, San Francisco	San Francisco, California	30	6
Brigham & Women's Hospital	Boston, Massachusetts	22	5
University of Texas/M.D. Anderson	Houston, Texas	21	4
University of Washington Medical Center	Seattle, Washington	19	6

Source: Adapted from *U.S. News & World Report. America's Best Hospitals.* 1996. New York: John Wiley & Sons, 56.

from a holistic health framework (Poole 1996). The 22,000-foot expansion and renovation updates the Adventists' ten-year-old East Pasco Health Center. A sun-filled atrium links three floors of ambulatory and inpatient services, which include:

- wellness center and fitness facility;
- children's (pediatric) gym;
- in-and-out ambulatory surgery;
- activities-of-daily-living rehabilitation unit;
- progressive patient care unit;
- medical information services;
- public-access medical library; and
- art and sculpture.

WILL CONSUMERISM PROVIDE NEW HOPE FOR SOLO HOSPITALS?

The consumer revolution may help solo hospitals retain their independence. A new study of 12 regional markets shows that nonaligned hospitals can be successful despite high consolidation among competitors (Oshnock and Moak 1996). Many of these freestanding hospitals are located in locations with excellent demographics. Consumer demand means that HMOs cannot leave these hospitals out, even if they are not part of regional systems. Statewide network manager David Wienstien of Georgia's Blue Cross/Blue Shield plan takes an independent stance on contracting: "My main concerns in determining whether or not to contract with a hospital are the entity's reputation in the community, its cost structure, and plans and vision for the future; not whether or not it's a part of a system" (Oshnock and Moak 1996, 9).

Stand-alone hospitals say they could not find a network with a good strategic fit with their consumer-driven "mission of excellence." North Memorial Hospital in the Minneapolis, Minnesota, suburb of Robbinsdale is a holdout in a market almost 100 percent consolidated. Its physicians wanted to be able to contract with multiple HMOs, so the hospital resisted affiliation overtures. North Memorial's strategy is both competitive and cooperative. The hospital is joint-venturing a medical office building with a local health system but has also developed its own network of ambulatory care centers. Management believes the hospital can remain solo by providing the best care and the best price. Patients are highly satisfied, with a recommendation rate of 98 percent. The hospital is participating as a local care system with the Buyers' Health Care Action Group's (BHCAG's) direct-contracting initiative, which was launched in 1997.

To attract and hold a loyal base, successful solo hospitals like North Memorial share a number of consumer-oriented characteristics:

- excellent clinical reputation;
- located in middle-class to affluent neighborhoods;
- medium size (200 to 600 beds);
- comprehensive services mix;
- good payor mix;
- investing in information systems and continuum of care;
- service- and consumer-driven; and
- physician friendly (most have not acquired physicians). (Oshnock and Moak 1996, 8)

SEVEN LEADING TRENDS IN CUSTOMER-FOCUS, SERVICE, AND QUALITY

You know consumerism has arrived when a cardiac surgeon complains he is losing patients to a hospital with more consumer amenities! Cardiac surgeon Scott Merrick, M.D., at the University of California–San Francisco complains that rival Stanford University Medical center can entice heart-surgery patients with "plush carpets and beautiful pictures on the wall"—even an atrium with a grand piano on which guest artists suffuse the hospital air with uplifting music (Weber 1996, 1). Sounds more like a Nordstrom's department store than a hospital, but that is consumer-focused competition in the 1990s. Here are seven key trends in healthcare's emerging consumer movement.

Trend #1—Choice, Choice, and More Choice

Consumers will choose their own local provider networks based on the latest information on quality, service, and customer satisfaction. In Minneapolis/St. Paul, the BHCAG is turning 100,000 enrollees into direct-access purchasers (McCafferty 1998). Employees, dependents, and company-sponsored retirees pick their own local care systems from more than a dozen regional choices. Doctors and hospitals are organized on a local basis. HMOs have put together some care systems, while others are provider sponsored. Employers pay a dedicated premium, and consumers may "buy up" to a more costly option from three tiers of choices.

Trend #2—Direct Access

Consumers want access to a broad array of physicians and hospitals, and they hate to wait! It's easy to improve access—just add more doctors and hospitals. HMO networks are reconsidering their narrow-panel models and reopening once-closed physician and hospital contracts. Provider-sponsored networks are expanding rapidly to provide short-drive access to their managed care enrollees. In Los Angeles, the UCLA Health Network has grown quickly since its 1995 acquisition of Santa Monica Hospital, creating a nucleus of hospitals on Los Angeles' west side (Bilodeau 1995). More importantly, Santa Monica Hospital brings a strong primary care base and a number of capitation contracts. UCLA now has a relationship with United Physicians of Santa Monica and the Santa Monica Medical Center Medical Group, two large physician IPAs. The UCLA Medical Group, a faculty practice plan, is establishing the first of four or five primary care satellites in a "hub-and-spoke" model to feed the two hospitals. UCLA is also establishing a strategic business relationship with the Huntington Provider Group, a 500-physician medical group widely used by southern California HMOs.

In response to consumer demands, HMOs are moving to cut red tape and improve access to referrals (Rundle 1996). California Blue Shield just offered a new option for consumers—an HMO without gatekeepers. This open-access product will cost more than Blue Shield's closed-panel model. Minnesota-based United HealthCare reports that its open access plan, which does not require specialty referrals, is the company's fastest-growing product, with a 44 percent increase in membership in five states. Southern California's PacifiCare offers an HMO point-of-service plan that lets patients choose any doctor for a premium of only $101 per member per month (PacifiCare 1996, A8).

Trend #3—Self-Care: Consumers Take Over Their Own Health

Consumers have their own remedy for rising health costs—self-care—especially when the HMO supports consumers in managing their own health. Industry giant Kaiser Permanente, the nation's largest HMO, is rethinking how to lower service costs while improving customer satisfaction. As a group-model HMO, Kaiser has relied almost exclusively on its own physicians and facilities. The result is a capital-intensive organization competing with network-model HMOs that can more readily accommodate consumer demands of choice and access. What Kaiser really needs is a new model of care. San Francisco consultant Wanda Jones, president of the New Century Healthcare Institute, urges: "If I was running Kaiser, I would not only downsize and get out of the hospital business, I would redesign the medical practice business to include a retail health and wellness designed to teach enrollees at the neighborhood level to become as independent from health professionals as possible" (Heimoff 1996, 25).

An experimental program of self-care handbooks and telephone advice cut demand for clinic visits by 21 percent in a group of HMO high users (Elsenhans 1995). In Washington, D.C., the Group Health Association targeted a limited number of its 145,000 enrollees who were high users of internal medicine units. Over 2,000 HMO members were sent a copy of *Healthwise Handbook*, a self-care manual. Staff nurses were trained to integrate the handbook into advice calls. Costs of the manuals plus staff training was only $16,000, and direct cost benefit was estimated to be at least 2-1, due to visit avoidance and improved member satisfaction. Demand for inappropriate time-limited acute symptom conditions fell by 33 percent, and total outpatient visits dropped 18 percent. Self-care can be very cost-beneficial to health systems.

Trend #4—Harnessing Technology

American consumers have a love affair with technology. Now health plans and provider organizations are recognizing that technology can be a powerful tool for enhancing quality and service. There are many ways in financing and delivering healthcare in which technology will be used to make services more consumer friendly:

- inform consumer choices on physicians and HMOs;
- provide report cards on provider performance;
- individualize treatment plans;
- personalize therapies (for example, patient-controlled medications);
- expedite care processes;
- reduce length of stay;
- reduce routine record keeping; and
- improve caregiver response time.

In Los Angeles, Salick Health Care, a national oncology service provider now owned by Zenaca Pharmaceuticals, is developing a computerized treatment approach that integrates patient data, clinical protocols, and physician profiles. Bringing the information revolution to healthcare is overdue, says founder and former owner Bernard Salick, M.D.: "Insurance companies can tell you the total members in their plan, and how much they spent for care, but they can't tell you how their patients are actually doing" (Olmos 1996, D8). Based on a patient's diagnosis and symptoms, the "SalickNet" system's database selects a physician for the patient. The selection is based on such factors as what type of cancer is suspected, whether it is an initial case or recurrence, and the patient's preference and location. After medical evaluation by a Salick physician, an approved treatment plan is computerized, including treatment guidelines, relevant treatment-quality studies, and efficiency criteria. Each new patient expands the Salick database for in-house clinical trials of new therapies.

Trend #5—Thinking Like a Patient

"Healthcare administrators must learn to take a consumer-centered approach," admonishes Mark Scott, CEO of Mid-Columbia Medical Center in The Dalles, Oregon: "What's wrong with hospitals is that the people in charge don't think what it's like to be a patient in that bed" (Dow and Cook 1996, 1). Mid-Columbia's obsession with customer service fits very well with the fundamental values of Planetree, a San Francisco–based nonprofit consumer organization. Planetree's emphasis on treating the whole patient includes physical, emotional, mental, and spiritual needs. The hospital built a complete healing environment with a strong focus on wellness, humanistic care, access to information, informed consumers, and healing all facets of patients' needs.

Trend #6—Seniors Are Number-One Health Consumers

The growing senior market is the number-one consumer group for health services and related products to assist with activities of daily living (ADL), according to predictions by ProMatura, a market research firm in Oxford, Mississippi (Rawson 1995). Today's 32 million Americans over age 65 will expand to 35 million by 2000. More than half (52 percent) are in the early-retirement category (65 to 74). Older (over age 75) seniors are even more likely to experience chronic illness, need acute care, and require some assistance with daily living. ProMatura reports that seniors are willing to pay more for high-quality health products and ADL support. "Opening a door or a jar is as important to seniors' independence as medical care," states Michael Zaifert, president of a pharmacy/ADL company based in southern California (Rawson 1995, 53).

Mass merchandising and retail firms are new competitors to traditional healthcare organizations and pharmacies. Eckerd Drug, based in St. Petersburg, Florida, is introducing Life Care Centers in its 450 to 500 drugstores across 14 states. The consumer-friendly centers are focused on seniors and will feature a pharmacy, a clinical lab, home medical equipment, and a home nursing program. Interactive video kiosks with toll-free phone lines to health professionals will answer consumer questions (Rawson 1995).

Medicare HMOs are competing aggressively for older consumers with low-copayment services and free benefits. Benefit-led marketing for seniors in southern California has taken pharmacy benefit limits from $500 per year to $2,500. Kaiser Permanente raised the marketing ceiling even higher with a recent ad for its Senior Advantage HMO, with a headline reading "Our New Prescription Benefit *with No Annual Maximum* Is Just What the Doctor Ordered" (Kaiser Permanente 1996, A11). Kaiser's senior plan has no monthly plan premium, 100 percent hospital coverage, and $3 doctor visits. Seniors lured by Kaiser's offer will also receive a 109-page self-health manual. Marketing seminars for participants are held at local restaurants as well as Kaiser clinics.

Trend #7—Paying for Service

Performance-based pay systems reward customer satisfaction. Variable pay systems reposition salaries based on such factors as patient ratings or the bottom line of the organization. Linking pay to a variety of performance outcomes reinforces the organization's concern for customers. A national study of trends in human resources by Lee Hecht Harrison, a New York–based consulting firm, predicted: "Health care professionals who wish to remain in the field will have to learn new skills, accept additional responsibilities, become team players, cultivate strong customer orientation skills, become conscious of bottom-line concerns, and prove they can do more with less" (Bailey and Hirsch-Overton 1993, 25).

The Hay Group, a national human resources consulting firm based in Boston, Massachusetts, predicts: "Next to technology, customers may be the most powerful force changing organizations" (Flannery, Hofrichter, and Platten 1996). Human resources experts believe as health organizations shift from a "process" culture to a "network" culture, they will increase the use of incentive-based compensation. New organizational designs and incentive-based compensation systems are being designed that emphasize the provider-patient partnership. Customer ratings help determine compensation. Healthcare providers have traditionally been conservative about incentive compensation and bonuses. Variable pay is dependent upon measurement systems that track "internal customers" as well as patients, physicians, and the public. In the future, it is likely that hospitals and health systems are likely to shift to outside, national consumer ratings companies that can provide comparative data with peer-group institutions in other markets.

LOOKING FORWARD: *THINK CUSTOMER* WHEN DOWNSIZING, RESTRUCTURING, AND REPOSITIONING

This is the time to renew the hospital's commitment to traditional values. It is not too late to send a message to nursing staff, physicians, and patients that the business of caring still puts caring first. Before the development of modern antibiotics and medical technology, hospitality was about all that a hospital could provide. But the fiscal squeeze of government budget cuts and managed care discounting has forced widespread layoffs. A recent national survey by Challenger, Gray & Christmas, a Chicago-based recruitment firm, found that hospitals had eliminated the jobs of 23,075 doctors, nurses, and technicians between 1993 and 1995 (Shuit 1996). Downsizing is not over. The consultants reported another 8,000 layoffs during the first five months of 1996.

Quality and personal service may among the casualties in the large-scale restructuring of the nation's medical system. Downsizing is raising concerns by patients and government policymakers: "The thinning of the nursing ranks, at a time when managed care is keeping all but the sickest patients out of hospitals, has raised questions about the quality of care in hospitals and whether they are adequately being staffed" (Shuit 1996, A1). Widespread layoffs in California triggered two patient protection ballot initiatives for November 1996, sponsored by the California Nurses Association and Service Employees International Union. The initiatives would require staffing minimums to be defined by state regulators, requiring hospitals to have consistent staffing mix depending upon patient severity. "There is no question that quality is being compromised," says Kit Costello, president of the 25,000-member nurses' union (Shuit 1996, A17). The California Nurses Union contends that UCLA, for example, is targeting more experienced nurses for layoffs as a cost-saving move. The hospital disagrees: "The care today is just as good as it was five years ago," argues Heidi Crooks, UCLA's director of patient care services. UCLA has cut 60 full-time positions down to 650 in the past half-decade.

Hospitalized patients may also complain about too many staffers, not too few. Robin Orr, a Monarch Beach–based consultant who worked with Mid-Columbia Medical Center, pointedly notes: "No wonder patients feel like no one really cares about them. They face a never-ending parade of fifty to sixty people a day coming in and out of their room" (Dow and Cook 1996, 106). She criticizes the patient-centered care movement as being more oriented to cost than service.

U.S. healthcare executives are not thinking about consumers right now. A recent survey by the American Hospital Association identified the top six concerns of hospital officials as managed care, Medicare and Medicaid policies, physician integration, restructuring the delivery system, capitation, and data and information (Green 1995). Note that there are no consumer issues. But healthcare organizations may be upgrading their market orientation in the future. The AHA survey of 152 healthcare administrators found that 80 percent would like more information about community health needs and health status.

Is this latest interest in consumers just another management fad? The new focus on customers comes ten years after "guest relations" and customer-based initiatives flourished in healthcare. That trend became part of total quality management and a variety of quality improvement initiatives, but the focus on consumers became blurred and lost. Downsizing and staff cutbacks sent another signal—management's attention was focused on the bottom line. It has been ten years since most hospitals conducted a customer relations training seminar.

Recent headlines about the "Best HMOs" and "How to Choose Your Doctors" are refocusing healthcare providers' attention on consumers (Spragins 1996). The new emphasis on consumers may be more than a fad if HMOs and employers are serious about selecting providers based on patient ratings. The National Committee for Quality Assurance is sending a strong message about customer satisfaction to HMOs and their provider networks. Maybe this time the "Think Customer" message will stick.

REFERENCES

Annison, M. 1993. *Managing the Whirlwind: Patterns and Opportunities in a Changing World.* Westrend Group.

Bailey, R. W., and J. Hirsh-Overton. 1993. "Health Care Careers in Transition." New York: Lee Hecht Harrison, 1–28.

Bilodeau, A. 1995. "UCLA Strengthens Physician Links to Prepare for Capitation." *Healthcare Systems Strategy Report* 12 (17): 1–2.

Colonial Life & Accident Insurance and Employers Council on Flexible Compensation. 1995. "Workplace Pulse National Survey on Health Care." Cited in *Medical Benefits* 12 (14): 1–2.

Dow, R., and S. Cook. 1996. *Turned On: Eight Vital Insights to Energize Your People, Customers and Profits.* New York: HarperCollins Publishers.

Elsenhans, V. D. 1995. "Use of Self-Care Manual Shifts Utilization Pattern." Cited in *Medical Benefits* 12 (14): 7.

Flannery, T. P., D. A. Hofrichter, and P. E. Platten. 1996. *People, Performance and Pay.* New York: Free Press.

Governance Institute. 1995. *Emerging from Shadow: Resurgence to Prosperity Under Managed Care.* Washington, DC.

Green, J. 1995. "Formal Trend Tracking Gives Way to Casual Methods." *AHA News* 31 (33): 1.

Heimoff, S. 1996. "Rethinking Kaiser." *California Medicine* 3 (4): 21–25.

Kaiser Permanente. 1996. "Our New Prescription Benefit with No Annual Maximum Is Just What the Doctor Ordered." *Los Angeles Times* (June 24): A11.

McCafferty, J. 1998. "Power to the Providers: Hospitals, Doctors, and Some Health Care Purchasers Are Finding Ways to Bypass the HMOs in the Middle." *CFO Magazine* (January).

Olmos, D. 1996. "Digital Medicine." *Los Angeles Times* (July 22): D1, D8.

Oshnock, M. D., and M. N. Moak. 1996. "Solo Hospitals: Sustainable Strategy or Passing Phase?" *Medical Network Strategy Report* 5 (5): 8–12.

PacifiCare. 1996. "Introducing a Health Plan for Individuals." (Advertisement). *Los Angeles Times* (June 24): A8.

Poole, C. D. 1996. "Something Old, Something New: Facility Expansion Emphasizes Holistic Health." *Healthcare Leadership* 1 (1): 9–10.

Rawson, R. 1995. "Getting Older and Wiser." *HomeCare* (August): 53–56.

Rundle, R. 1996. "Heeding Patients' Mounting Frustration, HMOs Move to Cut Referral Red Tape." *Wall Street Journal* (May 30): B1, B2.

Scott, K. 1996. "Allina Health System Revisited." *Health System Leader* 3 (4): 12–19.

Shuit, D. P. 1996. "Hospital Nurses Feel Pain of Restructuring." *Los Angeles Times* (July 1): A1, A17.

Spragins, E. 1996. "Does Your HMO Stack Up?" *Newsweek* (June 24): 56–63.

U.S. News & World Report. 1995. Cited in R. Selbert, "The Center Does Not Hold." *Future Scan* (August 21): 3.

U.S. News & World Report: America's Best Hospitals. 1996. New York: John Wiley & Sons.

Weber, D. O. 1996. "Aggressive Physician-Led Re-Engineering Helps University of California-San Francisco Medical Center Stay Competitive." *Strategies for Healthcare Excellence* 9 (5): 1–10.

Care by Design:
"Hospitals Without Walls," Healing
Environments, and Buildings That
Pay for Themselves

> *Organizations that value patients' lives, staff well-being, visitor participation and community health . . . articulate these values by creating a design that positively influences desired performance outcomes.*
>   —Wayne Ruga, *Innovations in Healthcare Design*
>   (Marberry 1997, 298)

The design of healthcare facilities is a management tool and competitive strategy. High-performance design can make facilities more responsive to the efficiency demands of managed care while increasing responsiveness to consumer needs and expectations. The best future-oriented facilities are being designed to optimize health and create a sense of well-being. An emerging body of research is illuminating what design aspects promote healing and patient satisfaction—and shorten hospital stays with lower treatment costs.

A number of trends are sweeping the field of health facility design and construction:

- *Bedless hospitals.* Large ambulatory care campuses are multiservice satellites that provide a wide range of outpatient diagnostic and therapeutic services with a high level of consumer amenities.

- *Low-tech centers of excellence.* Tomorrow's profit centers are subacute and women's units, not high-tech (and high-cost) centers like cardiology or orthopedics.

- *Patient-centered design.* Consumers are being involved early in the design of future facilities, and space planning is being oriented to bring services much closer to patients.

- *Long-term care facilities.* Expanded investments are now being made in long-term care facilities to build a continuum of care.

- *Critical care.* Rapid obsolescence in critical care units is accelerating the pace of redesign and expansion to accommodate new technology and growing patient volumes.

- *Outside-inside.* Bringing the outside (light, air, plants) into interiors is transforming institutional spaces, refreshing drab institutional settings, and renewing patient spirits.

- *Off-campus.* Ambulatory and long-term care facilities are moving to strategic locations, anchoring a regionally distributed care network.

- *Medical clinic.* Medical office buildings are designed for group practices owned by hospitals, health systems, and physician management companies.

- *Business planning.* Most health facility projects are now justified through a business plan, not a facility/site master plan.

- *Program managers.* Facilities are hiring outside program managers who are specialists in planning, organizing, and managing all aspects of a building program.

HOSPITALS OF THE FUTURE

Hospitals of the next century will be strikingly different from today's large multipurpose facilities. Many hospitals will be smaller, employing far fewer people and specializing in the care of the sickest patients. Other healthier patients will be cared for in a variety of alternate sites such as subacute facilities, ambulatory centers, physician offices, medical clinics, rehabilitation and other specialized units, skilled nursing facilities, and their own homes. Futurist Leland Kaiser of Kaiser Associates, based in Brighton, Colorado, anticipates a "hospital without walls, where care is decentralized outside the hospital and delivered in homes, churches, schools and other settings" (Olmos

1995). As the highest-cost setting, hospitals may be the facilities of last resort in many regional healthcare networks.

Demands of new models of healthcare and new technology will continue to drive future facility projects, despite capital and cost issues. The need to adapt outdated space for new delivery processes and equipment has increased renovation projects. St. Louis healthcare architect Bud Guest of Hosenstab & McCarthy notes, "If an organization built something 10 years ago, there will be a need for something in this space today" (Fitzgerald 1995, 2). Typical of today's healthcare building projects is the Columbus Children's Hospital, which recently completed a $17 million outpatient facility composed of 22 clinics and 7 physician suites. The Columbus, Ohio, health facility contains no inpatient beds and will expand the hospital's role as comprehensive ambulatory care provider with physician offices designed for group practice.

Constructing an ambulatory care facility for hospital-based medical groups is totally different than constructing a traditional medical office building for fee-for-service solo physicians and small groups. In Upland, Pennsylvania, the Crozer-Chester Medical Center has replaced its front door with a 96,000-square-foot ambulatory care pavilion (Saukaitis 1994). Hospital planners decided to position the five-story ambulatory center in front of the hospital's inpatient facility to provide the primary access for all patients and visitors, while symbolically redefining the core business of the hospital as ambulatory services.

Future-oriented facilities will service a cluster of specialized inpatient, ambulatory, and continuum-of-care programs and physician groups into an integrated healthcare campus. In Nashville, Tennessee, Columbia/HCA's Centennial Medical Center and Physicians Park is an $84 million project encompassing 691 acute care beds, 26 skilled nursing beds, a women's hospital, cancer center, extended care services, and a psychiatric hospital pavilion (Fitzgerald 1995). Freestanding ambulatory facilities and the Physicians Park are connected to the inpatient tower by enclosed aerial walkways.

HEALTH FACILITY CONSTRUCTION BOOM MAY BE WANING

Healthcare building was one of the few growth sectors for America's construction industry in the past 20 years. Now there are signs that the boom in new health facilities may be losing momentum, as hospitals fear the effect of managed care and federal budget cuts. The caution light is on for healthcare construction. Although health facility building totaled $11.9 billion in 1994—an increase of 6 percent over 1993—but only one percent of surveyed architects and designers believe that acute hospitals will be a construction opportunity for the future (Fitzgerald 1995).

Despite fears about managed care and Medicare cuts, more than 3,000 healthcare projects completed the design process in 1994, according to *Modern Healthcare*'s annual survey of healthcare design and construction (see Table 8.1). The hospital industry is still building hospitals: Some 29 hospital replacement projects were completed in 1994, while another 60 facilities are moving through the design phase. A majority of architects and designers (51.2 percent) predicted that outpatient care facilities would offer the biggest opportunities for construction in the future.

The five-year outlook for healthcare architecture and design is clouded by managed care's effect on hospital demand. The Sachs Group, in Evanston, Illinois, predicts that nationwide hospital bed demand may fall sharply by 1999, down some 34 percent from 1994 utilization levels (Sachs Group 1995). On the trendsetting West Coast, the Kaiser Permanente Health Plan has several built but unopened hospitals. Kaiser's enrollment in California of 4 million covered lives virtually stopped growing in the mid-1990s, and premium-based competition is forcing a rethinking of Kaiser's capital investment strategy in new facilities. FHP, one of southern California's largest HMOs, which merged with PacifiCare, sold its hospitals and switched entirely to a contracting strategy. It is a buyers' market in California, where hospitals average less than 50 percent hospital occupancy. The California Healthcare Association, in a forecast of healthcare's long-range outlook in

Table 8.1   Healthcare Design and Construction: Annual Survey 1993–1994

Survey Category	1994	1993	Percent Change
Architecture (square feet)	101,802	95,411	6.3%
Architecture (dollar volume)	$11,624	$11,042	5.3
Design/build (square feet)	5,546	4,523	20.5
Design/build (dollar volume)	$566	$457	23.7
Program management (square feet)	4,456	4,412	1.0
Program management (dollar volume)	$672	$647	3.8
General contractor (square feet)	8,282	8,703	−4.8
General contractor (dollar volume)	$739	$723	2.2
Construction management (square feet)	30,285	28,907	4.8
Construction management (dollar volume)	$3,837	$3,614	6.2

Source: Modern Healthcare's Design and Construction Survey, Mar. 27, 1995, 27–42. Reprinted with permission from *Modern Healthcare.* Copyright Crain Communications, Inc., 740 N. Rush Street, Chicago, IL 60611.

the Golden State entitled *California Health Care 1995–2005: A View of the Future,* predicts that bed demand will fall below one bed per 1,000 people, creating a surplus of 33,000 beds in California by 2005 (CHA 1995).

BUILDING PLANS DRIVE BUILDING PLANS

Costs are *the* major factor in planning and constructing future health facilities. Under fiscal pressure from managed care and government Medicare and Medicaid budget cuts, tomorrow's health buildings will be designed to pay for themselves with lower fixed, operating, and energy costs. A new generation of energy-efficient facilities are being designed with nature in mind. Incorporating natural light deep into spaces with ten-foot ceilings is reducing energy costs while improving productivity and patient ratings. More efficient layouts and ergonomics help pay back building costs by reducing transportation and communication efforts, cutting labor hours. Team-oriented configurations are designed for cross-trained, multilevel, self-directed work groups.

In an era of fiscal caution, every health facility project must demonstrate its cost-benefit. Hospitals and sponsoring health systems are asking:

- What is the return on investment?
- Can a new building significantly reduce operating, staffing, or energy costs?
- How is it going to benefit the future healthcare system?
- Will the new facility be a visible symbol of the system's mission and vision?
- How does this capital investment help position the system for managed care?
- Does the design of the facility support the system's "brand recognition" strategy with consumers?
- Will the design, circulation plan, public spaces, and amenities raise consumer satisfaction ratings?
- Are physicians and key medical groups significantly involved and strongly supportive of the project?
- Does it align with the priority goals of the strategic plan?

Health facilities projects are being viewed from a new perspective: How do they reduce clinical costs? Anthony Roesch, a principal with the Chicago office of Bobrow/Thomas and Associates, notes that less than 15 percent of total operating costs relate to capital maintenance costs such as facilities and equipment. More critical to facility designers is the challenge of obtaining reductions of 10 to 20 percent in the clinical costs of operating the facility, which average some 60 percent of a typical hospital's annual operating budget (Roesch 1994). For example, Roesch observes that each of the following items costs about the same—$1.5 million:

- total cost of electronic bedside charting for a 400-bed hospital;
- annual labor cost for a 35-bed nursing unit;
- annual energy cost for a 600-bed hospital in the Midwest;
- annual interest expense for a $30 million bond at 5.5 percent fixed rate of interest;
- total cost of equipping a single-plane cath laboratory; and
- annual cost for pharmaceutical and medical supplies for a surgical center with four operating rooms.

FLEXIBLE "UNBUNDLED" HEALTH FACILITIES OF THE FUTURE

A perennial problem for planners, designers, and architects is how to build flexibility into health facilities for a set of future functions and technologies that may be very different from today's. The average American hospital lasts 30 to 40 years, and some U.S. facilities have been used for more than a century. Bond financing is typically on a 30-year basis. Lenders and bond-holders assume a long lifecycle for hospital buildings, although remodeling often begins within ten years after the facility is opened.

Built to rigorous safety codes and building standards, hospitals are long-lived, even if their facilities become functionally obsolete after the first 15 years. Today's healthcare facilities, costing $50 to 200 million—with some over $1 billion!—won't soon be closed or demolished. San Francisco–based planning consultant Wanda Jones, president of the New Century Institute, observes:

> Most managers plan their facilities to solve today's space needs. While accomplishing that goal, many hospital designs "freeze in" today's orga-
> nizational patterns. Hospital administrators and their staffs share a medical culture bias toward consensus-building that is expressed through asking teams of people at the operating level to deal with day-to-day or month-to-month issues and annual budgets. Every seven to 15 years, however, a similar team will be asked to plan for a facility that may last 40 or more years and cause the generation of many millions of dollars of operating expenses. (Jones 1995, 12)

More than one-third of health facility projects often experience problems, according to a survey of health facilities managers by Princeton, New Jersey–based consultants CUH2A, Inc. (Ingalls 1993). Almost half (45 percent) of facility managers characterize their facility/real estate strategy as only loosely defined, and only 21 percent of the managers based their facility plans on a solid financial model for analyzing facility costs. Corporate-wide standards for design were lacking in a majority (60 percent) of systems and hospitals, and only 8 percent had a database for predicting future staffing and space requirements. The survey underscores the problem about lack of long-range planning, even by large systems operating more than one million square feet of health services and facilities.

Modern design concepts increasingly emphasize a flexible cluster of spaces that anticipate that many services will be brought to the patient. The goal is to minimize the time and expense of intrafacility travel for both patients and staff. The acute hospital may play a much lesser role in the health system of the future, a loosely coupled network of services that rely on ambulatory and in-home settings for many healthcare services.

Tomorrow's health facilities may be a "hospital without walls" of various settings and services spread across a broad market region. Information systems, fiber-optic cable, and microwave communications will make it possible to coordinate care across markets and even time zones. Hospital departments, often numbering 30 to 50, are rapidly becoming obsolete as diagnostic and care functions are cross-trained and flexibly provided by health teams. Ancillary departments occupying thousands of square feet will be replaced by off-site, centralized facilities complemented by small, often portable units located close to patients.

New "bedless hospitals" may be as large as 300,000 to 400,000 square feet of all-ambulatory facilities, with adjacent subacute, skilled nursing, rehabilitation, or specialized recovery facilities. Texas Medical Center's Methodist Hospital in Houston opened a new $50 million ambulatory care center with only 22 recovery beds in 1998. Hospital designers and architects are adjusting their vision of the hospital. The concept of bedless health facilities is the focus of a national conference in 1998 by the American Institute of Architecture.

Public hospitals are taking on a new look. In Lancaster, California, the High Desert Medical Center is a 550,000-square-foot replacement hospital designed by Los Angeles office of the architectural firm of Anshen + Allen (Anshen + Allen 1995). As a public hospital operated by Los Angeles County, the facility will provide a range of healthcare and health education services to a young, expanding population in the northeast corner of the county. Three core concepts were used in the design: (1) creation of a physical and psychological "oasis" to provide a place of healing, calm, and shelter; (2) layers of enclosure to integrate the facility with its desert environment; and (3) decentralized design that "unbundles" the buildings to separate inpatient, ambulatory, and support services. The 40-acre campus includes a main hospital building, clinic building, and general services and central plant facility. For its holistic approach, the project was awarded a Citation of Excellence Award from the American Institute of Architects.

TEN NEW TYPES OF HEALTH FACILITIES FOR THE FUTURE

There is definitely an upside outlook to health building. A new generation of hospitals, ambulatory centers, medical offices, and continuum-of-care facilities will be needed. Hospitals built in the 1960s and 1970s are already reaching technological obsolescence. Large outmoded inpatient facilities with surplus beds will be replaced with much smaller acute-care hospitals. Aging hospitals will be recycled into chronic care facilities or ambulatory centers. The slowdown of acute and ambulatory construction is being replaced by greater investment in long-term care. Despite a shrinkage in the size and scale of new projects in the next five years, health facility construction will total at least $10 to $12 billion annually, and possibly higher, for 1995 to 2000. Even if future facilities are smaller and more cost-efficient, there will still be building in the health sector.

Cost-cutting and consolidation may spur a new generation of health building projects that rationalize current overcapacity and provide sustainable spaces for health services under a managed care, cost-constrained scenario:

1. *"NewCo" hospital* will be built as a single replacement facility when two local hospitals have merged under a new identity (e.g., "NewCo").
2. *The downsized hospital* will be a new facility or radical re-do of an existing hospital with a small inpatient core, with 60 to 70 percent of the square footage dedicated to ambulatory and continuum-of-care services.
3. *The long-term care hospital* will redesign and convert a surplus acute-care hospital into a continuum-of-care facility, offering such services as subacute care, rehabilitation, skilled nursing, behavioral medicine, and chronic care programs like cardiac rehabilitation.
4. *An ambulatory surgical megafacility* will be a regional surgical center handling more sophisticated ambulatory surgical procedures with ten or more surgical suites, which may be supported by 10 to 20 post-surgical recovery beds for stays of 24 to 48 hours.
5. *The women's center* will "bundle" a variety of inpatient, ambulatory, and chronic care services for women, including obstetrics, gynecological surgery, cancer treatment, and specialized diagnostic services, such as mammography, diabetic care, and cardiac care.
6. *The birthing center* will perform short-stay (under 48 hours) normal vaginal deliveries for low-risk patients in hotel-like facilities.
7. *An ambulatory health campus* will provide a full spectrum of health services—except acute inpatient care—on campus settings of 25 to 40 acres. The campus will include medical office buildings, group medical clinics, ambulatory surgery facilities, diagnostic centers, outpatient rehabilitation, a pharmacy, and home care, in projects that may range from 400,000 to 500,000 square feet.

8. *Community health education* facilities may be constructed in sites that are easily consumer-accessible, such as ambulatory care centers, storefront retail spaces, shopping malls, and retirement centers.

9. *Health and fitness centers* will be designed to appeal to the baby boom generation, now reaching age 50, to maintain their vitality and well-being with a variety of exercise, weight reduction, and health promotion programs.

10. *Complementary therapy centers* may co-locate a variety of alternative medicine ambulatory, diagnostic, and therapeutic services, such as acupuncture, meditation, counseling, stress reduction, and a homeopathic pharmacy.

TWENTY-FIRST CENTURY DESIGN: REINVENTING HEALTH FACILITIES

If they hope to survive in a managed care market, hospitals and health facilities must be reinvented to be patient centered and cost effective. To become healing environments, hospitals and traditional healthcare settings will have to overcome significant environmental and procedural issues. A report in *U.S. News & World Report* observes:

> Most hospitals are dismally inhospitable. A weakened patient and traumatized family are greeted by harsh lights and cold stainless steel, labyrinths of white corridors, thumping equipment, and acrid mysterious smells. The sick rarely have access to information, privacy or a place for quiet talk and grieving. The resulting sense of anxiety and helplessness is the worst imaginable to promote healing. (Horn 1991)

It won't be easy. Hospitals are among the largest, most bureaucratic buildings-cum-organizations anywhere. Downsizing to meet shrinking inpatient demand is only part of the solution. There are still far more hospitals than the future market may support. If Michael Sachs of the Sachs Group is correct, only one bed in three will be needed by 2000 (Sachs Group 1995, 8). Does this mean only one hospital in three will survive into the twenty-first century? Hospitals and health facilities will have to become high-performance workplaces if they are to meet the tests of managed care and economic competition.

Designers are recognizing that space is the physical environment in which technology, work processes, management style, organizational values, and cost factors are expressed (Becker and Steele 1995). The environmental ecology is not a series of boxes and static work spaces but a single integrated system that efficiently advances the strategic goals, decision making, and business practices of the organization. In healthcare, the challenge is designing a high-performance workplace that optimizes patient health as well as cost efficiency.

A broader concept of healthcare design and architecture is now sweeping the health field. Hospitals will need more than geographic location and a reputation for clinical excellence. Even the latest technology may not be enough to attract HMO contracts and win high consumer ratings. Future-minded hospitals and health systems are designing new facilities that put the patient first:

- In Orlando, Florida, the Walt Disney organization has designed a home-based, computer-linked model of care in Celebration, a new town planned to house 30,000 to 50,000 residents.
- In San Diego, California, Sharp Healthcare opened a new institute in 1994 to promote alternative therapies and "body-mind" medicine.
- In Chicago, Illinois, two suburban hospitals have built a breast health and mammography center inside a Nordstrom store.
- In Palo Alto, California, the Stanford University Hospital built a health library in the Stanford Shopping Center serving 15,000 consumers; it recently opened a "branch" on-site library that includes a patient/family reading room and online access to computer networks. (Olmos 1995; Goodkind 1994)

Many models of futuristic healthcare have already been designed. The National Center for Health Design, in Martinez, California, annually conducts the National Symposium on Healthcare Design. In recent years, there has been a flurry of innovative design involving every category of health facility with a strong emphasis on alternative medicine, prototypes, and models. A design competition features dozens of entries of all types of health buildings and interiors. Interest in progressive healthcare design is international. More than a quarter of the National Symposium's attendees are from Europe, Asia, the Pacific Rim, and South America, and new facilities are being showcased on a global basis.

Contemporary health facility design is certainly more customer-sensitive than the "science laboratory" designs of the past. Wallpaper, carpeting, comfortable chairs, and art on the walls have contributed to a more homelike atmosphere in many hospitals and physician waiting rooms. But genuinely accommodating health consumers would go below the surface level and address the anxiety and discomfort that patients experience.

Architect Wayne Ruga asserts that in a really progressive healthcare setting, patients should be able to design their own environment, including controlling such factors as:

- air quantity, quality, temperature, humidity, and movement;
- quality and quantity of light;
- color;
- acoustical privacy and control;

- odor and fragrance;
- art;
- dietary selection;
- decoration;
- privacy;
- room size and shape;
- audiovisual media;
- bed adjustment; and
- room layout. (Ruga 1995, 298)

Healthcare designers are seeking input from research and from patient preferences in designing future facilities. An innovative contribution to healing design comes from the ancient Chinese art of feng shui, which integrates a broad range of concepts from the practical to the philosophical and mystical. Feng shui adherents believe that color inspires emotions and structures behavior. Color, they believe, influences life experiences. The wise arrangement of color can increase happiness, foster harmony, and improve feelings of life satisfaction and well-being. For example, feng shui master Lin Yun's guide to the art of color advises that physician offices be painted primarily in white, "a color of cleanliness and purity" (Rossbach and Yun 1994, 85). Doctors' offices would give patients a sense of hope and life, with light off-white colors, including apple green, light blue, or off-white with a pink hue.

CONSUMER-DRIVEN COMPETITION

Consumers may not know much about medical technology and disease, but they know what they like. One health planner observes, "The new emphasis on main entries, attractive public areas, and improved signage all reflects attempts to appeal to a public whose tastes have been largely conditioned by their experience as consumers and by their exposure to the architectural vocabulary of shopping malls and convention hotels" (Quebe 1985). Patients who are unable to judge the quality of their medical care are making choices based on the hospital's image.

Designing healthcare facilities and systems for the human experience is essential. Sending a *we care* message must be designed into the facility (Carpman and Grant 1993, 7). From the moment a patient or visitor arrives at a healthcare facility, the design will convey symbolic messages. These symbols, intentional or not, convey whether the facility is designed for staff concerns or from a mission of caring for the whole person. The facility design includes its color scheme, circulation pattern, furniture arrangements, windows, signage, and accommodations for visitors and family. The height of the counter at a nursing station sends a message, whether it is "we are here to help you" or "go away, we professionals are busy." The physical design can encourage or discourage certain behaviors, by staff as well as patients. The positive healing effects of design are now being discovered, including "wayfinding" (the ease with which people find their way around buildings), physical comfort, and regulation of social contact and psychological needs.

The concept of the healing environment is becoming accepted, and recognition of the link between design and healing is now a widely emerging trend. Patient-focused healing integrates caring and curing in healthcare, when all aspects of the medical, nursing, support, and facilities are intended to advance one purpose—producing a healthy person. Futurist Leland Kaiser admonishes healthcare executives and trustees to better understand "what lies beyond the numbers" (Kaiser 1993, xi). The traditional technology focus of modern medicine, combined with the economic imperatives of managed care, have created a distance between healthcare organizations and the patients they serve (Moore and Komras 1993). Kaiser believes that patient-focused healing is part of a new vision of healthcare in the United States. More fundamentally, Kaiser predicts that hospitals will only survive if they meet the most rigorous survival criteria, including the best patient-care environments.

The symbolic and physical effect of healthcare environment and design was overlooked until recent years. The "sick building" phenomenon has only recently been discovered (Holdsworth and Sealey 1992). Research has recently shown that design ignoring basic psychological needs may increase level of anxiety, elevate blood pressure, and increase the need for pain-relieving drugs. A warm, nurturing setting, on the other hand, can induce a relaxation response, reduce medication levels, and shorten patient stays (Ulrich 1991). The results of a controlled study that compared outcomes of patients whose room faced a wall with patients who had a view of natural scenery shocked hospitals, which generally assumed that modern medicine could be delivered effectively in any clean facility with reasonably modern technology and trained staff. Norman Cousins, whose works on the healing power of humor and hope became national bestsellers, once checked himself out a hospital to protest the constant noise and privacy intrusions (Cousins 1979).

HEALTHY SPACES AND HEALTHY COMMUNITIES

The coming architectural and design revolution in healthcare will refocus facilities to produce the ultimate outcome—health. Leanne Kaiser Carlson of Kaiser Associates, based in Brighton, Colorado, believes: "In the 21st century, the real architectural challenge will be the design of physical and social infrastructures that support health. If we want health, we must design total communities" (Carlson 1994, 37). She predicts the arrival of new models of healthcare delivery in the future, including:

- *Psycho-architecture* will progress beyond creating more comfortable environments to designing spaces that have an orchestrated, intentional effect on consciousness. A concept of health-promoting architecture will begin with healthcare facilities, such as healing gardens, but will ultimately recognize the contribution of schools, work sites, and homes to feelings of health, well-being, and spirituality.

- *Distance medicine* takes healthcare out of traditional settings and into rural areas, satellite clinics, and homes. Linked by computer and telemedicine technology, health is a community affair, driven as much by social and economic forces as by the availability of high-tech medicine.

- *The healing village* combines conventional and alternative therapies to promote health. In Hawaii, plans for a healing village are taking shape. The North Hawaii Community Hospital, now in the planning phase, will have a small inpatient core, with only one-third of the space being devoted to inpatient beds. The dominant emphasis will be placed on ambulatory care and alternative approaches such as acupuncture, massage, chiropractic, biofeedback, music, and vibrational therapies.

LOOKING FORWARD: HEALTH FACILITIES THAT PUT PATIENTS FIRST

Founded in 1978 by a group of activists, the Planetree program was a radical departure from healthcare as usual (Olmos 1995, A17). The concept was simple—put the patient first, in everything from putting medical records on bedside tables to telling patients about their disease in detail—with an armload of literature from the National Library of Medicine. The goal of Planetree founders like Angele Thierot and executive director Robin Orr was to create an informed patient who would be a therapeutic partner in their own health.

The Planetree ideals are no longer radical, but they are far from widespread. San Jose Hospital administrator Bob Bruckner says simply: "This [Planetree] is how we should have been doing it all along." Health Dimension executives Bruckner and John Aird installed Planetree in their health system, based in San Jose, California, in the 1980s and built a consumer health resource center with an extensive library compiled by Planetree staff. Despite pioneering efforts like these, only a handful of America's more than 5,000 hospitals have adopted similar programs.

Planetree's first model nursing unit, with 13 medical/surgical beds in the California Pacific Medical Center in San Francisco, created a sensation. After a Planetree-directed makeover, the unit eliminated its nursing station. A family room for patients and visitors had been created instead, with a kitchen for preparing snacks. Nurses did their paperwork from small workstations that were shared with physicians. Doctors had to sign a set of Planetree principles before being allowed to admit patients to the special unit. A full-time health educator helped patients understand their condition and treatment in full medical detail. Medical records were kept at bedside, and patients were encouraged to write their own progress reports.

Oregon-based Mid-Columbia is the most complete expression of Planetree's commitment to making health facilities less sterile and more humanistic. Administrator Mark Scott first heard of Planetree at a business conference assisting hospitals adapt to the managed care revolution. As the sole community hospital located 70 miles from Portland, Mid-Columbia faced an erosion of patients attracted to more modern facilities in the metropolitan area. Mid-Columbia chose to challenge this migration and undertook a $5 million remodeling that reduced the number of beds from 125 to 49, converted every patient room into single occupancy, and created a family atmosphere on every unit. Scott says, "We're trying to personalize what it is we do in this crazy business. We know how positive emotion helps people heal. I just want to enliven this place with positive emotion" (Olmos 1995, A16).

Mark Scott is right. Why not just put patients first? Architect Derek Parker argues for the creation of a patient's bill of rights in healthcare architecture and design (Parker 1996). This statement of patient-first design principles would feature the consumer's rights to natural light, privacy, quiet, and the ability to control his or her environment from bedside. Parker believes strongly that these design guidelines can be delivered in cost-effective health facilities. His firm, Anshen + Allen, is the designer of award-winning Lucille Packard Children's Hospital of Stanford. The entire facility was designed from a child's point of view. Architects and hospital staffers tested full-scale mockups of patient rooms and treatment facilities—on their knees, at child height, to experience the spaces from the same perspective as a pint-sized patient.

After almost 20 years, why aren't there more Planetree-like hospitals? Twenty-three hospitals have adopted Planetree principles for patient-centered care, from California to Norway and England. But this patient-oriented concept that seems so steeped in common sense has yet to gain acceptance from the mainstream. Only Mark Scott's Mid-Columbia Medical Center has been totally redesigned to put patients first. Planetree's former executive, Robin Orr, now a consultant with the Orr Group in Tiburon, California, suggests: "There's a lot of skepticism, and cost is an issue that people put up there as an excuse for not doing some of these things, but it doesn't cost more money to treat patients with dignity and respect."

If patient advocates like Robin Orr, Derek Parker, and Mark Scott have their way, every patient encounter should be a designed experience in which healthcare consumers would experience uniquely satisfying treatments and outcomes. Imagine that a trip to a hospital or physician office could be as satisfying as a week in fantasy baseball camp, playing baseball with major league greats and wearing an official uniform. Sounds too good to be true? Why not healthcare? Few services are as personal—and stressful—as a hospital stay or a medical examination. It is past time for America's hospitals, health systems, and HMOs to provide their services while putting the patient first.

REFERENCES

Anshen + Allen. 1995. *High Desert Medical Center Replacement Facility.* Los Angeles: 1–4.

Becker, F., and F. Steele. 1995. *Workplace by Design: Mapping the High-Performance Workscape.* San Francisco: Jossey-Bass.

California Healthcare Association (CHA). 1996. *California Health Care 1995–2005: A View of the Future.* Sacramento.

Carlson, L. K. 1994. "Designing Healthy Spaces." *Healthcare Forum Journal* 37 (2): 37–39.

Carpman, J. R., and A. M. Grant. 1995. *Design That Cares.* 2d ed. Chicago: American Hospital Publishing.

Cousins, N. 1979. *Anatomy of an Illness as Perceived by the Patient: Reflections on Healing and Regeneration.* New York: Bantam Books.

Fitzgerald, J. 1995. "Healthcare by Design." *Modern Healthcare* 25 (13): 27–39.

Goodkind, M. 1994. "Better Late Than Never: On-Site Library Provides Information to Everyone." *Health Facilities Management* 7 (7): 22–23.

Holdsworth, B., and A. Sealey. 1992. *Healthy Buildings: A Design Primer for a Living Environment.* Burnt Mill, England: Longman House Publishers.

Horn, M. 1991. "Hospitals Fit for Healing." *U.S. News & World Report* (July): 48–50. Cited in N. Moore and H. Komras, *Patient-Focused Healing* (San Francisco: Jossey-Bass, 1993), 75.

Ingalls, L. 1993. "Survey: Long-Range Facility Planning." *Facilities Planning News* 12 (9): 10.

Jones, W. J. 1995. "Acute Care Design: Emerging Trends." In *Innovations in Healthcare Design,* edited by S. Marberry, 12–21. New York: Van Nostrand Reinhold.

Marberry, S. O. (ed.). 1997. *Innovations in Healthcare Design.* New York: Van Nostrand Reinhold.

Olmos, D. R. 1995. "Hospitals Reinvent Themselves." *Los Angeles Times* (January 11): A1, 16–17.

Parker, D. 1996. Presentation to the Board, National Center for Health Design, Sausalito, California, August 11.

Quebe, J. L. 1985. "The Changing Landscape of Health Care." *Health Care Strategic Management* (December): 4–10. Cited in J. R. Carpman and M. A. Grant, *Design That Cares,* 2d ed (Chicago: American Hospital Publishing, 1995).

Roesch, A. 1994. "Facilities Solutions for Reducing Clinical Costs." *Facilities Planning News* 13 (4): 3, 20.

Rossbach, S., and L. Yun. 1994. *Living Color: Master Lin Yun's Guide to Feng Shui and the Art of Color.* New York: Kodansha International.

Sachs Group. 1995. *Health Care 1999: A National Bellwether.* Evanston, IL.

Saukaitis, C. A. 1994. "Ambulatory Care Pavilion Takes Its Place Out Front by Solving Multiple Needs." *Health Facilities Management* 7 (9): 20–21.

Ulrich, R. 1991. "Effects of Interior Design on Wellness: Theory and Recent Scientific Research." *Journal of Healthcare Interior Design* 3 (3): 97–109.

9

Strategic Planning: Building Stakeholder Commitment by Setting Future Directions

> *Like the Moon mission, a true BHAG ("big, hairy, audacious goal")*
> *is clear and compelling, and serves as a unifying point of effort—*
> *often creating immense team spirit. It has a clear finish line, so the*
> *organization can know when it has achieved the goal; people like*
> *to shoot for finish lines.*
> —James Collins and Jerry Porras (1994, 84)

The future should not be an accident. Healthcare organizations must plan their way into the millennium—and beyond. Failure to plan could result in slumping revenues, lost business opportunities, and unmatched competitor moves. It is not enough to imagine the future, advises C. K. Prahalad, coauthor of *Competing for the Future*, "you also have to build it" (Prahalad 1997, 67). The plan must be a combination of vision, market intelligence, strategy, implementation—all working to achieve a desired outcome. Organizations need a blueprint for building future businesses and expanding their existing service lines. A study by the Association of Management Consulting Firms reported in *Business Week* that "strategy is now the single most important management issue, and will remain so for the next five years" (Byrne 1996, 46).

Marketing experts believe the lack of planning is a growing problem in healthcare (Hemmasi, Graf, and Williams 1997, 38). Unless companies have a clear vision about how they are going to be different and unique, they may be trounced by their competition if they offer something different than their rivals to some different group of customers (Porter 1997, 49).

Planning is essential to grow revenues, create new products and services, and increase market share in the health field. Planning must be proactive, not reactive. Healthcare managers have been preoccupied with cost management for a decade, focusing internally while the outside world has changed substantially. The major transformations now taking place in the provision of health services demand a proactive approach and a renewed emphasis on strategic thinking. Fortune 500 companies are training thousands of managers to "think out of the box"—innovative thinking, abstract thinking, lateral thinking (Thompson and Brooks 1997, 20). The goal is to develop new and unique ways to gain competitive advantage.

THE COURAGE TO PLAN

With little time remaining until 2001, the official start of the next millennium, U.S. healthcare providers must soon rise to meet the challenge of the future. Strategic planning is not for the timid: Every assumption and tactic will be open to scrutiny, and an open planning process could tip off competitors. Planning requires the courage for administrators and boards to be forthright in their market predictions and self-assessment and lead with their chin—and their values—in tomorrow's competitive market.

Planning can be dangerous. A strategic plan puts everything on the table, where every stakeholder in the organization—and every competitor—can see where it is going. It is the blueprint of the architecture for building a desired future market position—the roadmap to the future. The plan sets forth the mission, markets, products, services, and specific objectives of the organization, often with detailed how-to tactics. The goals of planning are to reduce uncertainty, identify market opportunities and threats, and develop business strategies that will create sustained competitive advantage. Planning focuses the organization outward, compelling senior management and the board to recognize the challenges of the environment. A realistic plan also forces a tough internal assessment of the organization's capabilities and limitations.

The progressive healthcare organization will open itself to an internal and external assessment process that may challenge every assumption and basis upon which the hospital, medical group, or health plan has been successful in the past. Leaders are those executives who have the courage to make their ideas and ideals publicly accessible in a written strategic plan to every level of the organization. A reluctance to plan is actually risk-avoiding behavior. Planning takes courage because the leaders of the organization make their goals explicit. If they miss, everyone knows it. Those senior executives who "keep their options close to their vest" are ensuring that if their goals are not achieved, only a few will be aware of the failure.

WHY PLAN, ANYWAY?

Is a plan necessary for success? The planning literature is generally positive, but the actual evidence is thin (Bruton, Oviatt, and Kallas-Bruton 1995). After reviewing dozens of studies on the effect of planning, the evidence in service industries and healthcare is mixed. Research in other service industries suggests that planning processes can become bureaucratic, inhibiting an organization's flexibility and ability to respond quickly to market changes. In healthcare, planning has been shown to be helpful in adjusting to strategic change. Engaging in planning can enhance quality, as demonstrated in better patient rankings on customer satisfaction. Strategic plans help large health systems promote integration.

Too much emphasis on planning can be an impediment to rapid adaptation to market changes. Management guru Tom Peters is a supporter of "ready, fire, aim" (Peters 1987). He obviously has a bias for action. If Tom Peters is right, the modern company must learn to thrive in "chaos," a constantly swirling mix of market trends, competitor moves, government regulation, and consumer behavior. Who can plan when the assumptions are continuously changing? Better to "try it, do it, fix it," and try again, argues Peters, the best-selling author of *In Search of Excellence* and *Thriving in Chaos*. But past success is no guarantee of future success. Only a few of the 36 firms profiled in *In Search of Excellence* are still high-performers, and a few have fallen into bankruptcy (Makridakis 1996).

Strategic planning has had its ups and downs in corporate popularity. After a surge in the 1970s, with such planning fads as zero-base budgeting, planning fell out of favor in the 1980s, when many organizations fell back into a style of incremental decision making that Charles Lindblom (1965) characterized as "muddling through." The real issue was that operational management was divorced from the planning activities directed by nonoperational planning staff who were far from the factory floor or patient's bedside.

The culprits in the planning decline are global competition, new technology, and the increasing pace of change (Zeleney 1997, 77). Planners counter this criticism with the argument that planning will produce more thoughtful (and more accurate) strategies by which the organization will achieve its goals in the marketplace. Organizational psychologist Henry Mintzberg (1994) takes a frankly skeptical view of planning in *The Rise and Fall of Strategic*

Planning, asking, "Is strategy making simply a process of planning? Or is strategic planning an oxymoron, like 'jumbo shrimp'? Should strategies always be planned, never be planned, or sometimes be planned?" (Mintzberg 1994, 5)

A more balanced view is offered by Peter Senge. Planning is part of becoming a "learning organization," a term used widely by MIT's Peter Senge, author of *The Fifth Discipline* (1993). The information revolution has only accelerated the need to learn and plan. Being able to gather and send information in gigabytes may only make strategy development harder. Senge observes, "We are out of control, driving down a dark road with little or no light, and most technological progress amounts to speeding up" (Senge 1997, 125). Large complex healthcare organizations must develop a "global" view of their market and develop shared visions. Through systems thinking and understanding interdependencies in their markets, healthcare providers can develop innovative solutions, like virtual organizations.

RICHES IN THE NICHES

One good reason to plan is to sharpen an organization's focus on very specific customer segments. American healthcare is experiencing a revival in consumerism. After a decade of gatekeepers, choice and access are becoming easier for health plan enrollees, and HMOs and insurers are scrambling to expand provider networks and make it less difficult for consumers to see physician specialists. Consumer report cards are gaining popularity. Lists of the best hospitals and HMOs have been presented recently by *U.S. News & World Report* and *USA Today*, and President Clinton's commission is producing a "patient's bill of rights."

Assuming healthcare consumers may get greater flexibility in selecting providers and services, what would they like? Marketing consultant Philip Kotler, author of *Marketing for Healthcare Organizations*, has a number of market-savvy observations about the millennium marketplace:

- *Older consumers.* Mature consumers, those over age 55, will become the dominant consumers of many services and products.
- *Entertainment.* People will want to be entertained whatever they're doing, whether working, shopping, or consuming.
- *High-income consumers.* Marketing tactics will be targeted at the upper-income customer, who will demand high-quality products and personalized services.
- *Shrinking middle class.* The buying market will be segmented into high- and low-income consumers, with a declining number of true middle class, who will stretch their purchasing power by choosing basic, no-frills products and services at the lowest possible price.

- *Hassle-free.* Time-starved consumers with disposable income will respond positively to products and services that are made available in a hassle-free way.
- *Geoclustering.* Computer analysis of demographics, consumption patterns, and available income will give marketers very precise data on specific market segments.
- *Consumer types.* Market research firms will provide a rich database on consumer values, attitudes, and preferences, like the PRIZM lifestyle groupings developed by the Claritas Corporation, with such categories as "young influentials," "emergent minorities," and "shotguns and pickups."
- *Cause-related marketing.* Organizations can achieve differentiation for their products or services by sponsoring high-consensus social causes, such as the environment. (Kotler 1997, 198–201)

WHOOPS! THE ASSUMPTIONS WERE WRONG

Future assumptions are the bedrock that underlie any strategy plan. But lately, many assumptions are being challenged. Think about some of the predictions that have been widely used benchmarks in healthcare's strategic thinking.

- *Kaiser's staff model.* California's Kaiser model of medical organization was widely considered the most efficient in American medicine. How many physicians does a hospital need in the future? Just apply Kaiser's physician-population ratios by specialty. Kaiser in the 1990s was investing $4 to $6 billion in creating a company-owned network of facilities for the twenty-first century. But today, Kaiser is closing hospitals and outsourcing acute and physician services. Go figure!
- *Capitation.* Despite many predictions that capitation would dominate healthcare payment, this reimbursement model is taking hold slowly. Why? Because HMOs found out that physicians could make money under capitation, so the plans would like to regain control of the premium.
- *Primary care gatekeepers.* California HMOs extensively used primary care physicians (PCPs) as gatekeepers to the system, but attempts to apply the gatekeeper model in other markets have met with stiff resistance from consumers and specialists. The latest reports from California suggest that PCPs may be switched back to fee-for-service and capitation switched to subspecialist physicians.
- *Nonfunctional IPAs.* Market research organizations like the Advisory Group, based in Washington, D.C., considered IPAs (independent physician associations) as unlikely to have the capital, management, or discipline to be a factor in managed care, but market experience is demonstrating that IPAs can be very effective in assuming and managing risk and capitation.

This uncertainty is calling into question the whole process of strategic planning. Is it realistic to believe that a hospital or medical group can really predict its future? Many organizations are confining their assumptions and planning horizons to the immediate future—12 to 36 months, at most.

WHAT IS STRATEGY?

This is the era of hypercompetition. Markets and companies are moving fast, becoming leaner and more nimble, improving core processes, and slashing corporate overhead. Good ideas, all of them. But are they strategies that will yield sustained competitive advantage? Not if every other competitor is pursuing them at the same time. Harvard-based strategy guru Michael Porter argues that many of these operational effectiveness programs yield only temporary benefits. When companies immediately use their new cost advantages to engage in price competition, the benefits are short-lived. This may not be a long-term strategy that translates into sustainable profitability. The limitation of reengineering and operational effectiveness strategies are that competitors will quickly adopt them, too. Sustainable strategies are those that position the organization to perform *different* activities than rivals—or performing similar activities in *different* ways (Porter 1996, 61).

Real strategy development focuses on the ability to create a difference that an organization can preserve. Strategy rests on unique activities to create a mix of value that is different than the offerings of competitors. New York's Oxford health plan is attempting to create a sustainable advantage over traditional HMOs. The plan ran a two-page advertisement in the *New York Times* in early 1997 to broadcast its claim that it was different from gatekeeper-model HMOs like Aetna U.S. Healthcare. Oxford is offering a credentialed network of alternative medicine providers and easy access to specialists for consumers. The emphasis on exceeding consumers' expectations has allowed Oxford to grow quickly while achieving high customer satisfaction. But it has also created greater management challenges, trying to control medical costs while raising consumer expectations. Oxford's stock price fell sharply in October when its rising medical charges forced a major write-off against company reserves. Oxford's fast-rising enrollment outran its computer system and ability to track or pay provider claims.

Strategic positioning can be based on very different approaches to the market. Some basic strategic positions include:

- niche position servicing limited markets and customer segments;
- comprehensive supplier;
- low-cost competitor;
- quality/value-based premium-priced market leader; and
- innovative leading-edge provider.

METASTRATEGY—THE BROADEST PERSPECTIVE OF ALL!

The most inspiring lessons in strategy may not come from business at all. The concept of *metastrategy* is to look for strategic insights in all fields, not just the one in which the organization is competing (Makridakis 1997, 129). Even failures can be inspiring. Think of AT&T's acquisition of NCR, a manufacturer of computers, in a deal that led to a loss of $10 billion and the premature departure of AT&T's CEO Robert Allen. In the health field, Columbia HCA's recent attempt to buy a Blue Cross plan in Ohio was another failed attempt to create strategic synergies with a metastrategy.

Examples of innovative strategies may be found in many aspects of life, not just the business sector. In team sports, for example, cooperation and motivation are often as important as capital investment or process improvement. In the National Hockey League, the Colorado Avalanche was a losing franchise that moved from Canada to Colorado and subsequently won the Stanley Cup, inspired in part by the movie "Rudy," about a practice-team player at Notre Dame who became an example of courage and tenacity.

Healthcare executives should look broadly for strategic inspiration. How about toys? The success of electronic "nanopets" from Japan is a unique blend of high-tech, low-cost, and niche-creating strategies. It demonstrates that the human processes of needing and nurturing can yield new products with broad appeal to adults as well as children. Thinking metastrategically, do nanopets and patients have anything in common? The answer is that both thrive when given timely, frequent, and sustained attention and care.

MODERN METHODS FOR PLANNING: A 22-STEP PROCESS

Reliance on strategic planning is somewhat cyclical. Planning goes in and out of vogue, according to organizational life cycles and market trends. As American corporations approach the millennium, strategic planning is back— but with a difference. The changes include less bureaucracy, more emphasis on implementation and innovation, fewer staff planners, more involvement of line managers, and teams of employees (Taylor 1997, 334). Planning does not have to be slow or bureaucratic. Tom Peters encourages fast-paced innovation and admonishes organizations to "make faster mistakes" than competitors, learn from those mistakes, and modify plans and processes on the run (Peters 1987, 192).

Planning does not have to be complex, but it will be better if it is. Improving the depth of the analysis will make the plan more accurate, better estimate risks and rewards, and improve the prospects for successful implementation. Planning is a learning system that facilitates networking within the organization and captures knowledge every step of the way (Fuller 1996, 24). Taking more time, involving more people at deeper levels in the organization, and increasing the specificity of analysis and tactics—these activities will pay off with a plan that actually drives the operations, budgeting, and strategic choices of the organization.

In planning textbooks, there are five-step, seven-step, and ten-step processes for carrying out the core activities of strategic planning. Simplicity is valuable in providing an introduction to making strategic choices, but there is no substitute for solid market insights and tactics that are based on better data. An organizationwide planning process cannot be realistically completed within three months if in-depth analysis is to be done and broad involvement of key stakeholders is to take place.

Here, an unprecedented 22-step planning process is outlined—and more steps could be added!

1. *Value clarification.* Values are at the foundation of a strategic plan. Explicit articulation of the organization's values, vision, and aspirations provides a framework for making strategic choices.

2. *Holistic concept.* Healthcare needs a holistic approach to strategic planning. This "New Age" concept emphasizes a business development process based on the notion that the organization, its suppliers, and its customers are all part of an interdependent and balanced whole (Ginsberg 1997, 125). A holistic approach to planning requires the discipline of systems thinking to analyze the market and the organization in a holistic way. Thinking in terms of complex systems means seeing the business as part of a wider economic ecosystem. The huge potential of the postacute continuum of care services can be seen, for example, when taking a broad perspective of society, technology, government policy, and the economy.

3. *Planning horizon.* Set a time frame for strategic thinking to the edge of the horizon for which management is willing to make assumptions about future conditions. A three- to five-year planning horizon will extend management's outlook and help overcome the preoccupation with the present quarter-to-quarter business competition. Besides, many long-range strategies will take at least two to three years to implement fully.

4. *Market forecast.* Honestly examine the future market conditions in which the organization will compete. These predictions and future trends may be organized using the STEEP framework—social, technology, economics, environment, and politics. Hospitals and health systems do not have to start from scratch. Consulting firms, academic think tanks, and other competitors are sources for market forecasts.

5. *Consumer demands.* Identification of changes in consumers' wants, expectations, and potential prices is essential baseline information. This data may be obtained from market research techniques includ-

ing focus groups, survey research, and customer surveys such as patient satisfaction studies.

6. *Competitor assessment.* Developing market intelligence on competitors' market strategies is an underused method of strategic position. The organization's best strategy may be to position itself against the market thrust of a competitor. Otherwise, the hospital or health system may appear to be following a "me, too" pattern when other competitors have taken a lead.

7. *Regulation.* Calculating the role that government may play in the healthcare market is an important driver of the future market. Government payments typically comprise 40 to 60 percent of a healthcare provider's revenues. The current shift of Medicare and Medicaid into managed care will have significant consequences for providers.

8. *Purchaser/customer demands.* Healthcare has both wholesale and retail consumers. Separating the needs of "purchasers" (employers, government) from the desires and values of "consumers" (patients, family, the public) is necessary. Separate strategies for dealing with both classes of consumers is critical.

9. *Service and quality.* Planning to improve service and quality is a major strategy for differentiation. Providers should identify service barriers and sources of customer dissatisfaction. Service management plans can improve processes in aspects important to patients and families. Clinical quality will become a competitive arena within five years, as report cards become commonplace. Begin to monitor quality intensively and think of quality and service as strategic weapons.

10. *Utilization predictions.* Predicting use rates for all service lines will generate estimates of expected volume over time. But healthcare utilizations are currently in flux and may vary widely by market stage and managed care utilization. This makes past patterns of consumption and utilization less reliable as a predictor of future use rates (Kurtenbach and Warmoth 1995). Look at benchmark markets to provide indicators of future utilization under managed care. Healthcare organizations assuming risk for enrolled populations will need epidemiologic data and actuarial projections to predict the future health needs of covered populations.

11. *Adjusting demand projections.* Given the changes sweeping healthcare today, factoring in changes in utilization caused by such factors as payment patterns, managed care, capitation, shifting demographics, and new technology will provide a range of estimates for future utilization. These may be expressed as scenarios with varied assumptions built into the projections to create alternative forecasts of demand.

12. *Business plans.* Once the environmental assessment is complete and the major lines of strategy laid out for the parent organization, business goals and tactics in every service line must be developed. Business plans will have a shorter time frame, perhaps 12 to 24 months.

13. *Gap analysis.* Identifying gaps between strategy and execution requires asking the tough questions (Proctor 1997). What is the difference between the organization's market projections of sales, revenues, and internal estimates of costs and capital requirements? How likely is it that new technology will be developed or installed on time (e.g., information systems)? Are the most promising business development ideas accurately forecasted?

14. *Product elimination.* Willingness to drop an underutilized service, noncompetitive program, or obsolete facility requires a "tough love" approach to strategic planning. An organization must have the discipline to assess its service line portfolio regularly and make business decisions about maintaining excess capacity or below-margin programs.

15. *Participation.* Early and frequent involvement of the "doers" in the organization with the managers and planners will ensure that strategies and tactics are created by those who will implement the plans. A broadly based planning process may take a little longer, but the loss in time efficiency will be returned in more enthusiastic adoption of the plans, goals, and strategies by those at the front lines.

16. *Testing plans.* Testing market assumptions and plans with consumers—and revising them when customers provide their feedback—can save time and money. Don't make assumptions about what customers want without testing strategies and tactics thoroughly.

17. *Tradeoffs.* What compromises will be made in pursuing multiple markets, targets, and service lines? Strategy is about choices. What the organization chooses not to do is one of the essential components of strategy, advises Michael Porter, and may be one of the hardest steps in the planning process (Porter 1996, 70).

18. *Contingency planning.* Futurists use scenarios to estimate the effect of changes in the market. While all assumptions are open to revision by events, some market shifts are more likely than others. Strategy consultant Mark Fuller of the Monitor Company argues that contingency thinking is not just an intellectual exercise (Fuller 1996, 27). It is a means of increasing the organization's confidence in carrying out its objectives, whatever happens in the future.

19. *Change the plan.* Revise the plan as often as the market, competitors, or unexpected events dictate that the plan has become out of date. This ensures that the organization's strategies and services are very closely matched with the market. Continuous improvement of

the plan creates a "rolling" planning horizon where strategies and business plans are updated frequently.

20. *Board review.* Strategic planning is one of the most critical responsibilities of trustees, but experience shows that it is also the task they tend to perform the least effectively (Abendshien 1995, 1). Board involvement should begin early in the planning process. Think of the board as a community focus group and test ideas and scenarios with it well before those ideas and scenarios become the driving assumptions of the plan.

21. *Strategic audit.* Obtain a second opinion on the organization's strategy from an outside source that knows the company well—the board (Donaldson 1995, 100). Instead of rubber-stamping the CEO's strategic initiatives in all-too-brief planning retreats, restructure the board's role in strategic planning. Like a financial audit, a periodic strategic audit imposes a new discipline on management and the directors to treat strategy seriously. It would fix the leadership of strategic oversight in the hands of outside directors and provide the board with the authority and information to assess the organization's performance against its strategic plan.

22. *Make no small plans.* Think globally, long-term, and deeply about the future. Gary Hamel, an international business consultant and coauthor of *Competing for the Future* (Hamel and Prahalad 1997), calls strategy development a "revolutionary" activity (Hamel 1996, 69). Pursuing incremental strategies while others reinvent the market is like "fiddling while Rome burns."

LOOKING FORWARD: PLANNING IS A BRIDGE TO AN UNCERTAIN FUTURE

There is a lot more uncertainty about the future today than there has been in the past. Past assumptions about the future have turned out to be way off the mark. In the 1950s, futurists predicted that automation would enable the average citizen to double his or her leisure time while machines did the work. Today, 50 years after the invention of the computer, weekly work hours are going up, not down, and nearly 50 percent of women are in the workplace. Fewer than 25 percent of American households fit the 1960s stereotype of a married couple with children.

Health planning has not always been a success. In the 1970s, government planners estimated that the United States needed four hospital beds for every 1,000 residents. The federal Hill-Burton hospital financing program underwrote construction of thousands of hospitals across the nation. But the planners way overshot their target, leaving the nation with hundreds of thousands of beds that would never be filled. Despite a growing surplus of beds and facilities, in the 1980s hospitals were building so many "centers of excellence" that some facilities had a construction tower continuously on site for ten years. And hospitals could not expand their ambulatory care facilities fast enough, as more than half of all surgeries shifted to the outpatient setting.

Then came managed care and prospective payment, throwing all of yesterday's assumptions out the window. Hospital utilization slumped by 25 percent in the ten-year period between 1985 and 1995. Not using past experience to guide the future was a leading cause of today's glut of some 250,000 to 450,000 excess hospital beds. Most of the unused capacity still sits idle today, despite some conversion of inpatient hospital beds to long-term or ambulatory care. Hundreds of thousands of beds have been taken out of service, mothballed in hopes of a future time when a new wave of patients will fill them. Dealing with excess capacity will be a major planning and management challenge of the millennium.

So is planning a waste of time? Far from it. Planning is an essential discipline for facing the future with a questioning attitude. Leland Kaiser likes to challenge his healthcare clients to imagine any future *except being in the business they are in today*. Kaiser is a fierce believer in the opportunity that every organization has to design its own future. What kind of future might be possible for a children's hospital if it could provide any service except not to children? Or provide any health services to children except not in a hospital? That freedom of imagination can be terrifying if the organization cannot dream it might be forced to leave its core business for something completely different.

Principles may be one of the few anchor-points for planning in a world of uncertainty. Management consultant Stephen Covey, author of *Principle-Centered Leadership*, argues that ultimately, principles will rule (1997, 45). There is no easy way to create a high-trust culture in which employees and midlevel managers carry out their functions without higher supervision. It is the belief system of the organization, not its policies and procedures, that drives and shapes performance. A value-based strategic plan taps into those roots and lays out organizational tactics that are consistent with the principles of the organization. A well-communicated plan sends a message across the organization—*here* is where we're going. Warren Bennis defines leaders as those who have a dream, a mission, an explicit strategic intent, widely communicated and with meaning to everyone in the organization (1997, 155).

Strategic planning can provide a transition strategy—a bridge of anticipation and action—to carry an organization from today to tomorrow. Scenarios are a simple way to picture an alternative future. Best-case, worst-case, out-of-left-field images of future conditions let an organization's imagination soar. A healthy skepticism about future market conditions may give decision makers pause, but it can prevent costly mistakes. Five years ago, a large Midwest medical center in the midst of its strategic planning process faced a choice of reinvesting $100 million in its high-tech facilities or, instead, channeling $20 to $30 million in capital investments into growing its hospital-owned HMO and physician network. This was risky: investing heavily in businesses in which the hospital had little experience.

Today, it is very clear that the organization chose wisely in strengthening its HMO and medical organization when there was a window of opportunity to grow these new businesses in its Stage 2 market with less than 15 percent of the population enrolled in an HMO. At present, the hospital's HMO is the second-largest in the region, and the physician network is providing much of the primary care, all according to plan. Deferring major capital investment in the facility had another benefit that could not have been predicted five years before. It allowed the hospital's investments to soar with the stock market's rise. The rise in investment income was indeed a bonus, because the rise of the Dow Jones to over 8,000 had not been predicted. But it occurred when the hospital decided to protect its capital in its core business while engaging in some risk-taking in the HMO and physician network.

The midst of uncertainty is the best time to make plans. Many competitors will be sitting on the sidelines, waiting for conditions to restabilize. Bureaucratic organizations will move slowly, if at all. Risk-averse organizations will be playing it safe, watching others to learn what strategies are safe. Innovative organizations will be risking their futures by developing new services and new processes. Which would you rather be? Remember Yogi Berra's admonition: *The future ain't what it used to be* (Kotler 1997, 209). The millennium is no time to be without a plan.

REFERENCES

Abendshien, J. 1995. "Strategic Planning by the Board." *Trustee* 48 (7) (Supplement): 1–4.

Bennis, W. 1997. "Becoming a Nation of Leaders." In *Rethinking the Future,* edited by A. and H. Toffler, 148–63. London: Nicholas Brealey Publishing.

Bruton, G. D., B. M. Oviatt, and L. Kallas-Bruton. 1995. "Strategic Planning in Hospitals: A Review and Proposal." *Health Care Management Review* 20 (3): 16–25.

Byrne, J. A. 1996. "Strategic Planning." *Business Week* (September 2): 46–50.

Collins, J. C., and J. I. Porras. 1994. *Built to Last: Successful Habits of Visionary Companies.* New York: Harper Business.

Covey, S. 1997. "Putting Principles First." In *Rethinking the Future,* edited by A. and H. Toffler, 34–36. London: Nicholas Brealey Publishing.

Donaldson, G. 1995. "A New Tool for Boards: The Strategic Audit." *Harvard Business Review* 73 (4): 99–107.

Fuller, M. 1996. "Strategic Planning in an Era of Total Competition." *Strategy & Leadership* 24 (3): 22–27.

Ginsberg, A. 1997. "'New Age' Strategic Planning: Bridging Theory and Practice." *Long Range Planning* 30 (1): 125–28.

Hamel, G. 1996. "Strategy as Revolution." *Harvard Business Review* 74 (4): 69–82.

Hamel, G., and C. K. Prahalad. 1997. *Competing for the Future.* Boston, MA: Harvard Business School Press.

Hemmasi, M., L. A. Graf, and M. R. Williams. 1997. "Strategic Planning in Healthcare: Merging Two Methodologies." *Competitiveness Review* 7 (2): 38–51.

Kotler, P. 1997. "Mapping the Future Marketplace." In *Rethinking the Future,* edited by A. and H. Toffler, 196–210. London: Nicholas Brealey Publishing.

Kurtenbach, J., and T. Warmoth. 1995. "Strategic Planning Futurists Need to Be Capitation-Specific and Epidemiological." *Health Care Strategic Management* 13 (9): 8–11.

Lindblom, C. E. 1965. *The Intelligence of Democracy.* New York: Free Press.

Makridakis, S. 1996. "Factors Affecting Success in Business: Management Theories/Tools vs. Predicting Changes." *European Management Journal* 14 (1): 1–20.

———. 1997. "Metastrategy: Learning and Avoiding Past Mistakes." *Long Range Planning* 30 (1): 129–35.

Mintzberg, H. 1994. *The Rise and Fall of Strategic Planning.* New York: Free Press.

Peters, T. 1987. *Thriving on Chaos: A Handbook for the Management Revolution.* New York: Alfred A. Knopf.

Porter, M. 1985. *Competitive Advantage: Creating and Sustaining Superior Performance.* New York: Free Press.

———. 1996. "What Is Strategy?" *Harvard Business Review* 74 (6): 61–78.

———. 1997. "Creating Tomorrow's Advantages." In *Rethinking the Future,* edited by A. and H. Toffler, 48–61. London: Nicholas Brealey Publishing.

Prahalad, C. K. 1997. "Strategies for Growth." In *Rethinking the Future,* edited by A. and H. Toffler, 64–75. London: Nicholas Brealey Publishing.

Proctor, T. 1997. "Establishing a Strategic Direction: A Review." *Management Decision* 35 (1): 143–56.

Senge, P. 1997. "Through the Eye of the Needle." In *Rethinking the Future,* edited by A. and H. Toffler, 122–46. London: Nicholas Brealey Publishing.

———. 1993. *The Fifth Discipline: The Art and Practice of the Learning Organization.* New York: Doubleday.

Taylor, B. 1997. "The Return of Strategic Planning—Once More, with Feeling." *Long Range Planning* 30 (3): 334–44.

Thompson, P., and K. Brooks. 1997. "A Creative Approach to Strategic Planning." *CMA Magazine* 71 (6): 20–22.

Zeleney, M. 1997. "The Fall of Strategic Planning." *Human Systems Management* 16 (2): 77–79.

10

Corporate Soul: Seven Pathways to Organizational Enlightenment for Healthcare Organizations

It's frightening that many healthcare organizations can't seem to connect with anything more inspiring than preparing themselves to accept a capitated dollar.
—J. Daniel Beckham (1994)

A cross the United States, healthcare organizations are discovering a new set of values and vision—their "corporate soul." Health executives coming up in the 1980s and 1990s learned that success meant managing by the numbers. Now, facing the millennium, with managed care and government cutbacks driving down volume and profitability, healthcare managers are looking for a new conceptual footing. Many health professionals and boards are rediscovering their roots as social institutions and rededicating their healthcare organizations to putting patients first and improving the health of the community.

There is a quiet revolution going on in healthcare these days, claims healthcare consultant Erie Chapman, the former CEO of U.S. Health Corporation in Columbus, Ohio:

People are starting to talk about quality and service and value; about community, family and individual; about prevention and lifestyle and environment; about transforming our healthcare system from one that heals the sick to one that keeps people well. (Chapman and Wimberly 1994, 20).

In a compendium of community-based initiatives, the Healthcare Forum, a leadership development organization based in San Francisco, found dozens of hospitals, health systems, and community health programs energetically improving the health of their communities, including:

- Cambridge Hospital in Cambridge, Massachusetts, "reinvented" its hospital around community service, launching programs such as "House Calls for the Homebound Elderly" and a school-based "Teen Health Center."

- North Bay Healthcare System in Fairfield, California, founded a community collaborative with dozens of community organizations to address needs such as managed care for Medicaid, a health outreach system, and a business task force.

- Bexar County Medical Society of San Antonio, Texas, partnered with the local chamber of commerce and Trinity University's Department of Health Administration to organize an 800-volunteer task force to create community-based standards of care and a regional health information network.

- Ivinson Memorial Hospital of Laramie, Wyoming, started the "Well-Aware" civic project to improve the health status of rural and impoverished Laramie County, including community education programs and a 24-hour information and referral service. (Sasenick 1994)

DISCOVERING "CORPORATE SOUL"

A new wave of management literature encourages leaders and organizations to nurture their corporate soul, letting values drive the business strategy and market positioning. Tom Chappell, CEO of Tom's of Maine, defines the soul of a corporation as "how mind and spirit can work together to compete for profit and market share. It's about how to use the two sides of all of us, the spiritual and practical, and to achieve whatever business goals we set for ourselves" (Chappell 1995, ix). Tom's of Maine demonstrates that it is possible to combine a visionary spirit with bottom-line performance. Tom Chappell created a naturally based line of personal care products that earned the company awards for its commitment to the environment—and earned a 31 percent increase in sales and a 41 percent increase in profits in 1994.

Even among theologists, the concept of "soul" is difficult to define. Psychologist Thomas Moore describes the concept: "Tradition teaches that the soul lies midway between understanding and unconsciousness, and that its instrument is neither the mind nor the body, but imagination" (1995, xiii). Organizations with soul have fulfilling work and rewarding relationships and are free from strife. Moore advises that acting with soul is not looking for some future ideal but acting in the present in a way that is mindful of religion and spirituality.

Developing corporate soul will not be easy. The emphasis on quarterly financial goals in many U.S. corporations robs many organizations of the opportunity to focus on higher-order goals that may take years to accomplish (Secretan 1997, 7). Management consultant Stephen R. Covey (1995, 13), author of *The Seven Habits of Highly Effective People*, identifies tensions found in many organizations today:

- balancing personal and professional lives;
- being genuinely happy about the successes and competencies of another;
- maintaining control yet giving people the freedom to work;
- internalizing principles of total quality management while overcoming cynicism about past "programs of the month";
- giving priority to the urgent problem instead of the long-term goal; and
- sacrificing principles for expediency to meet business goals.

VALUE-DRIVEN MANAGEMENT IN THE PRIVATE SECTOR

Is it possible to mix business and social goals? Tom Chappell, CEO of Tom's of Maine and author of *The Soul of a Business*, thinks so: "Beliefs drive strategy. Your ethics *can* form the foundation of smart analysis and clear thinking. Your personal values can be integrated with managing for all the traditional goals of business—making money, expanded market share, increased profits, retained earnings, and sales growth. Not only can your personal beliefs be brought to work, they can work for you. You can be a hard-assed competitor and still run a business with soul" (1995, xiv).

A growing number of companies are demonstrating corporate soul with high-visibility commitments to objectives beyond the bottom line. Management consultants Lee Bolman and Terrence Deal (1995, 5–6) call for executives to "lead with soul," reinfusing the workplace with vigor and élan by "reclaiming the enduring capacity that gives our lives passion and purpose." To achieve an organization committed to values, senior managers must focus on rediscovering a different path and rekindling new meaning. Not surprisingly, one of the first questions the consultants were asked was: "What do you know about the meaning of life?" And implicitly, "Is spiritual growth necessary to make a profit?"

Becoming an organization with corporate soul is the challenge of leadership in the twenty-first century. California management experts Jim Kouzes and Barry Posner (1995) cite the five fundamental practices for exemplary leadership:

1. challenging the process;
2. inspiring a shared vision;
3. enabling others to act;
4. modeling the way; and
5. encouraging the heart.

A new path must be taken if modern corporations are to overcome stagnation, reflexive downsizing, and managing only for economic return. Traditional management focuses attention on the short term, but what is needed is a view to the horizon of global competition. In such a dynamic environment, leaders must venture out, not waiting for luck or being in the right place at the right time. Those who lead others to greatness seek and accept challenge. The challenge may be an innovative new product, world-class service, starting up a new company, or reinvigorating an old one.

Infusing a corporate soul in organizations means a return to traditional values of religion and spirituality, and managing a business according to high ethical standards. Leadership means steering by a spiritual compass in an uncertain environment, putting consumers and community above short-term returns. Sacred Heart Community Service team wrote a poem at a Kouzes-Posner workshop:

> "We are leaders one and all,
>   We invite you to the call.
> We ask you to dream our vision
>   As we share our joyful mission.
> Feed the hungry, clothe the needy,
>   Welcome strangers, one and all.
> Homeless, immigrant, children, poor
>   All find refuge at our door." (1995, 312)

BEN & JERRY'S INVESTS PROFITS FOR PEACE

Arguably the best-known example of a corporation with social responsibility is Ben & Jerry's. By now, the company is legendary for its commitment to social issues and environmental protection, with popular products such as Peace Pop and Rainforest Crunch ice cream (Lager 1994). Two counterculture people astonished America by taking a company with two employees and $8,000 in start-up capital from the Small Business Award to annual sales of $30 million and winner of the SBA's company-of-the-year award.

On the way up, Ben and Jerry never lost their core values. To help finance a campaign to reduce the government's military expenditures, the founders decided to donate one percent of the company's profits to peace. As they took their small company public, Ben and Jerry told Wall Street analysts they planned to succeed with a strategy of "linked prosperity." As the company grew, the benefits would accrue not only to shareholders but to employees and community. A nonprofit foundation was established with an initial donation of 50,000 shares plus a guarantee of 7.5 percent of the company's profits. The foundation would support community-based organizations that approached social and environmental issues in nontraditional ways. This decision was made while cash flow was almost nonexistent, as underwriters went through the roof, arguing that the donations policy would be "bad for the stock" (Lager 1994, 128).

The founders persisted in building a value-driven business, giving employees 5 percent of the profits while dealing with small, nontraditional suppliers such as Greystone Bakery, run by a Zen community. The company's six core values embraced a variety of causes, from human rights and the environment to reducing military spending. The result was customers who zealously purchased their products because the company's heart was as good as what it made.

A NEW PARADIGM FOR BUSINESS

A growing number of senior executives and midlevel managers recognize that the environment is changing—and rapidly. Michael Ray, professor of creativity and innovation in marketing at Stanford University, asks, "If you sense that a profound change is happening in the business world, but you're not quite sure what it is; if you've noticed that old visions and strategies don't seem to work anymore; if you feel deeply that you need to learn new ways to lead, to express and maintain values, be creative and foster community—you are not alone" (Ray and Rinzler 1993, 1).

Social scientists and organizational behaviorists believe that the United States—and the global marketplace—is experiencing a watershed paradigm shift in the fundamental assumptions about the world. Psychologist Marilyn Ferguson (1993, 28) argues that "making a life, not just a living, is essential to one seeking wholeness." The power of the transformative process is the shaking of traditional values, and therefore the economy, in ways that will change the individual's relationship to work and the organization's relationship with society and the environment. The new paradigm will place emphasis on values, not just economics. The changes are reflected in evolving lifestyles that take advantage of synergy, sharing, barter, cooperation, and creativity.

CHOPRA'S SEVEN SPIRITUAL LAWS OF SUCCESS

Deepak Chopra, author of *Ageless Body, Timeless Mind* (1995), blends philosophy and physics with Eastern religion and Western science. In cooperation with the Sharp Healthcare System, Dr. Chopra has developed a center for health and spirituality in La Jolla, California. Chopra identifies seven pathways to a spiritually-motivated success.

Law #1—Pure Potentiality

The first spiritual law of success is pure potentiality. Our spiritual essence, when internalized, produces an absence of fear, no compulsion to control, and no struggle for external power.

Law #2—Giving

The law of giving recognizes that the root word *affluere* means "to flow to," so money is a symbol for the exchange of life energy and service we give to others. The intention of giving is to create happiness, and the return is directly proportional to the giving when it is unconditional and from the heart.

Law #3—"Karma" or Cause and Effect

The term *karma* relates to the consequences of actions, that is, "what you sow is what you reap." All actions are karmic episodes. When we choose actions that bring happiness and success to others, the fruit of karma is happiness and success for ourselves.

Law #4—Least Effort

This is the principle of least action and no resistance and, therefore, the principle of harmony and love. When actions are motivated by love, there is no waste of energy, and you will experience life flowing with effortless ease.

Law #5—Intention and Desire

The principle of intention and desire is the basis for the organization of energy and information to a useful purpose. You can put the infinite organizing power of this "cosmic computer" to work for you.

Law #6—Detachment

In detachment lies the wisdom of uncertainty and the freedom to step into the unknown. Attachment to symbols such as money or material goods leads to insecurity, because these things are always changing. Letting go of attachments will free the self to be creative and to experience the fun of life.

Law #7—"Dharma" or Purpose in Life

Everyone has a purpose in life, a unique gift or special talent. When we blend this unique talent with service to others, we succeed by asking, "How can I help?" rather than, "What's in it for me?" The happiness that comes from serving others is the highest level of spirituality.

SEVEN PATHWAYS TO CORPORATE SOUL

They don't teach soul in MBA schools. Managers must discover their corporate souls through individual leadership or by learning under a visionary mentor. Healthcare executives must learn to do the right thing, advises ethicist Emily Friedman (1996). She challenges health executives to:

- open their minds and hearts to the "stories" of patients;
- share and learn from experiences;
- gain insights from the ever-changing world of healthcare;
- remember that behind the statistics there are real people; and
- make decisions based on ethical principles.

It is possible to learn how to practice "values-centered leadership" (Secretan 1997). There is much to be learned about how to make ethical choices in business situations, or the most effective ways of communicating a vision. *Kaizen* is a Japanese term for continuous improvement. Building strong relationships, inspiring the courage to make right choices, and infusing values into competitive strategies are all part of the repertoire of the values-centered executive. Here are seven pathways to developing corporate soul in healthcare organizations.

Pathway #1—Vision

Corporate soul needs a vision, a view of a future that energizes stakeholders, commits them to a higher purpose, and mobilizes enthusiasm and action. In recognition of the growing emphasis on customer and community service, the Marriott Service Excellence Awards for healthcare providers have been expanded to four categories, including: vision, internal service, values integration, and customer service. The annual competition recently drew 94 entries for the prizes and commendations offered by Marriott Corporation and *Modern Healthcare* magazine. Healthcare's interest in quality and service excellence is rising. Awards judge Arthur Sturm, Jr., a senior marketing consultant with Chicago-based Sturm Rosenberg Cafferata, commented: "The caliber of the entrants was much higher this year. People were more understanding of service than in the past. The winners stood out because they had done their research upfront to find out what their customers' interests were and put tracking mechanisms in place to make sure the programs were effective" (Snow 1995, 66).

Pathway #2—Symbolic Actions

Vision is most effectively conveyed to an organization by symbolic actions—"walking the talk"—that confirm the employees' trust in the correctness of management's vision path (Bennis and Townsend 1995). Trust in the vision comes with consistent actions, which reflect the expressed values and goals of the organization. Communicating a vision can most directly be done by actions that confirm the new values. Building a $1 million day care center for employees and the community affirms a community-minded vision far better than investing in a new $1 million device in radiology. The public—and the employees and medical staff—assumes that the hospital will maintain state-of-the-art technology. Building a day care center, reconstructing housing in poor neighborhoods, or creating health career summer jobs for youths—these are symbolic statements that say the organization cares about the community, above and beyond the public's expectations.

Vision cannot be driven top-down into the organization. Value-confident leaders must be willing to trust subordinates to follow the vision, each in his or her own way, harnessing personal values and creativity to achieving the vision. Leadership consultant Warren Bennis of the University of Southern California, in his book *Reinventing Leadership*, recalls the vision of the physician executive of a large New York hospital: "I spend most of my time reminding people what's important. Our job here is to get patients to be better, to be well. Everything else is a cost" (Bennis and Townsend 1995, 46).

Pathway #3—Patients First

For healthcare organizations, the secret of success should be very simple: "Rule #1—Put patients first" (Friedman 1996, xxi). For example, after the state of New Jersey legislated a 48-hour stay for normal deliveries, a number of hospitals across the United States announced they would allow a two-day stay for newborns, even if the hospital had to pay for part of the stay because the HMO would not authorize coverage (Malkin 1995).

Of course, there is more to it. Always giving priority to patients may compromise a physician or nurse's clinical authority. It may disrupt service workers' schedules, such as delivery of meals or housekeeping. Ethicist Emily Friedman strongly believes that the phrase "freedom of choice" is a fundamental principle and powerful concept for healthcare (Friedman 1994, 13). However, keeping patients informed takes more staff time and increases costs. Patients may prefer brand-name pharmaceuticals, even though generics or other prescriptions may be therapeutically substituted. Most facilities are designed to improve productivity, not to pamper patients. How would health facilities be different if they were designed with a patients-first orientation?

Healthcare has struggled to define its core constituency. The term *patients* has somehow suggested a dependent relationship with providers. According to various management slogans trendy in the past five years, patients have been redefined as *consumers, guests, clients,* or even *purchasers.* Physicians, nurses, and other health workers have always been more comfortable with putting the emphasis on *patients.* Care professionals have been somewhat dismayed when managers and marketers insist on using alternative terms that reconceptualized the patient as a market-driven consumer.

Pennsylvania Hospital in Philadelphia is committed to a patient-first philosophy, making information available and accessible for patients. They call it "information empowerment." For example:

- A video model has been developed for each major critical pathway to help patients understand the care process.
- A "consumer education telecommunication center" is being developed to meet the patients' full education needs at home.
- The "Positive Medicine" project uses a variety of multimedia products and links such as talk lines for consumers and providers on America Online.
- Home-based access to health information will permit patients to have a physician walk them through decision pathways by telephone or computer. (Magee 1995)

Pathway #4—Open Communications

Most doctors and healthcare workers have no idea how much it costs to produce a day of care, an emergency medical service, or a surgical procedure. Even fewer physicians or staffers know how much profit the hospital or medical group is making, per unit of service or on an annual basis. They are not alone. Most workers in large companies have little information on costs, strategy, or corporate goals. But a surprising 86 percent of the rank-and-file say they would be motivated to help their companies succeed if they were privy to financial data seen only by senior managers, according to a survey of major corporations by Ernst & Young, a Chicago-based management consulting firm (Jones 1995).

A corporate policy of open communication will reinforce a management trend called "open-book management." Management consultant John Case, author of *Open-Book Management,* calls for a "business revolution" in employer-employee communication: "Opening the books means a whole lot more than just announcing quarterly results the way publicly traded companies do. It means communicating all the relevant information, monthly, weekly or daily, to people in every plant or department . . . so people learn to follow the numbers and help make decisions. They learn to think and act like owners, and not like hired hands" (Case 1995, xvii–xviii).

The concept of open-book communication challenges the status quo in which only top executives are concerned about whether the business is succeeding. With continuous communication of key data, everyone acts as if they own the company. Case cites examples such as power company AES, which supplies its 1,000 employees with so much financial information that they are considered insiders by the Securities and Exchange Commission. There are limits, of course: Coca-Cola should not give its secret recipe to the employees. But employees feel a sense of commitment and empowerment when top management is willing to share information on financial and strategic performance.

Healthcare organizations could share much more information with the medical staff and employees to promote a shared entrepreneurial attitude of "ownership" toward cost containment and key strategic objectives. In an open-book environment, the medical staff and employees should know annual revenue, expense, and profit goals, with regular monthly or quarterly reports. At the departmental level, for example, share the following data with physicians and care workers:

- cost per case by diagnosis-related group (DRG), clustered by department;
- labor and supplies costs per case and patient day;
- pharmaceutical costs per case by DRG;
- costs of "outlier" patients;
- costs of errors, such as in medication or scheduling; and
- changes in volume indicators of utilization data.

Goal-setting at the departmental level should involve both physicians and staffers, not just the supervisors and middle managers. Use benchmarks from other peer institutions or medical groups. Consulting firms can provide an outside perspective and guidelines, such as actuaries Milliman & Robertson of Seattle, Washington, and management companies like Chi Systems of Ann Arbor, Michigan, APM of Walnut Creek, California, and Booz Allen in Chicago, Illinois.

Still skeptical? Many healthcare executives may be concerned about confidentiality of sensitive financial data. Most of this sensitive data is already public, anyway. Hospital annual reports provide a great deal of information on utilization and financial performance. Plans for expansion, new programs, and strategic directions are stated openly in in-house newsletters and the annual report. In large organizations like hospitals and health systems, it is difficult to maintain true data privacy. Most administrators believe that little financial data that has been shared with the medical staff is likely to remain confidential very long. Forget about confidentiality except for genuinely sensitive issues, such as patient protection and personnel matters, and otherwise practice open-book communication to gain trust and commitment.

Pathway #5—Restructuring Economics

Vision is not enough, challenges Leanne Kaiser Carlson, a Denver-based consultant on health futures and design: "Most healthy communities initiatives exist on the periphery of the healthcare system, bundled either from the profits made by the 'real' business of healthcare system—illness—or dependent upon voluntary initiatives" (1995, 15). Until the payment system is fundamentally restructured, health expenditures will continue to flow into provider services, not health promotion. As Dan Beckham suggests, to see where healthcare sets its priorities, just "follow the money" (1995, 36).

Health insurance is basically hospital-physician insurance, with minimal coverage for any health risk reduction or health promotion. Over half of the risk factors influencing health are related to lifestyle rather than heredity or environment. Payors are more committed to controlling dollar flows than managing health improvements. Some employers and business coalitions are forcing more attention to health by requiring HMOs and insurers to develop report cards on health indicators such as child immunizations and prenatal care (Addleman 1995). Government could help by assisting to identify the populations most at health risk and by designing outreach and compliance strategies to build a healthier population.

Despite the implied promise of health maintenance, few HMOs give more than lip service to health improvement strategies. Healthcare payments focus on treatment, not prevention or health promotion. Roger Greaves, the former chairman of Health Net, California's second-largest HMO, comments: "Fifty percent of all healthcare dollars are spent on the sickest five percent of patients. Health prevention and education can help balance this ratio" (1995). Greaves recommends that hospitals be decentralized into small disease-management units, with legislation allowing hospitals to share resources with one another.

The next step is to redesign the system to fundamentally change the way health services are financed and delivered, in ways that incent both providers and consumers to emphasize health, and reward based on health outcomes. Capitation provides many of these incentives. Under capitation, all resources for care are prepaid, placing providers at risk for all costs and care. The ultimate cost-reduction strategy is healthy enrollees.

But will capitation work in less favorable circumstances, like urban poverty neighborhoods or rural areas? That is why health-minded organizations such as Mid-Columbia Medical Center in The Dalles, Oregon, and

Commanche County Regional Hospital in Lawton, Oklahoma—both more than 70 miles from the nearest metropolitan area—are accelerating the arrival of capitation in their rural markets. CEOs Mark Scott of Mid-Columbia and Randy Curry of Commanche believe they are making a long-term investment in the health of their rural populations, an investment that will pay off with reduced health costs and healthier consumers.

Pathway #6 —Healthy Communities

The wave of interest in healthy communities is taking healthcare organizations back to their social-institution roots. The notion that a hospital or health system has a social responsibility for the health of its community is heartening to industry critics who feared that health executives were preoccupied with finances and economic competition. The notion of promoting community health also aligns well with the incentives of capitation, which reward at-risk providers for keeping consumers healthy and out of the hospital.

Catholic healthcare is an important health sector that has taken the lead in the arena of community commitment. Former CHA chief executive Jack Curley commented: "We are going to have to do more with less, and I believe this can only be done through cooperation and collaboration between the public and private sectors" (1995, 2). The Catholic Health Association's "Social Accountability Budget" issued a call to public and private organizations to cooperate to fill service gaps jointly. CHA has followed with *Community Accountability in Integrated Delivery*, a workbook that focuses on how to achieve the objectives of the federal government's Healthy People 2000 report. Seven Catholic healthcare organizations were among the selected project sites for the Kellogg Foundation's Community Care Network Demonstration Program.

Imagine a healthier future, then create it. Futurists Trevor Hancock, M.D., a founder of the "Healthy Cities" and well-being. To achieve these outcomes, it will be necessary to bridge health services with movement in Canada and Europe, and Clem Bezold, director of the Institute for Alternative Futures, call for development of community-based "health futures" (Hancock and Bezold 1995). Their efforts at the community level to bring together health officials with consumers and elected officials have a broad policy and societal focus. The concept of community-focused "health futures" is the creation of a design for the future that envisions higher levels of health community efforts in environmental improvement and social support networks.

Pathway #7—Corporate Citizenship

The ultimate symbolic acts are those of corporate citizenship, which demonstrate the corporate soul of the healthcare organization to the entire community. The public expects that hospitals will provide charitable care to the poor and the uninsured. Nonprofit hospitals provided $9.2 billion of uncompensated care in 1993, according to the American Hospital Association (Greene 1995). For-profit healthcare companies like Columbia/HCA have launched a strong challenge to hospitals' tax-exempt status. Federal tax experts calculate the value of nonprofits' tax exemptions at $8.5 billion in 1988, the most recent IRS study of this issue. In a strong critique by the General Accounting Office in 1990, federal auditors estimated that 15 percent of the nation's 3,000 nonprofit hospitals provided less uncompensated care than the value of their tax exemptions.

Community charitable care may not be enough to ultimately justify tax-exemption for healthcare providers. These acts of corporate citizenship go beyond uncompensated services:

- corporate tithing of a percent of the profits;
- subsidies for community outpatient clinics;
- taking responsibility for special populations;
- legislative advocacy on health-related issues;
- membership on community boards;
- support of economic development activities;
- housing for the elderly;
- transportation for the homebound;
- community health education programs;
- disease screening and follow-up with no financial criteria;
- civic initiatives to address local issues;
- community-based coalitions for health and civic improvement; and
- consumers and employees on the board.

Across the nation, hospitals and health systems are reaching outside of their walls to make a difference in the community. In Chicago, for example, hospitals and healthcare providers played an active support role in a city-sponsored heat emergency plan (Friedman 1995a). The program radically reduced heat-related morbidity, after a heat wave in 1995 led to the deaths of 1,500.

Many hospitals are wearing their community hearts on their sleeves. The Catholic Health Association sponsors an annual Achievement Citation awarded to providers demonstrating special community initiatives:

- In Spokane, Washington, the Sacred Heart Medical Center formed the Domestic Violence Task Force in 1991; its in-service training program raised the rate of identified domestic violence from 4 percent to 28 percent of assault cases seen in the hospital's emergency department.
- In Belleville, Illinois, the Teenage Grief Support Group was formed by the St. Elizabeth Hospital Pastoral Care Department, offering teens a safe place to grieve in close cooperation with local high schools.

- In Swainton, New Jersey, a community food bank was established by the Holy Redeemer Visiting Nurse Agency of New Jersey; in 1993, the program distributed 126,656 meals and 18 tons of food. (CHA 1995)

CASE STUDY IN ENLIGHTENMENT: BAYSTATE MEDICAL CENTER

As the first multihospital system in the commonwealth of Massachusetts, Baystate has a reputation for innovation. Its regional flagship hospital in central Massachusetts is the hub to two smaller community hospitals. Baystate started an HMO in 1981, well before the rest of the state's providers could spell "HMO." Its for-profit Health New England is the fastest-growing managed care plan in western Massachusetts, using a network of 1,200 physicians and nine area hospitals. So far, CEO Mike Daly has been successful in positioning Baystate as an "all-payors" organization, contracting with multiple HMOs and insurers for 250,000 enrollees.

Baystate Medical Center is a 741-bed teaching hospital that serves as the western campus of Tufts University. Daly knows that academic medical centers must compete on price. Baystate's costs are 30 to 50 percent lower than comparable Boston-area prices for similar services. Daly is stubborn enough to believe that teaching improves quality, worth subsidizing despite the federal government's cutbacks: "There is a halo of concern for quality" in academic centers (Coile 1995, 74). Baystate cares about the community. It is the second-largest Medicaid provider in the state. Baystate is now developing a broadly decentralized continuum of care, mostly through strategic partnerships: "We don't have the capital—or the need—to own it all," says Daly (Coile 1995, 75).

Baystate takes its social obligations seriously: "The weakness of America's healthcare management profession is not asserting themselves in community leadership" (Coile 1995, 75). Mike Daly chairs the Pioneer Valley Economic Development Council, a local committee working to build the economic health of the region. Among the Council's plans are the development of a high-speed rail connection between western Massachusetts and Boston. Daly talks about his vision for sustaining academic medicine while still providing community service: "Isn't community care why we got into this in the first place?" (Coile 1995, 75)

PITFALLS AND PROBLEMS IN BECOMING VISION-DRIVEN

Creating a vision-driven organization involves more than a weekend retreat or catchy slogan on employee uniforms. Management consultant Dan Beckham of the Beckham Company, based in Whitefish Bay, Wisconsin, alerts vision-minded executives of the potential hazards and pitfalls of developing a corporate soul:

- *Unrealistic expectations.* Traveling too far ahead can leave an executive—and his or her vision—ahead of the stakeholders. A vision that is unconnected to the organization's environment or circumstances is going to be a hard sell. One visionary hospital had a model made of its ultimate "footprint," a five-block Taj Mahal that was totally unrealistic and unfundable. The organization overextended itself in debt trying to build its dream. The next CEO banished the model to a remote storeroom and made no such grand designs.

- *Early failure (or early success!).* A good vision will contain "stretch goals" that will be hard to achieve. But early failures may lead stakeholders to lose their confidence. Conversely, early success may embolden an organization to do too much too soon—another route to disaster and unmet expectations. Creating a vision is a continuous balancing act of risk-taking and incremental progress.

- *Diversions.* A successful vision creates a priority order to strategies and budgets. Don't be distracted by diversions, like responding to competitor moves. Putting patients first will mean that the interests of employees and physicians must sometimes be compromised. Putting the community first may mean not acquiring new technology already installed by a competitor.

- *Language.* Visions can become simplistic slogans. Skeptical employees may wear the "button of the month" but may give it little heed (1994).

IS "CORPORATE SOUL" JUST ANOTHER FAD?

The resurgence of interest in values, vision, and healthy communities is heartening to all those who feared that hospitals and physicians were losing all motivations except economic maximization. But will this only last as long as profits are plentiful? Do values get cut with the budget? Do vision-driven community projects have to "take their hit" in across-the-board budget reductions? And are management bonuses appropriate in a time of staff layoffs and no increases? The larger question is whether value-based management—corporate soul—is just another fad?

For the consumers' sake, ideally not. The public would like to redefine the role of health institutions toward a far greater health emphasis. In a 1994 poll sponsored by the Healthcare Forum with the National Civic League and W. K. Kellogg Foundation, the American public feels the nation is in decline, and a majority (52 percent) believes that substantial sacrifices will be needed to get the country back on the right track (Roberge 1994). A large majority of the public agrees they can help reduce health costs through prevention and cost-conscious use of the health system, but fewer than one in four Americans expect health reform to benefit their community or themselves.

Healthcare ethicist Emily Friedman (1995b) is also skeptical. She asks: "Are healthy communities just another fad?" There are many reasons to build a compelling rationale for community involvement by hospitals and physicians, including the aging of America, federal budget cutbacks, and justification for tax-exempt status. But Friedman fears that ". . . the commitment may not be there; instead, it may be a case of follow-the-leader, or else opportunistic exhortations by consultants and others who see a gold mine in this movement" (1995b, 10).

CAN "SOUL" EQUATE WITH PROFITABILITY?

In all this talk about corporate soul, what about the profit motive? The short answer is, profit as a goal works. Just look at the top 100 hospitals in America, selected by HCIA and William R. Mercer & Co. Some 100 hospitals in five categories of size and location were selected for outstanding financial performance (Morrissey 1995). More than one in four of these 100 were managed by Columbia/HCA, the nation's largest for-profit hospital chain. Comments Jean Chenowith of Baltimore-based HCIA, a financial consulting firm: "It's fair to say that Columbia has provided significant benefit to their institutions through their tough dealing with vendors, and their ability to go out to the capital markets" (Morrissey 1995, 55).

Setting high profitability goals can spur increases in performance. Columbia dominated the large nonteaching hospitals category. Its top performers achieved a commendable 23 percent return on assets, with cash flow margins of 23 percent. Equity growth was the highest of any of the comparison groups—a startling 35 percent. Not all the gains appeared on the bottom line. An attention to efficiency also helps quality. Benchmark hospitals in the top 100 had lower mortality figures, while demonstrating the lowest lengths of stay and expense per discharge.

Financial success is an opportunity for ethical action. Hospitals that made a profit are confused by the public with for-profit investor-owned hospitals (Friedman 1996, 299). Consumers seem to think that all healthcare organizations are profit driven. In the face of public attitudes that health organizations are too business oriented, healthcare organizations need to demonstrate their community conscience. Management and trustees can decide how to invest surplus revenues, choosing among priorities such as new health facilities and equipment, upgrading wages and staffing levels, or addressing unmet community health needs. Profitable healthcare organizations can publicly demonstrate their corporate soul with visible initiatives that benefit patients and the community. Oregon's MidColumbia Medical Center wears its community heart on its sleeve with an annual tithe to health-promoting community projects. In recent years, this 49-bed community hospital has built a community swimming pool, constructed a running path along the Columbia River, and furnished a health resource center for community health education.

LOOKING FORWARD: IS TRANSFORMATION POSSIBLE? OR LIKELY?

Bureaucracy may be the enduring legacy of the twentieth century. Transforming it won't be easy. Organizational behaviorist Russell Ackoff argues for a more "democratic corporation" that works for its shareholders, both internal participants and external customers. The organization is a social system that must emphasize the quality of work life as well as the quality of its products. To build a new style of "multidimensional corporation," work must be decentralized through a system of organizational democracy and stakeholder cooperation. Is such a transformation possible? Ackoff is skeptical: "There are not enough institutional and organizational leaders in America who understand the prevailing mess, let alone know how to deal with it" (1994, xii).

There is evidence of a new consciousness emerging that attempts to blend tough, market-driven management with a genuine concern for people and the environment. Denver-based futurist Michael Annison, author of *Managing the Whirlwind*, argues that organizations are discovering they can "do well by doing right" (Annison 1996, 137). Proponents of corporate soul cite examples like Johnson & Johnson, Tom's of Maine, or Ben & Jerry's as companies where doing well—growing the business and making a profit—can happily coexist with doing good—making a demonstrated commitment to the community and the environment. Those are for-profit, entrepreneurial companies that have also managed to demonstrate social responsibility. Should not America's 3,000 nonprofit, tax-exempt hospitals set an even higher standard?

REFERENCES

Ackoff, R. L. 1994. *The Democratic Corporation.* New York: Oxford University Press.

Addleman, R. A. 1995. "Value-Driven Healthcare." 38 (6): 46–50.

Annison, M. H. 1996. *Managing the Whirlwind: Patterns and Opportunities in a Changing World.* Englewood, CO: Medical Group Management Association.

Beckham, J. D. 1994. "The Vision Thing." *Healthcare Forum Journal* 37 (2): 60–68.

————. 1995. "Follow the Money." *Healthcare Forum Journal* 38 (6): 36–44.

Bennis, W., and R. Townsend. 1995. *Reinventing Leadership: Strategies to Empower the Organization.* New York: William Morrow & Co.

Bolman, L. G., and T. E. Deal. 1995. *Leading with Soul: An Uncommon Journey of Spirit.* San Francisco: Jossey-Bass.

Carlson, L. K. 1995. "The Next Step." *Healthcare Forum Journal* 38 (3): 14–18.

Case, J. 1995. *Open-Book Management: The Coming Business Revolution.* New York: Harper Business.

Catholic Health Association (CHA). 1995. "1995 Achievement Citation Winners and Nominees." *Health Progress* 76 (7): 41–72.

Chappell, T. 1995. *The Soul of a Business: Managing for Profit and the Common Good.* New York: Bantam.

Chopra, D. 1995. *The Seven Spiritual Laws of Success.* San Rafael, CA: Amber-Allen Publishing.

Coile, R. C., Jr. 1995. "A Visionary Executive." *Healthcare Forum Journal* 38 (3): 74–75.

Covey, S. R. 1995. "Principle-Centered Leadership." New York: Simon & Schuster.

Curley, J. E. 1995. "Building Bridges: A New Era in Collaborative Healthcare." *Catholic Health World* 11 (21): 2.

Friedman, E. 1994. "Freedom of Choice." *Healthcare Forum Journal* 37 (2): 13–17.

————. 1995a. "If You Really Mean It." *Healthcare Forum Journal* 38 (3): 9–12.

————. 1995b. "Never Again." *Healthcare Forum Journal* 38 (6): 10–12.

————. 1996. *The Right Thing: Ten Years of Ethics Columns from the Healthcare Forum Journal.* San Francisco: Jossey-Bass.

Ferguson, M. 1993. "The Transformation of Values and Vocation." In *The New Paradigm in Business,* edited by M. Ray and A. Rinzler. New York: Jeremy P. Tarcher/G.P. Putnam's Sons.

Greaves, R. F. 1995. "What's Right and Wrong with Our Healthcare System." *California Medicine* 2 (10): 42.

Greene, J. 1995. "Tax-Exempts Feeling the Heat." *Modern Healthcare* 25 (47): 46–52.

Hancock, T., and C. Bezold. 1995. "Possible Futures, Preferable Futures." *Healthcare Forum Journal* 37 (2): 23–29.

Jones, D. 1995. "Open-Book Policy Can Motivate Employees." *USA Today* (December 14): B1.

Kouzes, J. M., and B. Z. Posner. 1995. *Credibility: How Leaders Gain and Lose It, Why People Demand It.* San Francisco: Jossey-Bass.

Lager, F. C. 1994. *Ben & Jerry's: The Inside Scoop.* New York: Crown Trade.

Magee, M. 1995. "Information Empowerment of the Patient: The Next Payer/Provider Battlefield." *Journal of Outcomes Management* 2 (3): 17–21.

Malkin, M. 1995. "The Costly Motherhood Mandate." *Wall Street Journal* (November 16): A20.

Moore, T. 1992. *Care of the Soul: A Guide for Cultivating Depth and Sacredness in Everyday Life.* New York: Harper Perennial.

Morrisey, J. 1995. "The Best-Run Hospitals." *Modern Healthcare* 25 (49): 54–64.

Ray, M., and A. Rinzler (eds.). 1993. *The New Paradigm in Business.* New York: Jeremy P. Tarcher/G.P. Putnam's Sons.

Roberge, H. 1994. "What Creates Health?" *Healthcare Forum Journal* 37 (3): 16–17.

Sasenick, S. 1994. "On Healthier Communities" (Special Insert). *Healthcare Forum Journal* 37 (3): 56–72.

Secretan, L. H. K. 1997. *Reclaiming Higher Ground: Creating Organizations That Inspire the Soul.* New York: McGraw-Hill.

Snow, C. 1995. "Provider See Rewards of Superior Service." *Modern Healthcare* 25 (49): 66.

11

Excess Hospital Capacity:
Recycling, Retrofitting, or Closure—
Alternatives for Surplus Inpatient Beds

The issue is not how to fill or reuse empty beds. In this changing environment, hospitals and health systems must focus on streamlining and simplifying operational processes, facilitating case management, promoting the least costly setting for care delivery, and optimizing resource sharing among departments. When hospitals have addressed these issues, then the solutions to the "bed problem" will be obvious.
　　　—Cynthia Hayward, "Recycling the Hospital"
　　　(Nadal 1996, 36)

What *will* we do with the excess hospital capacity? Across the United States, there are hundreds of thousands of empty hospital beds, and acres of square footage, that are underused or sitting idle. Inpatient demand is shrinking. If everyone belonged to a managed care plan, the number of excess inpatient beds could be 450,000, according to a study by the Washington, D.C.–based AmHS Institute (*Hospitals and Health Networks* 1994). Hospital use rates in the four years between 1992 and 1995 dropped from 122 to 110 per 1,000 population and could fall to 85 by 2000 (Nadal 1996, 35). The number of available hospital beds has steadily fallen, from 923,000 in 1992 to 700,000 in 1995. At this rate, based on an average of 100 square feet per bed, U.S. hospitals might have to decide what to do with 42 million square feet of available vacated space by 2000.

There are possibilities for recycling, retrofitting, and even closure for these empty beds:

- alternative acute care use, such as step-down or rehabilitation;
- continuum of care substitution, such as subacute care, skilled nursing care, and hospice care;
- remodeling of multibed rooms to single-patient accommodations;
- consolidation of inpatient rooms to suite concept;
- conversion of traditional inpatient rooms to newer designs, such as labor-delivery-recovery-post partum rooms;
- recycling of acute inpatient space for expanded ambulatory care programs;
- retrofitting for nonpatient care uses, such as office space or visitor hotel rooms;
- conversion of the entire facility to other social purposes, such as senior housing; and
- closure and divestiture for nonpatient care uses, such as office buildings, retail, or housing.

The costs of excess capacity are more than simply subsidizing underused capacity. The huge surplus of hospital beds has created a disequilibrium between the supply and demand, giving HMOs and insurers enormous leverage in negotiating managed care contracts. The overcapacity situation pits one community hospital against another in a cutthroat war to survive. Payors get the lowest prices, sometimes below cost. One California CEO complains, "Until those excess beds come out, you're going to see hospitals pricing on the margin, not covering fully allocated costs" (Cerne and Montague 1994). This "war of the balance sheets" will be won by deeper-pocketed hospitals and health systems, but it will be a sad outcome for communities that invested in their local facilities but could not outspend community rivals in matching subsidies. Is this unfair market warfare or simply an exercise in enterprise economics that will reduce marginal players and strengthen the surviving health systems?

PREDICTIONS OF DECLINING DEMAND

Will only one in three hospital beds be needed in the twenty-first century? If Michael Sachs is right, the demand for U.S. acute hospital beds may fall by 34 percent between 1996 and 2000 (Sachs Group 1995). The Sachs Group, a national market research firm based in Evanston, Illinois, has developed a computer-based forecast for hospital bed demand for dozens of major DRG clusters. From a baseline of 1994, the five-year forecast offers this outlook:

- Total patient days will decline nationwide by 34 percent from 1994 to 1999, in all 30 major product groups.

- Most of the decline will be lower volume; in 26 of the 30 product groups, discharges will drop by 26 percent overall.
- All regions will experience decline in varying levels; the Northeast will potentially see the greatest drop in utilization, while the West will have the lowest drop.
- Average hospital stays will fall to 5.5 days; the Northeast will experience the steepest drop, plunging 22 percent, while the West will increase slightly, up 5 percent.

The Sachs Group's "bellwether" forecast for 1996 to 2000 makes it perfectly clear—there are far too many hospital beds for tomorrow's market conditions. Today's hospitals account for 1.2 million beds. In 1994, the effective demand for hospital beds was 664,000. By Sachs Group indicators, demand will fall to only 424,000 in 2000. Sachs assumes that regional differences in hospital bed use will disappear for many procedures and DRG groups. Today, length of stay varies by two days, highest in the Northeast and lowest in the West, which has been substantially affected by managed care.

Such a huge surplus of unused hospital beds will not last. The Sachs Group assumes substantial consolidation of traditional providers will occur in the next five years. Excess bed capacity will be corrected by mergers and downsizing. Fewer beds means fewer staff, and cuts in nursing and support staff are expected as demand shifts from traditional inpatient facilities and into nonacute alternative settings such as subacute, ambulatory, and home care. Integrated health systems will rely on primary care physician networks, case managers, and alternative settings to meet the demands of their enrolled populations under a managed care scenario. Affiliations with continuum-of-care providers and home care agencies will develop cost-effective services that are coordinated and managed by networkwide information systems. The reengineering of America's hospital-dominated industry will be far along by 2000.

The full effect of managed care is accelerating a steep decline in the effective demand for inpatient beds and facilities. Total HMO enrollment has reached more than 50 million, more than 20 percent of the U.S. population, according to St. Paul, Minnesota–based InterStudy, a market research organization that tracks the HMO industry (Hamer 1997). Heavily affected services are among the most strategically important product lines for many U.S. hospitals, including cardiology, general surgery, orthopedics, psychiatry, and open-heart surgery. The Sachs Group's outlook clustered DRGs into 30 market clusters and predicted substantial declines in most sectors (see Table 11.1):

- cardiology days will slump 32 percent from 23.4 million to 15.9 million;

Table 11.1   Changes in Total Patient Days: 1994–1999
(Days in Millions)

Product/DRG Cluster	1994	1999	Percentage Change
Cardiology	23.4	15.9	−32%
Pulmonary	18.0	12.5	−31
Psychiatry	18.6	9.2	−50
Orthopedics	16.9	10.5	−38
General Surgery	16.4	13.9	−15

Source: Sachs Group. 1995. "Healthcare 1999: A National Bellwether." Chicago, 4.

- pulmonary days will decrease 31 percent from 18.0 million to 12.5 million;
- psychiatry days will decline 50 percent from 18.6 million to 9.2 million;
- orthopedic days will plunge 38 percent, falling from 16.9 million to 10.5 million;
- general surgery days will slip 15 percent, down from 16.4 million to 13.9 million;
- otolaryngology days will fall by more than half, down 51 percent;
- endocrine days will erode by 47 percent; and
- open-heart days will drop by 39 percent. (Sachs Group 1995)

All regions will feel the effect of falling demand for hospital services, but regions that have experienced the highest rate of admissions and longest lengths of stay will feel it the most. The Northeast, for example, accounted for 27 percent of all discharges in 1994. By 2000, that could fall to only 20 percent of the national total. In the West, in contrast, California and other western states will feel the effect less because its use rates and lengths of stay are already heavily affected by managed care. As a result, the West may account for more bed days by the end of the decade, up to 21 percent from 15 percent in 1994.

Hospitals in these regions will all be vulnerable to patient day declines:

- The Northeast will be hit hardest, with bed demand plunging steeply by 49 percent, from 52.9 million days to 26.8 million.
- Patient days and bed demand in the South will drop sharply, down 35 percent from 70.9 million to 46.2 million.
- The Midwest will experience a significant loss of patient days, down 31 percent from 45.5 million to 31.6 million.
- The West will slip only 8 percent, falling from 30.2 million days to 27.8 million.

REASONS FOR THE DECLINE

The Sachs Group predicts a nationwide decline in hospital bed need, despite the general aging of the population and increases in total population. Only a few product groups, such as vascular surgery, will see an increase in hospital need because of aging. The continued spread of AIDS will produce increased bed need by at-risk populations. General medicine days will hold relatively constant, with only a one percent drop, down roughly 78,000 patient days by 2000. Average length of stay will extend by 20 percent, to 8.2 days, and psychiatric stays will also stretch by 20 percent, to 12.9 days. By the twenty-first century, patients will generally be older, sicker, and will require longer stays.

There are compelling forces that will drive hospital demand down so rapidly, in the Sachs' view:

1. *Managed care* will continue to convert more of the population from fee-for-service and traditional government health programs to HMOs, such as Medicare and Medicaid HMOs.
2. *Capitation* will place more providers and integrated health systems at risk, which shifts the economic incentives to reduce inpatient care and shifts the emphasis of care to ambulatory and home-based services.
3. *Case management* and clinical pathways will effectively control the care of more patients, distributing them across the continuum of care and away from traditional inpatient settings.
4. *Alternative settings* that are less expensive but equally effective will be progressively substituted for inpatient care; this will be especially evident in orthopedic, ophthalmology, and other surgical services.
5. *Chronic care* will be increasingly treated in nonacute settings, even as hospitals convert beds to subacute and other specialized programs to manage the health needs of chronically ill patients.
6. *Technology* and new pharmaceuticals will reduce or eliminate the need for some inpatient procedures, accelerating the shift to ambulatory and in-home settings.

The Sachs Group's bellwether study for 1999 provides an important benchmark in the transition of U.S. healthcare to a managed care scenario for the national market. Take note that the Sachs Group calls its predictions conservative. Projections are based on current use rates in managed care markets, and Sachs' market researchers believe that, over time, managed care may diminish inpatient utilization even further. The overall trend is toward a leveling of demand rates and lengths of stay, but healthcare is still a local business. Regional differences in use rates for various medical and surgical product lines is predicted to vary significantly.

COSTS OF EXCESS INPATIENT CAPACITY

Capital expenditures for facilities account for some 6 percent of the average hospital's budget. In a $500 million multihospital system, the annual capital costs of acute facilities could represent $30 million of hard-to-reduce expenses. Downsizing and reengineering have left many hospitals with dozens, sometimes hundreds, of regularly vacant beds. Sunk capital costs, interest expenses, and nonreduceable overhead costs add to the burden of carrying unused capacity. Hospital mergers and acquisitions have raised the visibility of the capacity issue. Should health systems eliminate entire excess hospitals rather than satisfy local desires to keep a symbol of community healthcare open? These are tough political issues that are often not resolved based on rational economic analysis. Which still leaves the question, what will we do with America's 450,000-bed surplus hospital capacity?

Managed care plans exploit the surplus of hospital beds by offering discounted reimbursement rates, even rates below the hospitals' costs. Hospitals are thus faced with the choice of selling inpatient services at managed care discounts and making a marginal revenue contribution to overhead, or turning business away. Chief financial officers know there are real costs of carrying excess capacity. CFOs cannot "make it up on volume" when reimbursement is below cost, unless improved efficiency drives the hospital's per-bed expenses below the discounted reimbursement.

How much does an empty bed cost? It depends, say the accountants. The marginal cost of holding unused capacity is different for each facility. Current accounting practices may overstate the cost of an unused hospital bed. Conventional hospital accounting practices divide yearly fixed inpatient costs—for example, depreciation and property taxes—by the number of patient days expected to be provided. According to this formula, if bed use declines, the fixed cost per patient day increases. Another method for calculating the cost of carrying underused capacity suggests a practical approach that focuses on the maximum feasible patient days as a more realistic measure (Sopariwala 1996). As a practical reality, most hospital beds and units are unlikely to be operated at 100 percent capacity. Even with this more conservative approach, the costs of keeping unused beds available may range from $35 to $65 per day, or $12,775 to $23,725 per bed per year. Multiply those figures by 450,000 empty beds, and American healthcare may be subsidizing $51 to $106 billion of excess capacity annually.

INTEGRATED DELIVERY SYSTEMS MUST CONFRONT POLITICAL AND ECONOMIC FACTORS

Integrated delivery systems (IDSs)—not government—will be the organizations that address the issue of excess capacity. The IDS movement is gaining steam, thanks to unprecedented consolidation activities. In 1996, the number of hospitals involved in merger and acquisition activities increased 4.5 percent to a record 768—some 15 percent of the nation's nonfederal hospitals—according to *Modern Healthcare*'s annual list of merger and acquisition activities (Cochrane 1997). In the three-year period from 1994 to 1996, nearly two out of five U.S. hospitals were involved in mergers, acquisitions, or joint ventures. The busiest merger states were California, with 30; Texas, with 20; New York, with 19; and Florida, with 13. The result is that many major metropolitan areas have consolidated into three to four regional provider networks.

Excess capacity will not be easy to eradicate. Deeply entrenched economic interests and local politics are serious considerations that any healthcare executive must overcome when recommending consolidation or closure. Key factors that must be addressed include:

- *Attorney general.* Activist state attorneys general are inserting themselves with growing frequency in hospital decisions for consolidation or closure—especially when the situation may involve a conversion to for-profit status. In 1996, some 68 hospitals were changing from nonprofit to for-profit, or 8 percent of all hospitals involved in mergers (Cochrane 1997). In San Diego, California state attorney Dan Lungren derailed a proposed acquisition of the nonprofit Sharp Healthcare System by Columbia/HCA. Sharp cancelled the deal.

- *Community opposition.* Strong local opposition is a powerful factor in healthcare consolidations or closures. Community uproar about the Sharp acquisition in San Diego resulted in the involvement of the state attorney general and legislative enactment of a new law that now gives the state the right to veto such a transaction in the future.

- *Displaced workers.* The jobs issue is now a primary factor in hospitals' decisions to downsize, restructure, or close. As healthcare organizations shed thousands of jobs in between 1990 and 1995, the organized opposition of workers has grown (Coile 1997). Two ballot initiatives in California that would have curbed hospital downsizings or for-profit conversions were labor-sponsored, although neither proposal succeeded in the November 1996 election.

- *Economic impact.* Do not underestimate the effect of hospitals upon the region's economic vitality. In many markets, hospitals are among the top five employers. In a recent Economic Summit sponsored by the West Virginia Chamber of Commerce, hospitals were recognized as the state's third-ranking employer.

- *Local elected officials.* Hospital consolidations and closures can provide high drama and political conflict. Some local elected officials may see these decisions as an opportunity to gain political visibility for future elections.

- *Legislation/regulation.* California, Nebraska, and Rhode Island are among a growing number of states that are raising regulatory hurdles for hospital decisions to merge, acquire, or close a facility. Some of the initiatives are clearly intended to block for-profit companies from acquiring local nonprofit hospitals. Rhode Island's law drew a gubernatorial veto, all part of a major controversy over Columbia/HCA's offer to acquire 152-bed Roger Williams Medical Center for $50 million (Japsen 1997). The offer has since been withdrawn.

- *Philanthropy.* Raising the issue of consolidation or closure can have a chilling effect on local philanthropy. Community sponsors resent the loss of their community capital when hospitals are threatened to be closed, even if closure would clearly be the most cost-effective strategy. Local leaders, community groups, and civic leaders will certainly be cooler to future requests for philanthropy after seeing "their" hospital closed or converted.

- *Public relations.* The PR aspects of conversion or closure are sensitive and hard to handle. Taking the options public is likely to spark community opposition. But what is the choice? Hospitals that attempt to keep such discussions private can be embarrassed when they leak to local media. And it is almost impossible to keep such hot topics from public view.

- *Unions.* As controversy has grown about consolidations or closures, so has the involvement of unions. In New York, federal bailout funds will be used in part to build networks of primary care centers. The National Health and Human Services Employees Union, Local 1199, lobbied hard for federal assistance in creating alternative employment for thousands of union workers. (Hernandez 1997)

HOW MUCH CAPACITY IS RIGHT?
PROJECTED UTILIZATION FOR 200,000 MANAGED LIVES

How many hospital beds does the United States really need? Government facility planners once targeted hospital development based on an assumption of 4 beds per 1,000 people, and government subsidies and grants allowed hundreds of local communities to build hospitals in a 20-year period in the 1950s and 1960s. On a national basis, U.S. current hospital capacity is 3.6 beds per 1,000 people.

But managed care is changing all that—and rapidly. Capitated physicians are slashing hospital use rates, reducing admissions, and shortening length of stay. In California, hospital demand has fallen to 1.06 beds per 1,000, according to a recent forecast for the California Healthcare Association (Coile and Menkin 1997). Chi Systems of Ann Arbor, Michigan, a national healthcare strategy and facilities planning firm, has a model for projecting demand under managed care assumptions that demonstrates how a population of 200,000 could be effectively served by fewer than 220 beds, or about 1 bed per 1,000 (see Table 11.2).

PRIME TARGETS FOR CONSOLIDATION

Medicare budget cuts and managed care discounts will force hospitals and health systems to reassess their facilities investments. To close or not to close—these are difficult questions. Boards of trustees and senior managers will be moving into murky waters here. There are no hard-and-fast rules on hospital obsolescence, short of failure to meet local or state building code requirements. These guidelines for identifying excess capacity do not have to be terribly precise. There is so much excess capacity in most markets that any rational observer can easily spot targets for consolidation, conversion, or closure.

Here is a list of potential targets for downsizing or divestiture in markets with excess capacity:

- *Academic medical centers.* The Pew Commission recommended closing 20 to 25 percent of the nation's 125 medical schools and academic medical centers. Mergers are already taking place on a voluntary basis in Boston, Philadelphia, and San Francisco.

Table 11.2   Projected Utilization for 200,000 Managed Lives

Market	*Demand*	*Key Resource Requirements*
200,000 population	692,500 physician visits	240 exam rooms
	45,400 emergency visits	23 treatment bays
	21,900 surgery cases	20 operating rooms
	3,000 births	2 delivery rooms, 7 LDR rooms, 25 ante/post-partum beds
	46,170 medical/surgical days	158 medical/surgical beds
	10,920 behavioral health days	38 behavioral health beds
	5,080 acute rehabilitative days	18 acute rehab beds
	34,260 subacute days	117 subacute beds
	423,580 skilled nursing days	1,290 skilled nursing beds
	5,795 home health patients	165,700 home health visits

Assumptions: Medicare and Medicaid aggressively managed; commercial market moderately managed; 15 percent of population is over 65; 80 percent occupancy is assumed except for skilled nursing facilities (SNFs) at 90 percent.

Source: Hayward, C., and R. C. Coile, Jr. 1997. *What Are We Going to Do with All Our Surplus Capacity?* Palm Springs, CA: Society for Healthcare Strategy and Market Development.

- *Acute general hospitals closer than three miles.* In urban markets, the average travel time to establish local service areas for hospitals is 20–30 minutes. Health systems and integrated delivery networks may want to take a hard look at overlapping facilities that service shared local markets.

- *Emergency rooms.* Not all hospitals need to subsidize the provision of maximum-level emergency services. The high cost of subsidizing emergency services demands a regional perspective in assessing health system or network capacity. This is a ripe area for consolidation and conversion.

- *Campuses smaller than 30 acres.* Hospital sites with little room for expansion have limited flexibility in redeveloping acute inpatient facilities for ambulatory or postacute care. Small, land-locked campuses are especially difficult to reengineer. These small sites are leading targets for consolidation onto roomier campus settings that can flexibly accommodate multiple levels of care and a large number of hospital-based physicians and groups.

- *Facilities built before 1975.* Although many pre-1975 facilities still have useful life, they will not compete or perform as well as more modern units. Consumers associate up-to-date facilities with quality care. Older hospitals also have performance limitations, such as limited floor-to-ceiling height, that make it difficult to accommodate modern infrastructure such as information technology or upgraded heating and cooling systems.

- *Floors with 3- to 4-bed units.* Today's consumers prefer single-room accommodations. Multibed units are less flexible for patient assignment, gender considerations, infectious disease prevention, and isolation needs.

- *Hospitals with more than 33 percent of beds out of service.* When a lot of beds are routinely out of circulation, warning flags go up. Hospital capacity is clearly out of balance with community need. The hospital may be in danger of falling below a critical mass of patients. Even flexing the staff cannot compensate for subsidy costs of operating a substantially underused facility.

- *Programs below national minimums.* When clinical service use rates fall below nationally recommended minimums, alarm bells should ring. These rules of thumb are surrogate criteria for a well-managed program. Below-minimum services may not cover their overhead costs. Worse yet, quality problems may lie ahead.

- *Inpatient surgical services more than 50 percent ambulatory.* Is an acute hospital really in the acute-care business when more than half of all surgery is performed on an ambulatory basis? Historically, surgery was a hospital's bread-and-butter revenue source. Now the surgical demand is migrating to outpatient settings. Big shifts in surgical acuity are signals of change. In the context of a health system or regional network, these "lite" hospitals with high levels of outpatient surgery may be in transition, eventually being replaced by ambulatory care centers.

- *Units with fewer than 25 beds.* Small inpatient units with few beds have limited flexibility for accommodating the range of high-acuity patients that modern hospitals with larger nursing units can handle more easily.

FINDING SOLUTIONS FOR UNDERUSED RURAL HOSPITALS

More than one-third of U.S. hospitals may be classified as rural. They serve the 20 percent of the nation's population that lives in small-town markets with low population densities. Some 2,200 of the nation's 5,200 community hospitals are classified as rural (Rene 1997). Many of these rural facilities are small, fewer than 50 beds—some with only 25 beds. But small towns stubbornly protect their health facilities. Hospitals are economic anchors for community development. Can they survive into the twenty-first century under Medicare budget cutbacks, dwindling physician support, and the need for replacement capital?

Realistically, the rural hospital of the future in many communities may be an urgent care center with skilled nursing beds. Will it still be a licensed hospital? To gain Medicare reimbursement, rural hospitals must meet an ever-rising number of requirements for staffing, information systems, and quality assurance. JCAHO accreditation is expensive for rural facilities. Diversification into ambulatory and postacute services can provide diversified revenues for rural facilities. Half of all rural hospitals now operate home health agencies, one-third have nursing homes, and almost all have outpatient clinics, according to the 1995 survey of rural facilities by the American Hospital Association (Rene 1997).

ALTERNATIVES FOR RECYCLING AND REUSE OF EXCESS CAPACITY

Downsizing has negative connotations. Creative healthcare executives should place excess capacity in a positive context. Bring together the medical staff, nursing and professional staff, middle managers, and trustees to brainstorm new ways to recycle, redevelop, or profitably divest underused facilities and square feet. Addressing the capacity issue will create opportunities for enhancing customer satisfaction, staff productivity, program development, and quality improvement, as well as cost reductions.

1. *More space.* Instead of closure or conversion, one tempting alternative for the affluent hospital or deep-pocketed system is remodeling to give the many cramped functions of the average hospital what they have been craving—more space! This scenario assumes that the hospital or health system can afford to carry underused facility space without closing it or finding another revenue-generating use. If your facility falls in this category, now is the opportunity to expand facilities for such new functions as:

   • less-cluttered hallways;
   • extra work space and counter space;
   • increased number of computers and related information technology;
   • storage for supplies, records, and equipment;
   • family and visitor waiting spaces, library, kitchen;
   • expanded administration, communication, and recordkeeping space;
   • conference rooms and meeting spaces;
   • on-site physician offices and examining rooms;
   • mini-labs, pharmacies, and x-ray facilities on nursing units; and
   • dramatic interior space, such as atriums and skylights.

2. *Consolidation into new facility.* Closure is easier to take when a system can consolidate two or more surplus facilities into one new "rightsized" facility that the community will share. The consolidated facility can be located on one of the existing campuses or be newly built on a compromise location that may include a bigger or more accessible site. Consolidation and closure must deal with deep-seated community attachment. These "cornfield" hospitals can be situated halfway between two towns or in a completely neutral setting. Michigan's Genesys Healthcare System recently closed four community hospitals after opening a new "hospital of the future" with just half the bed capacity of the replaced facilities (Havighurst 1997).

3. *Reengineered capacity.* A systemwide reengineering can lead to reduction or elimination of excess capacity. A reengineering analysis will demonstrate opportunities to streamline and simplify operational processes. Options for substitution of other lower-cost settings should be considered. The goal is expedited care delivery at the most efficient costs. Reengineering can identify ways to optimize sharing of resources. A thorough reengineering project will focus upon such aspects as:

   • operational/systems problems;
   • customer service/marketing issues;
   • poor functional layout;
   • wrong location;
   • inappropriate traffic mix;

- equipment/technology constraints;
- image/interior design concerns;
- physical plant issues; and
- code/regulatory noncompliances.

Academic medical centers are prime targets for integration. In Boston, a recent report by the Massachusetts Business Roundtable, "Reengineering for the Future," called for the region's academic medical centers to become "lean and productive," although the report stopped short of calling for closure (Cochrane 1996). Confronting a glut of half-empty facilities in many regions like Boston, this type of marketwide reengineering analysis is likely to lead to more recommendations for closure, assuming the provider network has sufficient capacity in the remaining facilities and the closure option does not eliminate strategically located hospitals that may be needed for managed care contracting or to provide consumer choice in a provider-sponsored HMO. In Detroit, the Oakwood Health System voted recently to close two of its ten local hospitals after a systemwide reengineering initiative. Greater Detroit Area Health Council's president and CEO, James B. Kenney, told local employers, "the reality is that we need to take out entire hospitals" (Havighurst 1997, 1).

4. *Redesign.* Like other buildings, architectural designs for hospitals have generally evolved following the dictum that form follows function. But it is no longer financially feasible to design hospitals under that premise because the functions are changing too rapidly. The problem today is that the core business—acute inpatient care—is often secondary to ambulatory care and postacute services, which are rapidly becoming the new core functions. Many of yesterday's hospitals need to be redesigned to recognize their rapidly evolving uses for a variety of outpatient and continuum of care programs.

    Healthcare facility design is changing, but not fast enough. Healthcare architect Pat Kennedy of Baltimore-based Kennedy Architects and Interiors argues that "we must accept that hospitals must be retooled periodically, just as an auto assembly line must be revamped to accommodate new models and manufacturing processes" (1994, 38). Redesigning health facilities for greater flexibility can be achieved by using concepts such as "open architecture," which is widely used in modern office buildings and light industry. Healthcare architects are using consumer-oriented design models such as shopping malls or hotels for inspiration as they redesign healthcare facilities for future market demands and technology that are expected to change continuously.

5. *Alternative inpatient uses.* Many hospitals are finding alternative inpatient services can be housed if conversion costs are not excessive. Hospital executives see this strategy as a way to recapture revenues

from services such as subacute care. In California, almost 7,000 subacute beds were licensed by the state between 1985 and 1995, many
of them in hospitals (Coile and Menkin 1997). Subacute care uses
more space. About 25 to 35 percent fewer beds can be accommodated
when converting an acute care unit to subacute care (Kennedy 1996).
Given longer stays, averaging 15 to 20 days for subacute care, the
costs of the conversion are not always profitable. Skilled nursing conversions assume longer days of 20 to 60 days.

It is very tempting for hospital administrators to renovate older,
vacant hospital units in search of new revenues and new uses for sunk
capital. But that strategy may not work. Facilities retrofitting for subacute or skilled nursing may trigger the need to meet modern building
codes and standards, which can push the costs past break-even levels.
A comprehensive bed-need analysis can identify other potential
options. Instead of bringing obsolete units out of mothballs, it may be
more cost-effective to convert younger facilities to subacute or skilled
nursing, where the units already meet code and require less capital to
retrofit for new uses.

6. *Think ambulatory.* Tomorrow's hospital may have no acute inpatient
   beds at all. A variety of experiments are now under way that stretch
   the concept of a hospital to the limits. In California, the state legisla-
   ture authorized up to 12 pilot projects to test the concept of the postsurgical center (Hinz 1991). These nonacute recovery facilities are
   authorized to hold patients up to 48 hours after surgery. Most of the
   recovery centers are associated with ambulatory surgery facilities, but
   several have been created in hospitals adjacent to in-and-out surgery
   programs. Proponents argue that the postsurgical recovery center could
   safely accommodate as many as 20 to 30 percent of all surgery
   patients. After five years of pilot-testing, however, the postsurgical
   recovery concept is still experimental and has not gained mainstream
   acceptance from physicians or payors. Costs are not much lower than
   conventional inpatient care, and patients who recover rapidly could
   be cared for at home more cheaply.

7. *Residential conversion.* Some aging hospitals may see new life as
   housing units rather than health facilities. Across the nation, older
   hospitals are being considered for a variety of new uses. Housing is
   one alternative. In San Francisco, two Catholic facilities have been
   recycled, one as senior housing and another as condominium apart-
   ments. Residential conversion of a hospital can be part of community
   redevelopment. On the Mississippi River, an abandoned municipal
   hospital, Natchez General, was retrofitted to provide transitional housing and services for the homeless (Andrews 1996). Architects have
   revived the hospital's graceful 1925 exterior, while refitting its interior for social service programs, using funds from several state and

federal agencies. The hospital's redevelopment is part of a neighborhood rehabilitation effort to revive an aging neighborhood adjacent to the city's historic district.

8. *Closure.* Closing the doors on an underused hospital may be the most cost-beneficial way to address the issue of surplus capacity. The largest markets may also be the biggest targets for reducing excess capacity. New York, for example, could close 10,000 beds. A study of bed demand in New York state found a maximum need for 44,000 beds, at least 20 percent below the supply of 55,000 beds (Lagoe, Marshall, and Norman 1995). There were sizable local differences in hospital use. A few counties had over a 100 percent excess capacity. But other markets, such as Rochester and Syracuse, were quite efficient, with a surplus of less than 7 percent.

Despite falling revenues from Medicare and managed care, the widespread closure of American hospitals has not occurred. Closing a hospital is not easy. Since 1980, about 40 hospitals a year have closed, rising to 81 shuttered facilities in 1988, according to the American Hospital Association (Burda and Weissenstein 1996). The number of closed facilities fell to 17 in 1994, then jumped to 30 in 1995. Eventually, about half of all closed hospitals return to healthcare uses, such as long-term care, home health care, and ambulatory services.

LOOKING FORWARD: WHY AREN'T WE CLOSING THOSE EMPTY BEDS?

There are understandable reasons why the U.S. health system is in no hurry to get rid of excess capacity. As Geoffrey Harris, author of *Patients, Profits and Health System Change*, notes: "Hospitals aren't doing so badly right now, particularly on Medicare. And if you're making money, the impetus to sell [convert, or close] goes down" (1995, 2). Today, the hospital industry accounts for almost $400 billion of America's $1 trillion health industry. Hospitals are powerful economic drivers in many communities, often ranking in the top five employers. Overcapacity was not built in a day. Putting the current bed surplus in perspective, there were powerful forces at work that drove hospitals to expand capacity in the 1980s:

- cost-based reimbursement and capital "pass-through";
- anticipated unbounded growth;
- diversification for new revenues;
- marketing to patients and physicians;
- recruiting specialists to staff clinical centers of excellence;
- "medical arms race" competition with other facilities;

- double-digit inflation in healthcare expenditures;
- easy access to capital; and
- community pride and philanthropic capital.

Heading into the twenty-first century, U.S. healthcare is a completely different market. Managed care dominates provider payment, and capitation is spreading. Healthcare spending is barely rising at the rate of consumer inflation. Admissions and length of stay have slumped by a third and could fall another 15 to 20 percent in many local regions. Relentless pressures by payors to reduce demand have left many hospitals half empty. There is a surplus of specialists, while primary care gatekeepers are given incentives to further reduce costly hospitalization and ancillary procedures. High-tech towers built to house centers of excellence now impose a heavy burden of capital debt, while ambulatory care has doubled its space needs. New treatment paths now bypass hospitals, with extensive substitution of ambulatory care, outpatient testing, and in-home therapies.

Critics of America's largely nonprofit hospital industry, like Richard Scott, the former CEO of Columbia/HCA, argue that healthcare executives of tax-exempt facilities do not have to operate like a for-profit business. With more than 80 percent of all U.S. hospitals operating on a tax-exempt basis, they pay no taxes, a sizable subsidy in comparison with for-profit companies like Columbia/HCA. Without shareholders, nonprofit hospitals are not under the same quarter-to-quarter pressure for financial results. Nor do they need to throw off 10 to 20 percent of their profits to satisfy investors. Their nonprofit status provides a financial safety net that allows even marginal hospitals to survive. But in the long term, market forces will compel all hospitals to address the issue of excess capacity.

How about a federal bailout to buy back excess capacity? Public funding could provide a cushion for hospitals caught in a downspin of falling utilization and revenues. Just as Congress subsidizes farmers not to plant, Washington could give hospitals a subsidy to reduce capacity, a "Hill-Burton program in reverse." Federal aid could help hospitals plan an orderly transition. In New York, the city's aging hospitals facing massive Medicaid cuts have been thrown a federal lifeline. A federal grant of $1.15 billion in aid is being sent from Washington to assist New York hospitals to reinvent themselves for a managed care future.

The money may only postpone the problem, critics argue: "The question is, does this money just subsidize an inefficient system, or will it truly help provide a smooth transition for these hospitals to provide care for the poor?" (Hernandez 1997, A11). The New York situation is a symbol of how the old system must address the new market demands. And there is not enough federal money to bail out every empty hospital. Integrated health systems and provider-sponsored networks must deal with the issue of excess capacity, or it will badly hamper our ability to reengineer the U.S. health system for the millennium.

REFERENCES

Andrews, J. 1996. "Natchez Hospital Conversion Sparks Residential Revival." *Planning* 62 (11): 23.

Burda, D., and E. Weissenstein. 1996. "Hospital Closings Up for the First Time." *Modern Healthcare* 26 (48): 2, 3.

Cerne, F., and J. Montague. 1994. "Capacity Crisis." *Hospitals & Health Networks* 68 (18): 30–40.

Cochrane, J. D. 1996. "Massachusetts Prescription for Academic Medical Centers." *Integrated Healthcare Report* 4 (7): 14–15.

———. 1997. "Healthcare Megatrends." *Integrated Healthcare Review* 5 (1): 1–16.

Coile, R. C., Jr. 1997. "Workplace Revolution: Management, Morale and Motivation in the Era of 'Future Work.'" *Health Trends* 8 (10): 1–8.

Coile, R. C., Jr., and H. L. Menkin. 1997. "California Health Care 1997–2005: A Millennium View of the Future." Sacramento, CA: California Healthcare Association.

Havighurst, C. 1997. "Rational Capacity: Right-Sizing Delivery in the Health Systems Era." *Health Systems Review* 31 (1): 25–30.

Hinz, C. A. 1991. "Recovery Centers Rx for Excess Beds in Hospitals." *Health Care Strategic Management* 9 (1): 19–22.

Hospitals & Health Networks. 1994. "Confronting Overcapacity." 68 (19): 34.

Kennedy, M. 1996. "Converting Acute Care Units to Subacute." *Planning Cost-Effective Health Care Facilities Newsletter* 1 (6): 4.

Kennedy. S. P. 1994. "As Care Delivery Evolves, Facility Design Must Change." *Modern Healthcare* (March 21): 38.

Lagoe, B. H., R. J. Marshall, and O. Norman. 1995. "Excess Acute Care Capacity and Its Causes: The Experience of New York State." *Health Services Research* 30 (1): 115–31.

Japsen, B. 1997. "Will Veto Stand?" *Modern Healthcare* 27 (28): 24.

Nadal, B. A. 1996. "Recycling the Hospital." *Health System Review* (2): 35–39.

Rene, S. 1997. "Rural Routes." *Hospitals & Health Networks* 71 (15): 44–46.

Sachs Group. 1995. *Health Care 1999: A National Bellwether.* Evanston, IL: 1–17.

Sopariwala, P. R. 1996. "How Much Does Excess Inpatient Capacity Really Cost?" *Healthcare Financial Management* 51 (4): 54–58, 60, 62.

12

Anticipating the Millennium: Healthcare Environment Will Be Driven by Consumerism, Cyberhealth, and Co-Opetition

New financing and risk management schemes, restructured delivery systems, advanced therapeutics, sophisticated information technology and profound demographic shifts are among the forces that will lead to very different healthcare systems in the first part of the 21st century.
    —Clem Bezold, *Future Care* (1996a, 1)

Tomorrow's healthcare executives, trustees, and middle managers will face a very different set of market trends and management challenges in the twenty-first century. The best conventional wisdom on managing healthcare organizations is rapidly eroding, while new arrangements compete for dominance. The assumptions of the past are breaking down. Major questions are being asked about the best thinking that has driven healthcare strategy for a decade:

- Are HMOs a failed model whose cost-management strategies have been exhausted?
- Are vertical integration or economies of scale among large provider networks only elusive dreams that cannot be achieved practically?

- Will health plans and insurers really share risk and premium with providers in capitated arrangements, or will the payors continue to grasp for control even in the face of decline?
- Are employers sufficiently sophisticated to demand accountability for quality or to contract directly with providers?
- Are provider networks and health plans wasting millions of dollars on information systems that will be replaced by low-cost telecommunications on the Internet?
- Will Wall Street turn its back on healthcare companies and HMOs that cannot achieve double-digit profits?
- Can hospitals and physicians create sustainable business relationships, or are they doomed to squabble about ever-dwindling payments?
- Will hopes for health promotion and self-health be dashed against the reality of mass noncompliance and unhealthy lifestyles?
- Is a government takeover of the health system the next logical step, assuming that managed care and the enterprise model cannot hold down health spending?

THE MILLENNIUM ARRIVES

No need to wait for 2001. Tomorrow's trends are here, at least in the pilot stage. Innovative healthcare providers are retaking control of their health system. With the United States now entering managed care's fourth stage, where 25 to 40 percent of residents are enrolled in HMOs, very large provider organizations are going head-to-head with the biggest health plans in the market (Coile 1997). HMOs are in retreat, suffering declining public relations as well as profitability. Provider-sponsored organizations are tightening their grip on market share, building bigger networks that cover entire market regions. Dominant providers are stretching the definition of cooperation, such as Connecticut's Hartford Health Care Corporation, a statewide network model of community hospitals, physician organizations, and an academic medical center based on partnering, not merger (Droste 1997a).

"CO-OPETITION"

Today's market collisions may pave the way for business collaboration tomorrow, a revolutionary concept labeled co-opetition (Brandenburger and Nalebuff 1996). When competitors reach a standoff in market advantage, they can switch to cooperation to increase their mutual strengths and benefits. In Houston, Terry Ward (1997) of the Ward Group is working to develop a local cooperative joint venture involving some of the market's biggest competitors. By refocusing these traditional competitors into a shared business alliance, the Ward Group hopes to reduce their development and operating costs and share a better level of profitability than any could have achieved independently.

The benefits of collaboration and co-opetition include:

- shared capital investments;
- special expertise of the partners;
- broad regional distribution system;
- closer to the customer locations;
- market reputations;
- combined marketing and advertising efforts;
- reduction of costly competition;
- better focus on the customer and service;
- shared processes and systems;
- expanded databases; and
- leveraged market contacts and contracts.

HMO MARGINALIZATION

Perhaps it is time to think beyond managed care. The traditional HMO model of limited provider networks, gatekeepers, and low-rate reimbursement is no longer working. Provider claims, pharmacy costs, and HMO medical loss ratios are rising. HMOs would like to recover profitability quickly by increasing premiums, but employers are resisting big price hikes. One scenario for HMOs predicts that business could cut out HMOs and deal directly with providers. While a few employers are banding together in powerful coalitions to demand better deals from HMOs, others are making an end run around traditional HMO plans and their capitated gatekeeper models. They are working directly with providers in new ways to lower costs and improve care, creating an opening for provider-sponsored networks efficient and gutsy enough to step in (Meyer 1996, 34)

In the next five to ten years, the HMO industry will enter a rocky new phase, according to a recent front page story in the *New York Times* (Kilborn 1997, A1). The HMO industry is under continuous attack from consumer groups, plaintiffs' attorneys, and the media. Stock prices are slumping, with New York's Oxford Health Plan's stock plunging more than 60 percent in one day after reports of computer problems and underestimated medical expenses. The spate of criticism comes despite signing up more than 66 million Americans and holding national healthcare inflation under the consumer price index.

Rising medical loss ratios signal that HMOs are losing their grip on provider utilization and healthcare expenditures. The plans continue to hold a dominant position with millions of enrollees, but employers are openly questioning whether HMOs should be taking 15 to 20 percent of the premium off the top for administration, marketing, and medical management. A growing number of HMOs are abandoning efforts to compete with providers as integrated delivery networks.

Evidence from a number of markets around the nation suggests that the plans' initiatives in vertical integration are failing (Kilborn 1997, A1). In the West, California's Kaiser Permanente is contracting out hospital services to community facilities. In Kansas City, the local Blue Cross–Blue Shield organization is closing 11 of its 22 clinics and laying off half of its 65 primary care practitioners. Cross-town rival Humana is also dismissing physicians and will slash salaries of cardiovascular surgeons by 40 to 50 percent next year.

Employers are rethinking their reliance on HMOs and adopting more flexible, provider-friendly arrangements. Electronics giant Motorola launched a nongatekeeper preferred provider organization (PPO) last year with 100,000 participating physicians and 450 hospitals (Meyer 1996). In the first open enrollment, 59 percent of employees dumped their HMOs and switched to the company-backed PPO, which is managed by a third-party administrator (TPA), Private Healthcare Systems. Employer discontent is not the end of the line for HMOs, which can stay in the managed care game by broadening their product lines, such as providing TPA services. In Illinois, United Healthcare set up a self-insured point-of-service plan for the Whitman Corporation in Rolling Meadows. The plan provides an unusually high level of coverage—80 percent—of payment for services provided out-of-network.

MANAGED MEDICARE

The shift to managed Medicare is on! Some 12.6 percent of Medicare beneficiaries have already switched to managed care, doubling in the past five years, according to St. Paul, Minnesota–based InterStudy (Hamer 1997a). Enrollment in Medicare HMOs is climbing rapidly, up 27.8 percent in 1997, and could reach 11.6 million enrollees, about one-third of all seniors, by the end of 2001 (see Figure 12.1). Only four states still have no Medicare HMOs— Alaska, Missouri, Tennessee, and South Carolina. That should change swiftly with the changes that Congress made boosting Medicare HMO reimbursement for many areas.

Seniors accustomed to choice of providers and easy access will demand similar accommodation from Medicare HMOs. Planning consultant Dan Beckham, based in Whitefish Bay, Wisconsin, predicts: "The elderly will receive whatever they want. There is no way this group isn't going to vote for their interests when it comes to healthcare . . . . Baby Boomers also have the clout to ensure their parents are treated well by health plans" (Droste 1997b, 2).

Figure 12.1 Medicare HMO Forecast

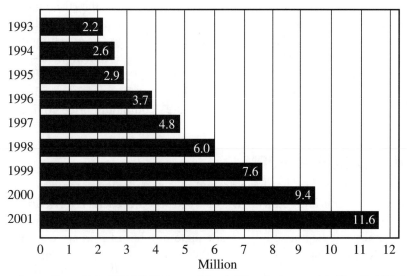

Source: Hamer, R. L. 1997. "HMO Facts and Trends." Presentation materials. Nov. 12, 1997, 6.

HEALTHCARE SPENDING

Despite rising HMO premiums, the likelihood of double-digit increases in health spending is low. The core rate of healthcare inflation will remain low to moderate, with increases in the range of 3 to 4 percent. The economics of competitive managed care will ensure that healthcare expenditures do not rise out of control in the near future. Washington, D.C.–based health economist Paul Ginsburg (1997) credits employer willingness to switch health plans to get a competitive price as a major factor insuring low inflation.

Inflation concerns arise from the current status of the HMO industry. Slumping profits in publicly traded HMOs are worrying Wall Street and HMO executives. The pall on managed care plans is affecting even successful HMOs like California's Wellpoint, despite 24 percent net income growth recently reported (Freudenheim 1997). Wellpoint's good news came a day after New York's Oxford Health Plan share price was hammered down 60 percent, after the company announced unexpected medical expenses and lower enrollment due to computer system problems. HMOs will attempt to boost prices 4.6 percent, according to the annual HMO pricing survey by Sherlock Company in Gwynedd, Pennsylvania (McGuire 1997). But the plans will run into price resistance from major employers, predict industry observers, with actual increases more likely to fall in the range of 2 to 3 percent.

HMOs are caught in the six-year insurance cycle of pricing, which averages three years of premium competition and lower prices, followed by three years of rising premiums in an effort to improve profits. The current pricing pattern appears to be part of a rising premium cycle. America's 651 HMOs are being squeezed by slowing rising medical expenses and employer resistance to price hikes. According to InterStudy, which tracks the HMO industry, the medical loss ratio for HMOs is now averaging 86 percent, up almost 3 percent in three years (Hamer 1997a, 49–50). HMO profits are slumping. The top 25 percent of HMOs—generally larger, more efficient plans—are still making money, in the range of 1 to 2 percent, but smaller, newer HMOs are experiencing losses ranging from 5 to 9 percent. The arrival of 53 new HMOs, many established by providers, ensures continuing price competition.

MANAGED CARE REFORM

A "patient bill of rights" has been drafted by a presidential commission on consumer protection and quality that is likely to become federal law (Rodrigue 1997, A1). The proposal would guarantee that health plans must pay for prudent emergency care, supply an adequate number of primary care and subspecialty physicians, and eliminate the "gag rules" by health plans that would prevent a doctor from discussing treatment options with patients. Managed care industry opposition to the new "ClintonCare" proposal is already forming, as the Health Insurance Association of America fired back with a threat to fight the proposal. Republican lawmakers like Richard Armey (R-TX) predicted that employers could drop their health coverage rather than comply and criticized the commission for driving up the costs of health insurance and increasing the number of medically uninsured.

The threat of Congressional action comes at a time when HMOs have already signed up 66 million Americans, predicted to grow to more than 100 million enrollees by January 2001 (see Figure 12.2), according to InterStudy (Hamer 1997a, 2). HMOs have become the health plan choice of the middle class and growing numbers of Medicare and Medicaid beneficiaries. The public may fear government regulation even more than its concerns about tight-walleted HMOs and insurers. The public overwhelmingly favors placing more controls over the health plans—84 percent to 16 percent—but they are divided on who should take control. A recent survey by the Kaiser Family Foundation found that only one in five Americans favors federal regulation, while another 20 percent wanted states to take a role, and another 33 percent want an independent oversight commission (Rodrigue 1997, A12). Support for regulation dropped to 52 percent when survey interviews told consumers that regulation could raise healthcare prices.

Patient concerns about privacy and security are likely to regulate the use of electronic medical records by managed care organizations. The American Psychiatric Association is concerned that "electronic peeping Toms" in man-

Figure 12.2 HMO Enrollment Forecast 1997–2001

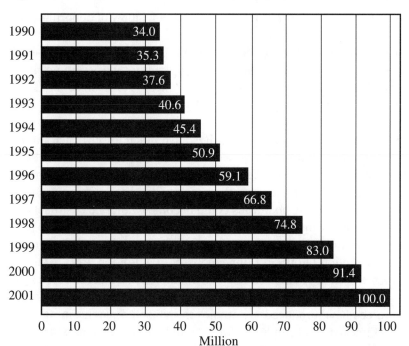

Source: Hamer, R. L. 1997. "HMO Facts and Trends." Presentation materials. St. Paul, MN: InterStudy Publications, Nov. 12.

aged care organizations and government will have access to patients' confidential records (Wechsler 1997, 16). The Clinton Administration has a medical records privacy proposal, and 12 health information security measures were introduced in Congress in 1997. Some federal legislation is likely in 1998, possibly teamed with antidiscrimination protections. A number of the proposals would require that managed care organizations keep a record of information disclosures that would be available to patients, which would be a costly nightmare for the plans to administer. The debate is complicated by the need for federal preemption of existing state laws, which could tie up medical confidentiality issues in the courts for years to come.

To help reduce the threat of regulation, the managed care industry is responding actively to consumer concerns. After years of frustration, healthcare patients are getting what they want in the managed care era: access to specialists, fewer gatekeeper requirements and HMO hassles, and new benefits like alternative medicine and podiatry. Stingy HMO attitudes and limited provider panels are being replaced by consumer-friendly service and open-access products.

PSOs/DIRECT CONTRACTING

Provider-sponsored organizations (PSOs) have a window of opportunity for direct contracting in Medicare, Medicaid, and self-insured ERISA health plans. Congressional action on PSOs opens the door for providers to participate directly in managed Medicare, signing up seniors and assuming risk at the local Medicare capitation rate beginning in 1999. Midsized and small markets may be the best targets for PSOs. Big HMOs already dominate large markets, increasing their market from 23.2 percent to 31.2 percent in just the last three years (Hamer 1997b, 1). HMOs have much lower penetration—20.8 percent—in medium-sized markets of about 500,000 population. PSOs in local markets would have the advantages of high visibility and market recognition, potentially reducing selling costs to recruit seniors.

Employer healthcare coalitions could become wholesale customers for direct contracting. In the future, business coalitions unhappy with HMO price increases could turn to provider-sponsored organizations, just as the Buyers' Health Care Action Group in Minneapolis–St. Paul did in 1997. Stanford economics professor Alain Enthoven has championed a market-based solution he calls "managed competition" (Enthoven 1997, 21). In California, market forces have produced six employer-sponsored purchasing groups, including three for small employers, one for midsized employers, and two for large employers (one public, one private). Enthoven serves on an advisory board to the California Public Employee Retirement System (CalPERS), the largest managed care buyer in California.

The trend to direct contracting is still more potential than actual, but signs of employer discontent are widespread. Employer groups in Wisconsin, Iowa, Illinois, and Texas are also rethinking their reliance on HMOs. Corporate health benefits managers are unhappy with HMO premium increases, which are averaging 5 percent for 1998 for large employers and 6 to 12 percent for smaller firms (Kilborn 1997). In Houston, the Health Care Purchasing Organization (HCPO) represents 40 large companies and 2,500 smaller ones. The employers' group contracts directly with a network of providers. HCPO president Ralph Smith complains: "The HMO middleman sets a fixed premium for employers, pushes the risk onto the providers, and then any gain goes to the HMO while providers and employers take all of the downside risk" (Meyer 1996, 36).

MARKET CONCENTRATION

Market concentration means "suppliers' clout" in dealing with health plans and economies of scale to slash overhead and operating costs. Hospitals and physicians are consolidating at an ever-increasing pace. Regional markets are consolidating to two to three competing provider-sponsored networks that may each control 25 to 35 percent of the market share—or more. Economics is the driving force leading to increasing concentration of power in hands of a few provider-sponsored organizations. In a national survey by TriBrook/AM&G in Westmont, Illinois, the top five reasons for consolidation were reducing operating expenses, attracting more managed care contracts, improving community health, reducing capital expenditures, and responding to employer/business coalition pressures (Japsen 1997).

Industry consolidation is steamrolling American hospitals, physicians, and health plans. Hospital mergers went up by 44 percent from 1994 to 1995 (Monroe 1996). In trend-setting southern California, a record 29 hospitals completed mergers, acquisitions, or formal affiliation in 1996, a pace that was twice the volume of consolidations in 1995. One survey indicated that another 28 hospitals planned to affiliate or merge in 1997 (Wall 1997, 34–35). More than half of these transactions involve for-profit hospitals that became part of larger chains. Five hospitals converted from tax-exempt to for-profit status, and two former for-profit facilities switched back to nonprofit status.

Vertical integration is still a prominent strategy driving merger mania. A recent industry survey showed that hospitals, physicians, and managed care organizations (MCOs) are planning to acquire each other in record numbers (see Figure 12.3). Nearly one-third of the surveyed hospitals had been part of a consolidation in the past five years, while one-third of the health plans had acquired another HMO in the same period (Greene 1997b). Half of the surveyed medical groups had been involved in a transaction with a for-profit physician company or nonprofit hospital or health system. Hospitals were still interested in buying medical group practices, despite reports that 80 percent of hospitals were losing money on the physician deals.

MEGA-MEDICAL GROUPS

Very large physician groups are rising to take charge of their markets. A new generation of mega-medical physician organizations are larger, better capitalized and managed, and broadly distributed to provide regional coverage. Many more physician organizations are now taking capitation. Large market-savvy medical groups have the capabilities that managed care organizations are seeking, including:

- geographic distribution with physicians within 10 to 15 minutes of all enrollees;
- ability to manage risk for professional services and, with some plans, global risk for inpatient and outpatient services;
- effective governance and management systems;

Figure 12.3 Who Plans to Do What with Whom? Future Healthcare Partnership Strategies

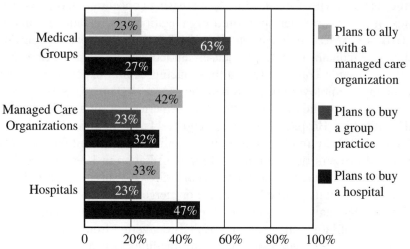

Source: Adapted from Jay Greene, "1997 Leadership Survey." Cited in *Medical Benefits*, (September 15), 8.

- financial strength to accept capitation and various payment options;
- a primary care orientation; and
- ability to document quality indicators including patient satisfaction and clinical outcomes. (Holm and Zuza 1997).

Physician groups are merging to create market-dominant organizations that have real clout. In the past three years, there was a 58 percent rise in physician group linkages (Monroe 1997). Bigger medical groups have more leverage in managed care contracting, but there are other reasons for physician consolidation. Sharing the cost of upgrading information systems is a major factor, cited by 61 percent of the groups. Only 4 percent of physicians are submitting claims electronically, mostly larger groups (Slepin 1996). Another benefit the merged physician groups are finding is the ability to compare practice patterns, lowering costs and improving productivity.

A second generation of independent practice associations (IPAs) is demonstrating that the network model of organization can successfully assume and manage capitation for large enrolled populations (Lowes 1997). In San Francisco, an IPA originally started by the California Pacific Medical Center was restructured as a physician-owned entity, the Brown & Toland Medical Group. The IPA's 1,250 physicians now have 172,000 covered lives under capitation. Brown & Toland recently became the first IPA in California to obtain a "limited Knox-Keene" state license to accept global capitation for both inpatient and outpatient services.

But it is not just California. In Milwaukee, the Wisconsin Independent Physicians Group has organized 1,050 physicians to service 45,000 Medicaid patients under a global risk contract. The IPA is capitated, but physicians are paid on a fee-for-service basis. The group is using a population health approach to reduce risks and utilization. To control costs, the doctors own a freestanding imaging center and channel all testing through a commercial lab. The IPA describes its fee schedule as "generous" to physicians and relies on education, rather than discipline, to manage costs. The IPA uses peer pressure to control utilization. Physician performance data systems regularly profile every doctor's costs, with the name of the physicians left on the reports so that colleagues can compare performance.

FOR-PROFIT BACKLASH

Wall Street may not be welcome on Main Street, at least not to operate hospitals and health plans. A growing backlash of media criticism, public concern, and state regulation is slowing the growth of for-profit healthcare companies. Public confidence in for-profit HMOs and healthcare companies is dropping. A random poll of 1,000 Americans by the Kaiser Family Foundation showed that the percentage who thought that for-profit organizations provided better care fell from 55 percent to 42 percent in 1997 (Walker 1997, 8).

Columbia/HCA's troubles with the FBI and Justice Department have been widely chronicled, including a fresh update of a best-selling exposé by Sandy Lutz and Preston Gee. Under a cloud of massive Medicare fraud investigation and falling profits, the dismemberment of Columbia and the sale of all but its core hospitals is now under way, with two or more new companies likely to result (Sharpe 1997). Columbia has announced plans to spin off some 108 hospitals that do not fit Columbia's long-term strategy (Woodyard and Findlay 1997, B1). Other Columbia facilities outside of markets in which Columbia now has a critical mass could also be sold.

Troubles for the for-profit healthcare industry are far from over. Columbia/HCA suffered another blow when several states joined a shareholders' lawsuit against the company. California, New York, Louisiana, and several municipalities have entered the fray, charging that Columbia management had allowed Medicare fraud to "flourish" (White and Lagnado 1997, B5). (CalPERS) suffered a $50 million loss because Columbia's shares sank in the wake of Medicare fraud investigations.

There are echoes of the "Wal-Mart wars" in rising public antipathy toward for-profit healthcare companies. Even well-managed companies like Tenet, HealthSouth, and PhyCor may find growing opposition to acquisitions and new development. State attorneys general have discovered the publicity value of opposing for-profit takeovers of nonprofit providers. Several states, including California, Rhode Island, and Nebraska, have recently passed legislation making for-profit conversions subject to state review. Despite the negative publicity and regulatory hurdles, CEOs of nonprofit hospitals expect that for-profit hospital chains will expand their market share to 20 percent by 2000, further rising to 29 percent within ten years, according to a national survey (Greene 1997).

CYBERHEALTH

Information technology is the fastest-growing American industry. According to a national study entitled *Cybernation* by the American Electronics Association and the NASDAQ stock market, computing and telecommunications has grown 57 percent since 1990 (Lohr 1997, C12). The high-tech sector generates 6.4 percent of America's gross domestic product (GDP) and employs 4.2 million workers. Cyberhealth information systems today include electronic medical records, enterprisewide information linkages, Internet and intranet connections, data warehouses, distributed PC networks, remote-site telecommunications, and even in-home patient monitoring systems.

Online consumers are leading a revolution in patient care. Informed consumers tap the World Wide Web to gain sophisticated information about diseases and treatments, including the latest research protocols and findings. The availability of information to the average consumer may radically reshape the patient-physician relationship. Tom Ferguson, M.D., the editor of the *Newsletter of Consumer Health Informatics and Online Health*, predicts that some patients will find more help in cyberspace than in their own physicians' offices (1997, 29). Patients are getting more than the latest medical research. Consumers with health problems are tapping into the experiences of fellow patients, who evaluate treatments and providers with an open candor. Support groups provide advice, counseling, and practical information for patients trying to manage their disease. Already widespread, these online health groups may have millions of members on a global basis in the millennium.

Healthcare information systems are essential for managing costs through disease management programs. In Falls Church, Virginia, the Innova Health System is creating a data repository to track more than 500,000 inpatient and outpatient visits per year (Hornung 1997). The end products will include clinical analysis, quality assurance, and outcomes assessment. Financial connectivity is another important area for automation. Providers are learning to make effective use of the information systems investments in areas such as claims processing and electronic data interchange. Submitting claims electronically can save $2 to $4 per claim, with some integrated systems experiencing savings of 75 to 90 percent in business office's claims costs that average $7.50 per bill (Slepin 1996, 48).

Information systems are expensive, and many buyers are still skeptical of the return-on-investment. The payoff comes from doing things differently, not just faster. Computerized analysis of cost variation can help repay information system investments. In South Bend, Indiana, the Holy Cross Health System saved $4.5 million by reducing variation in the pattern of care for 36 case groups (Appleby 1997). Holy Cross information specialists also predicted the effect of managed care for the system's 11 facilities, finding that it had to cut $80 million out of operating expenses or suffer major losses. The wake-up call was painful but timely.

Although most healthcare providers still only dream of a "paperless" information system, electronic medical records are making headway. A national survey of nearly 500 physician group practices found that 22 percent of the groups had some or all of their records computerized (Montague and Pitman 1996). Managed care transactions such as claims processing, eligibility verification, access to health plan enrollment lists, and submission of monthly encounter lists are a fast-growing target for automation. For capitated physicians, automating to reduce the cost of these "back-room" functions means more net income for the doctors.

The application of cybernetics to patient care is widening rapidly—even to promote patient satisfaction. Computer-based instructions are targeting physician-patient communications, creating messages in electronic medical records that remind physicians to respond to patient concerns. In Indianapolis, doctors at the William N. Wishard Memorial Hospital are responding to cues that are embedded in the hospital's intranet-enabled clinical information network. The messages are based on patient satisfaction surveys that identified communications concerns on a disease-specific basis. For example, doctors treating colonoscopy patients are reminded: "Before you order this colonoscopy, consider that patients often report they were not warned a test might cause pain or discomfort" (*Health Data Network News* 1997, 5).

RETAIL MARKETING

Consumers will have more choices in healthcare. Retail marketing strategies will target them like guided missiles. Media campaigns by hospitals and health plans are revving up market warfare for consumer preferences. In New York, Aetna US Healthcare purchased a full-page ad in the *New York Times*, with a photo of a large apple dominating a table of oranges (Aetna 1997). Aetna boasted that it was the first HMO in New York City to win full accreditation from the National Committee for Quality Assurance as well as the Sachs "seal of excellence" based on consumer satisfaction, awarded by the Sachs Group of Evanston, Illinois, based on a national comparison of consumer ratings.

Retail marketing gives providers an opportunity to "grow the business" with creative approaches to revenue growth and emerging customer trends. Marketing consultant Ellen Goldman of GrowthPartners in Reston, Virginia, and Karen Corrigan (1997) of Sentara Health System in Norfolk, Virginia, recommend three retail marketing strategies:

- *Enhance the customer's experience* by focusing on the "atmospherics" of the point of service—creating an environment where people want to purchase services—including decor, displays, signage, selling techniques, and customer service. Waiting areas that look like hotel lobbies, not airport waiting areas, are an illustration of how healthcare providers can enhance atmospherics. Winners of *Modern Healthcare*'s 1997 Design Awards for health facilities were praised for their "patient-driven architecture" that featured residential characteristics and a family orientation (Pinto 1997, 47).

- *Meeting the customer's related needs* is the opportunity to present and sell related products or services. Stimulating additional spending responds to customers' needs for convenience. Situating a home health agency outlet adjacent to heavy hospital traffic by patients and visitors may stimulate additional business.

- *Product and market segmentation* are opportunities to identify unmet needs of specific age, sex, ethnic, income, or other demographically defined subgroups in the market. Marketers look for product or service variations that are tailored to a specific set of customers, such as small businesses. Gaps are unrecognized segments or products. In healthcare services, for example, adolescent medicine is aimed at the youth market aged 14 to 19 that may be too old for pediatrics but may not want to share their parents' family practitioners.

COMPLEMENTARY MEDICINE

No longer categorized as alternative medicine, a marketing blitz by health plans and hospitals intends to capture consumers who have been spending $10 billion a year of out-of-pocket cash for health promotion and wellness. To help boost medical and consumer acceptance, many once-alternative or unconventional therapies are being relabeled as complementary medicine. Acupuncture, biofeedback, chiropractic, herbal remedies and homeopathy, nutrition, osteopathy, and yoga have arrived to join mainstream medical care. HMOs like New York's Oxford used a two-page advertisement in the *New York Times* to announce "A different philosophy, a different attitude .... Did we say it was different?" Oxford was trumpeting a newly credentialed network of alternative medical providers. In Dallas, Texas, the "new medicine" featured on the cover of *D Magazine* was the subject of a widely attended medical conference sponsored by the University of Texas' Southwest Medical School, which drew 1,200 participants (Peterson 1997).

The payoff from complementary medicine may be more than creating a marketing advantage. HMOs experimenting with alternative therapies are finding real cost benefit. According to Dr. Herbert Benson, head of Boston's Mind/Body Medical Institute, HMOs can experience a 50 percent reduction in stress-related injuries and 30 percent fewer visits for chronic back pain by training patients in self-relaxation and stress management (Montague 1996, 26).

The public's interest in health and wellness may have profit potential. Former Columbia/HCA executive Richard Scott is reentering the health industry from an unexpected direction—consumer health information. Scott and former second-in-command David Vandewater have purchased a majority stake in America's Health Network, a Florida-based cable channel that features such programs as "Ask the Doctor" (Lagnado 1997). The network currently reaches about 6.5 million households and was the target of a Columbia acquisition offer until Richard Scott's departure as head of Columbia.

LOOKING FORWARD: ALTERNATIVE SCENARIOS FOR THE MILLENNIUM

There is, of course, more than one future. Tomorrow is alive with potential and possibilities. Futurists use scenarios to create images of the future. They are learning tools for strategic decision making. Scenarios can stretch the imagination and also set some boundaries for future actions. Some future scenarios are more plausible and are extensions of the status quo. Other scenarios may be more philosophical or may present a point of view. Scenarios can be used for policymaking to generate consumer interest in health issues or to anticipate scientific breakthroughs.

Futurist Clem Bezold, Ph.D., director of the Institute for Alternative Futures in Alexandria, Virginia, has been developing healthcare industry scenarios for more than a decade. Some of the nation's leading futurists, including Roy Amara, Clem Bezold, Russell Coile, Jr., Jeff Goldsmith, and Leland Kaiser, participated in formulating scenarios for a national study, *Bridging the Leadership Gap*, sponsored by The Healthcare Forum, based in San Francisco, California (Healthcare Forum 1992). Bezold has distilled many future assumptions into four compelling alternative scenarios for healthcare in 2010 (Bezold 1996b).

Scenario #1—"Business as Usual"

In this scenario, national health reform is sent back to the states, resulting in great diversity of approaches to the medically uninsured. Expensive technology and new therapeutics, including function-enhancing bionics, boost health spending. Technology advances are widespread, including the information revolution, which provides new tools for personal health management. Healthcare's share of the GDP increases to 17 percent by 2005. To help offset rising costs to care for an aging population, healthcare providers shift to forecasting and managing illness for enrolled patients. Problems of poverty persist, despite a healthy economy, and the number of uninsured rises to 50 million. Some states adopt Oregon's Medicaid program with rationing of some services. Healthcare delivery becomes more efficient and effective. Multispecialty physician groups direct most care, aided by other healthcare providers and supported by expert systems. Demand for hospital beds shrinks, and the number of inpatient beds falls to 450,000 in 2001 and 300,000 by 2010. Economists and ethicists in 2010 argue that the percent of GDP devoted to healthcare could be reduced further if the nation did not spend so much on life-extension and performance enhancement, especially among the elderly.

Scenario #2—Hard Times/Government Leadership

A tightening economy sparks a political revolt to bring health spending under control, leading to a Canadian-like healthcare system. Economic recession combined with public concerns about for-profit companies in healthcare triggers legislation to curb America's enterprise model of health financing and delivery. Many states follow Oregon in consciously setting priorities. Heroic measures for terminal patients decline, and more frugal approaches to delivery of medical care are adopted. Healthcare's percentage of the GDP declines to 11 percent. Thirty percent of Americans spend their own money to "buy up" to affluent, higher-tech care, and two different health systems emerge. Spending on health technology slows, as governmental controls limit reimbursement for expensive new pharmaceuticals and high-tech treatments. Some people are better off under the new system. The uninsured are now guaranteed government-sponsored coverage. By 2010, policymakers are coming under increasing pressure to ration healthcare or face rising health costs driven by the age wave as baby boomers reach age 65.

Scenario #3—Buyer's Market

In this scenario, consumers take direct control of their own health spending. A coalition of consumer groups, employers, and government policymakers take radical action to take health spending away from intermediaries and third parties. This new consumer-driven market competition works to lower prices and increase consumer choices. Providers now compete on quality as well as cost. All consumers are required to carry some form of health insurance or managed care plan. Government-funded universal coverage for the uninsured allows all consumers to participate in the healthcare market. With consumers spending their own money on healthcare, many patients turn to nonphysician providers and alternative medicine services, which are less expensive than conventional medical care. Online health information systems allow consumers to evaluate medical providers, quality performance, and treatment outcomes. Incentives for individuals and employers reinforce prudent purchasing of health services. Not all consumers are comfortable with such a direct competitive environment for health, but it does hold down costs. Price competition among surplus providers drives health spending down to 12 percent of the GDP by 2010.

Scenario #4—Health Gains and Healing

This scenario for American healthcare is the result of a powerful shared vision about reinventing the healthcare system to emphasize health promotion and health improvement. Healing the mind, body, and spirit becomes the important goal of community-based health systems. New players like Microsoft, Disney, and AT&T help create a smarter market for healthcare in which millions of online-informed consumers evaluate the outcomes and quality of various medical approaches. Healthcare's emphasis on community health issues places greater priority on addressing underlying health threats such as unemployment and environmental pollution. Health organizations become involved in broader missions such as community development. Better nutrition, community health initiatives, and health-promoting behaviors lead to longer, healthier lives and lower health costs. Health spending shrinks to 10 percent of the GDP by 2010.

The most likely scenario for American healthcare in the millennium is probably some blend of features of all four scenarios that Clem Bezold and the other futurists have projected. Economics will be an important factor in all potential futures for healthcare, but so will technology, consumerism, and politics. Healthcare providers will shape their own futures by aligning their vision, mission, and business goals to meet evolving market conditions. "Wild card" factors such as the genetics revolution will play a major role in ways that can only be speculated today. New therapies, elimination of birth defects, and entirely new treatments are possible.

Millennium managers will succeed in the twenty-first century healthcare environment if they build learning organizations and flexible teams of managers, professionals—and patients—who share a goal of optimizing every patient's well-being and the community's health. The future is not a puzzle to be solved. It is a doorway to new possibilities for those with the leadership and courage to take new directions and see old problems in a fresh way. Managing the "age wave" of the baby boom is the obvious challenge of the millennium. Finding innovative ways to provide healthcare and promote health with limited resources is the challenge of millennium management.

REFERENCES

Aetna US Healthcare. 1997. "The More You Compare Health Care Companies, the More You Realize There Is No Comparison." *New York Times* (November 12).

Appleby, C. 1997. "Payoff @ InfoTech.Now." *Hospitals & Health Networks* 71 (19): 59–60.

Bezold, C. 1996a. "Future Care: Overview." In *Future Care: Responding to the Demand for Change,* edited by C. Bezold and E. Mayer, 1–8. New York: Faulkner & Gray.

———. 1996b. "Four Futures." In *Future Care: Responding to the Demand for Change,* edited by C. Bezold and E. Mayer, 63–80. New York: Faulkner & Gray.

Brandenburger, A. M., and B. J. Nalebuff. 1996. *Co-Opetition.* New York: Doubleday.

Coile, R.C., Jr. 1997. *The Five Stages of Managed Care.* Chicago: Health Administration Press.

Droste, T. M. 1997a. "One System Relies on Partnering as a Strategy to Build a Statewide Network." *Medical Network Strategy Report* 6 (10): 1–3.

———. 1997b. "Health System Marketers Must Learn From Past Mistakes So History Won't Repeat Itself." *Medical Network Strategy Report* (September):1–4.

Enthoven, A. 1997. "There's Gold in Them Thar' Coalitions." *Managed Healthcare* 10 (7): 21–24.

Ferguson, T. 1997. "Health Care in Cyberspace: Patients Lead a Revolution." *The Futurist* 31 (6): 29–33.

Freudenheim, M. 1997. "Wellpoint Shares Sink Despite Profit Gain." *New York Times* (October 31).

Ginsburg, P. B., and J. D. Pickreign. 1997. "Tracking Health Care Costs: An Update." *Medical Benefits* 14 (17): 7.

Goldman, E. F., and K. V. Corrigan. 1997. "'Thinking Retail' in Healthcare: New Approaches for Business Growth." *The Healthcare Strategist* 1 (1): 1–9.

Greene, J. 1997. "1997 Leadership Survey." *Medical Benefits* 14 (17): 8.

Hamer, R. L. 1997a. "HMO Facts and Trends." Presentation materials. St. Paul, MN: InterStudy Publications. November 12.

———. 1997b. "Small Markets Present Opportunities for Provider-Sponsored Networks." Cited in *Healthcare Leadership Review* 16 (9): 9.

Healthcare Forum. 1992. *Bridging the Leadership Gap.* San Francisco, 1–16.

Holm, C. E., and D. J. Zuza. 1997. "Positioning Primary Care Networks: Understand What Managed Care Organizations Really Want." *Health Care Services Strategic Management* 15 (8): 1, 22–23.

Hornung, K. 1997. "Tap into Patient Data to Bolster Your Disease Management Program." *Healthcare Demand & Disease Management* 3 (7): 97–101.

"Hospital to Test Use of Computer-Based Reminders." *Health Data Network News* 6 (10): 5, 7.

Japsen, B. 1997. "Survey: Money, Not Mission, Driving Mergers." *Modern Healthcare* 27 (41): 14.

Kilborn, P. T. 1997. "Health Care Plans Are Seen Entering Rocky New Phase." *New York Times* (November 22).

Lagnado, L. 1997. "Ousted CEO of Columbia Leads Cable Buy." *Wall Street Journal* (November 12).

Lohr, S. 1997. "Information Technology Field Is Rated Largest U.S. Industry." *New York Times* (November 18).

Lowes, R. L. 1997. "The Second-Generation IPA: Will It Save Independent Practice?" *Medical Economics* 74 (16): 182–91.

McGuire, J. 1997. "HMOs Expect Significant Premium Hikes for 1998." *Managed Care Outlook* 10 (20): 7.

Meyer, H. "Beyond HMOs: The Tide of the Times." *Hospitals & Health Networks* 70 (8): 34–40.

Monroe, S. 1996. *Health Care Merger and Acquisition Report.* New Canaan, CT: Irving Lewis Associates. Cited in "Mergers: The Center of the Storm." *Hospitals & Health Networks* 70 (8): 10.

Montague, J. 1996. "Mind Over Maladies." *Hospitals & Health Networks* 70 (8): 26–27.

Montague, J., and H. Pitman. 1996. "Currents: Information Systems." *Hospitals & Health Networks* 70 (8): 10–11.

Peterson, S. 1997. "Can the New Medicine Heal You?" *D Magazine* (November): 80–91.

Pinto, C. 1997. "1997 Design Awards." *Modern Healthcare* 27 (41): 47–62.

Rodrigue, G. 1997. "Panel Calls for HMO Changes." *Dallas Morning News* (November 20).

Sharpe, A. 1997. "Columbia/HCA Weighs Plan to Spin Off One-Third of Company's 340 Hospitals." *Wall Street Journal* (November 11).

Slepin, R. E. 1996. "EDI Translates into Big Savings." *California HFMA Journal* 9 (4): 48–49.

Walker, T. 1997. "Kaiser Poll Pans Forprofit Plans." *Managed Care* 10 (7): 8.

Wall, P. 1997. "Consolidations Accelerate, Nearly Double in 1996." *California HFMA Journal* 10 (1): 34–36.

Ward, T. 1997. "Co-Opetition: An Innovative Strategy Which Combines Cooperation and Competition." Houston, TX: The Ward Group.

Wechsler, J. 1997. "Proposal Struggles with Privacy and Practicality." *Managed Healthcare* 7 (10): 15–16.

White, J. B., and L. Lagnado. 1997. "Columbia/HCA Dealt Sharp Blow by CalPERS Move." *Wall Street Journal* (October 21).

Woodyard, C., and S. Findlay. 1997. "Columbia to Dump a Third of Hospitals." *USA Today* (November 18).

INDEX

Acacia Venture Partners, 99
Academic medical center (AMC)
   closure recommendations, 169
   cost competitiveness, 55, 154
   reengineered capacity, 173
Access, 103–4
Access Health, 6
Access managers, 74, 83
Ackoff, Russell, 157
Activities of daily living (ADL), 106
Adhocracy, 81
Advanced practice nurse, 68, 74–75, 81
Adventist Health System/Sunbelt Healthcare Corporation, 100, 102
Advisory Group, 131
AES, 150
Aetna US Healthcare, 132, 191–92
Ageless Body, Timeless Mind, 146
AHA. *See* American Hospital Association
Aird, John, 123
Alignment, 11
Allen, Robert, 133
Allina Health System, 100
Alternative medicine, 5, 192–93
Alternative settings, 165
Amara, Roy, 193
Ambulatory care centers, 112, 113, 117, 118
Ambulatory surgical care center, 118, 170–71
AMC. *See* Academic medical center

American College of Healthcare Executives, 96
American Electronics Association, 190
American Group Practice Association, 87
American Hospital Association (AHA)
   financial performance data, 55
   hospital closures, 175
   officials top concerns, 108
   rural hospital survey, 171
   uncompensated care, 153
American Institute of Architecture, 117
American Management Association, 82, 83
American Medical Association (AMA), 57, 87
American Medical Information Society, 8
American Psychiatric Association, 184–85
America's Health Network, 193
AmHS Institute, 161
Andersen Consulting, 54
Annison, Michael, x, 96, 157
Anshen + Allen, 117, 124
APM, 150
Apple, 8
Apple University, 98
Armey, Richard, 184
Ask-a-Nurse call center, 6
Association of Management Consulting Firms, 127
At-risk pay, 28

AT&T, 8, 82, 133, 195
Attitude, 91

Baby Doe, 14
Bank One, 18
Baptista, Joao, 82
Barner, Robert, 27
Baystate Medical Center, 154
Beckham, J. Daniel, 141
  corporate soul hazards, 154–55
  healthcare priorities, 151
  senior market, 182
Beckham Company, 155
Behavior, 23
Benchmarks, 34, 42, 46
Ben & Jerry's Homemade Ice Cream, 13,
  144–45, 157
Bennis, Warren
  adhocracy, 81
  leadership, 138, 148
  organizational change, 1
Benson, Herbert, 193
Berra, Yogi, 139
Bexar County Medical Society, 142
Beyond Reengineering, 38
Bezold, Clem
  future scenarios, 179, 193–96
  health futures, 152
  leadership gap, *x*
BHAG (big, hairy, audacious goal), 41,
  127
BHCAG. *See* Buyers' Health Care
  Action Group
Billingsley, Anne, 25
Birthing centers, 118
Blue Cross/Blue Shield, 102, 104, 133,
  182
Board review, 137
Bobrow/Thomas and Associates, 115
Boland, Peter, 56
Bolman, Lee, 143
Booz Allen, 44, 150
Bridges, William, 12
Bridging the Leadership Gap, 193

Broadbanding, 28
Brookwood Medical Center, 36, 38
Brown & Toland Medical Group, 188
Bruckner, Bob, 123
Buerhaus, Peter, 67, 75
Burfitt, Gregory, 38
Business plan, 112, 136
Business process reengineering, 34, 40
Business Week, 127
Buyers' Health Care Action Group
  (BHCAG), 102, 103, 186

California Healthcare Association,
  114–15, 168
California Nurses Association, 108
California Pacific Medical Center, 123,
  188
California Public Employees Retirement
  System (CalPERS), 60, 186, 189
Cambridge Hospital, 142
Capitation, *xii*
  assumptions, 131
  hospital demand, 165
  integration issues, 61
  rural market, 151–52
Care management programs, 8, 9
Care pair, 98
Care partners, 98
Carle Clinic, 57
Carlson, Leanne Kaiser, 122–23, 151
Carolinas HealthCare System, 60
Case, John, 149–50
Case management, 75, 165
Catholic Health Association
  achievement citation, 153–54
  cost competitiveness, 56
  social accountability budget, 152
Catholic Health Corporation, 56
Catholic Health Initiatives (CHI), *xii*,
  56, 61
Cedars-Sinai, 56–57
Centennial Medical Center, 113
Centers of excellence, 112
Challenger, Gray & Christmas, 34, 108

Change, 6–7
Chaos, 6, 20, 129
Chapman, Erie, 141–42
Chappell, Tom, 142, 143
Chenowith, Jean, 156
Chi Systems, Inc., 33, 45, 150, 168–69
CHI. *See* Catholic Health Initiatives
CHIN. *See* Community health
   information network
Chopra, Deepak, 146–47
Chronic care, 75, 165
Claims processing, 190–91
Clark, Jim, 99
Clinical Cost-Reduction System, 57
Clinical costs, 41
Clinical Pathway Constructor, 57
Clinical pathways, 6
   development, 41
   expansion, 9
   video model, 149
ClintonCare proposal, 184
Coastal Physician Group, 60
Coca-Cola, 150
Coddington, Dean, 49
Cohen, Ben, 13
Collaboration, 86, 180–81
Collins, James, 127
Colorado Avalanche, 133
Columbia/HCA, 176
   acquisitions, 167, 168
   acquisition targets, 193
   cost management model, 29
   future-oriented facilities, 113
   hospital closures, 59
   megastrategy, 133
   profitability goals, 156
   tax-exempt challenge, 153
   troubles, 189
Columbus Children's Hospital, 113
Commanche County Regional Hospital,
   152
Communication, 149–51
Community Accountability in
   Integrated Delivery, 152
Community-based health systems, 195

Community health
   education facilities, 119
   improvement programs, 14, 52
   initiatives, 142, 153–54
   promotion, *xi*
Community healthcare organization, 53
Community health information network
   (CHIN), 59, 69
Compensation
   affiliate, 89
   associate, 88–89
   competency-based, 28
   executive, 80, 88
   performance-based, 10, 27–29, 107
Compensation, Challenges and
   Changes, 28
Competing for the Future, 127, 137
Competition
   challenges, 2–3, 7, 12
   competitor assessment, 135
   consumer-focused, 103–7, 121–22
   economic, 72
   new rules, 3–11
   price-led, 98
Competitive advantage, 3, 5, 128
Complementary medicine, 192–93
Computer networks, 25
Confidentiality, 150–51
Consolidation, 51, 187
Consumer
   choice, 95–96, 98, 103
   demands, 134–35
   direct access, 103–4
   dissatisfaction, 96
   expectations, 7, 8, 132
   experience enhancement, 192
   focus, 61, 84
   high-income, 130
   informed, 190
   importance, 39
   needs, 192
   satisfaction, 92
   self-care, 104–5
   senior market, 106–7, 130
   sociopolitical groups, 97

telecommunications, 149
time constraints, 131
trends, 5, 96–97, 103–7
types, 131
Continental, 4
Contingency planning, 136
Continuous quality improvement, 34, 86
Continuum of care, 55
Control, 20
Cook, Susan, 95, 98
Cooper, Richard, 86
Co-opetition, *xii*, 180–81
Corporate citizen, 14, 152–54
Corporate culture
    change, 22–23, 90–91
    customer-driven, 17–18
    reengineering, 39–40
    shared vision, 93
Corporate soul, 29, 141–43
    commitment, 155–56
    definition, 142
    development, 142–44
    hazards, 154–55
    pathways, 147–54
    profit motives, 156–57
Corporate vacuum, 12
Corrigan, Karen, 192
Cost, 3
Cost competitiveness, 55–56
Cost management, 74–75
Costello, Kit, 108
Cousins, Norman, 122
Covey, Stephen R., 30, 138, 143
Critical care facilities, 112
Crooks, Heidi, 108
Crozer-Chester Medical Center, 113
CUH2A, Inc., 116
Curley, Jack, 152
Curry, Randy, 152
Curtin, Leah, 72
Customer. *See* Consumer
Customer service, 45, 106
Cyberhealth, 190–91
Cybernation, 190

Daly, Mike, 154
Davis, Stan, 21
Deal, Terence, 143
Decision float, 26
Deinstitutionalization, 97
Demand projections, 135
Detachment, 146
Dignity, 92
Direct contracting, 55, 60, 102–3, 186
Disease management programs, 56–57
Disney (Walt), 120, 195
Distance medicine, 123
Distribution channels, 7
Diversity, 9–10, 27
D Magazine, 193
Dow, Roger, 95, 98
Downsizing, 35–36, 40
    concerns, 62, 108
    current trends, 82
    definition, 34
    morale, 79–80
    targets, 169–71
    trend, 8, 34
Duke University Medical Center, 100

East Pasco Health Center, 102
Eckerd Drug, 106
Ecology of Commerce, The, 13
Economic patterns, *xii*
Eco-social responsibility, 13
Efficiency, 3
Elaboration, 6, 19
Electronic monitoring, 85
Emergency services, 170
Employee. *See* Workforce
Employer healthcare coalitions, 186
Employer-sponsored purchasing
    groups, 186
Employment, changes, 12
Employment Policy Foundation, 28
Empowerment, 10
End of Work, The, 80
Entertainment, 130

Enthoven, Alain, 186
Environmental issues, 12–14
Ernst & Young, 149
Esalen Institute, 20
Ethical issues, 14, 67
Excess capacity, 161–62
  alternatives, 171–75
  costs, 166
  forecasts, 162–65
  integrated delivery systems, 166–68
  integration issues, 61
  managed care, 165, 166
  realignment, 59–60
  utilization projections, 168–69
Executive compensation, 80, 88
Extension, 6, 19

Facilities. *See also* Hospital
  building plans, 115–16
  business plan, 112
  capital expenditures, 166
  construction, 113–16
  consumer-driven competition,
    121–22
  cost-benefits, 115
  design, 111–12, 119–21
  environment, 192
  flexibility, 116–17
  future types, 118–19
  nonacute recovery, 174
  off-campus, 112
  operating costs, 115–16
  patient-oriented, 123–25
  planning issues, 116–17
  program managers, 112
  redesign, 173
  sick building phenomenon, 122
Family structure, 96
Farson, Richard, 20, 21
Fee-for-service arrangements, 55
Feng shui, 121
Ferguson, Marilyn, 145
Ferguson, Tom, 190
FHP, 26, 114

Fifth Discipline, The, 130
Financial data, 149–51
Financial float, 26
Fisher, Donald W., 87
Fixed-base salary, 28
Ford, Henry, 35
For-profit healthcare companies,
  189–90
Foundation Health, 50
Foundation/HSI, 49
Fourth Wave, 13
FPA, 58
Fragmentation, 53
Friedman, Emily
  corporate soul, 147, 156
  ethical issues, 14
  freedom of choice, 148
Fuller, Mark, 136
Future Care, 179
Future Perfect, 21
FutureScan, 96

Gag analysis, 136
Gag rules, 184
Gainsharing, 28
Gatekeeper model, 131
GDP. *See* Gross domestic product
Gee, Preston, 189
Geneen, Harold, 18
General Accounting Office, 153
Generation X, 89–90
Genesys Health System, 44, 172
Genetic testing, 3
Geoclustering, 131
Geographic domain, 4
Gertz, Dwight, 82
Ginsburg, Paul, 183
Girl Scouts, 18
Givens, Sage, 99
Giving, law of, 146
Goals, 41, 150
Goldman, Ellen, 192
Goldsmith, Jeff, *x,* 30, 193
Government Institute, 95–96

Gray, Steve, 33, 45
Greater Detroit Area Health Council, 173
Greaves, Roger, 151
Greenfield, Jerry, 13
Greystone Bakery, 145
Gross domestic product (GDP), 190, 194, 195
Group Health Association, 105
Group model HMO, 104
Grove, Andrew, 7
Growth opportunities, 82–83
Growth Partners, 192
Growth strategies, 34–35
Guest, Bud, 113
Guest relations programs, 6, 44, 108

Halloran, Tom, 1
Hamel, Gary, 137
Hamilton (James A.) Book of the Year award, 96
Hammer, Michael
  beyond reengineering, 33, 58
  one-shot improvements, 39
  reengineering targets, 35
  stretch goals, 41
Hancock, Trevor, 152
Harbor Hospital, 98–99
Harris, Geoffrey, 175
Hartford Health Care Corporation, 180
Harvard Nursing Research Institute, 67
Harvard Pilgrim Healthcare, 4
Hawken, Paul, 12–13
Hay Group, 43, 107
Hayward, Cynthia, 161
HCIA, 156
Healing village, 123
Healthcare
  ecology, 12–14
  economic evolution, 2–3
  expenditures, 183–84
  future scenarios, 193–96
  marketplace, 2–3
  redefinition, *xi*, 7–8

transitional, 14
trends, 179–96
Healthcare Financial Management Association (HFMA), 58
Health Care Financing Administration, 100
Healthcare Forum, *x*, *xi*, 142, 155, 193
Health Care Purchasing Organization (HCPO), 186
Health Dimension, 123
Healtheon Corporation, 99
Health and fitness centers, 119
Health improvement plans, 8
Health insurance, 151
Health Insurance Association of America, 184
Health maintenance organization (HMO)
  alternative therapies, 5, 193
  business relationship, 52
  consumer demands, 104
  cost reduction, 75
  enrollee satisfaction, 45
  enrollment, 52, 66, 163, 180, 184, 185
  excess capacity, 59
  future market assumptions, 2, 181–82
  health improvement strategies, 151
  integration, 60, 182
  market penetration, 47, 186
  medical loss ratio, 184
  Medicare plans, 182–83
  models, 26
  open-access plans, 6, 12, 104
  point-of-service plan, 104
  premium increases, 186
  pricing patterns, 183–84
  provider relations, 60
  risk management programs, 76–77
Health Net, 26, 151
Health New England, 154
Health Plan Employer Data and Information Set (HEDIS), 95
Health plans, 2
Health Policy Institute, 86

Health promotion/prevention, *xi*, 75, 100, 102, 151
Health reform, 76
HealthSouth, 4, 189
Health teams, 86, 87–88
Healthwise Handbook, 105
Healthy communities, 152
HEDIS. *See* Health Plan Employer Data and Information Set
Hesselbein, Frances, 17
HFMA. *See* Healthcare Financial Management Association
Hickey, Martin, 86
High Desert Medical Center, 117
Hill-Burton program, 137–38
Historic patterns, 6
HMO. *See* Health maintenance organization
Holistic healthcare, 100, 102, 106, 134
Holy Cross Health System, 191
Holy Redeemer Visiting Nurse Agency, 154
Horizon/CMS, 4
Hosenstab & McCarthy, 113
Hospice, 6
Hospital
  acute general, 170
  alternative use, 173–74
  ambulatory care, 170–71
  bedless design, 112, 117
  capital costs, 166
  closures, 59–60, 175–77
  consolidation, 67, 167–68, 169–71
  construction, 114, 137–38
  conversions, 173–75
  customer service, 107–9
  demand, 162–65, 194
  downsized, 118
  excess capacity, 119, 161–77
  facility's age, 170
  future forecast, 2, 81–82
  future-oriented facilities, 112–13
  integration role, 61
  job eliminations, 108
  layoffs, 8

  managed care issues, 67–68
  management services organization, 57, 58
  mergers, 118, 187, 188
  nursing extender use, 67
  patient day declines, 163–64
  program minimums, 170
  public, 117
  public funding, 176–77
  rankings, 99–100, 101
  redesign, 172, 173
  reengineered capacity, 172–73
  rural, 171
  site size, 170
  solo, 102–3
  staffing, 84
  unit size, 170, 171
  utilization, 67–68, 138, 161, 168–69
  without walls, 117
Humana, 182
Huntington Provider Group, 104

IBM, 8
IDS. *See* Integrated delivery system (network)
Incentives, 43, 47, 88–89, 107
Indemnity health plans, 6
Independent practice association (IPA), 26, 131, 188–89
Industrial model (of work), 22
Industry standards, 7
Information, 92
  empowerment, 149
  online medical, 99
  technology, 24–25, 42, 87, 190–91
Information-based networks, 21
Information systems
  expenditures, 51, 52
  integration strategies, 58–59
  return-on-investment, 191
  strategic plan, 51
Innova Health Systems, 190
Innovation, 3
  continuous, 5–6, 47

strategic timing, 7
technological, 25
Innovations in Healthcare Design, 111
In Search of Excellence, 129
Institute for Alternative Futures, *x*, 152, 193
Integrated delivery system (network) (IDS), 36
   excess capacity issues, 166–68
   focus, 50
   future, 76
   management functions, 68–69
   management positions, 70–71
   nurse role, 74–75
   performance strategies, 68
Integration, 12
   implementation, 49–62
   issues, 61
   national study, 52–54
   stages, 50–52
   strategies, 54–60
   success factors, 60–62
Intel Corporation, 7
Intention and desire principle, 146
InterMountain Health Care, 1
Internet, 58–59
InterStudy, 163, 182, 184
IPA. *See* Independent practice association
ITT, 18
Ivinson Memorial Hospital, 142

James, Jennifer, 6, 19, 23
Jersey Shore Medical Center, 42
Job Shift, 12
John Hopkins Hospital, 100
Johnson, Kathryn, *x*
Johnson & Johnson, 157
Joint venture, 58
Jones, Wanda, 104, 116
Justice Department, 189

Kaiser Associates, 112, 122

Kaiser Family Foundation, 184, 189
Kaiser health system, 49–50
Kaiser, Leland, *x*, 193
   hospital without walls, 112
   patient-focused healing, 122
   strategic planning, 138
Kaiser Permanente, 104
   employment flexibility, 90
   facility construction, 114
   integration initiatives, 182
   primary care extenders, 74
   Senior Advantage HMO, 106–7
Kaizen, 147
Karma, 146
Kellogg (W.K.) Foundation, 152, 155
Kennedy, Pat, 173
Kennedy Architects and Interiors, 173
Kenney, James B., 173
Kiely, Robert, 41
Kleinman, John, 100
Knowledge-based work, 22
Kodak Foundation, *x*
Kotler, Philip, 130–31
Kouzes, Jim, 144
KPMG–Peat Marwick, 53

Labor costs, 35
Labor- and delivery-recovery rooms, 6
Labor Department, 27, 85
Labor Statistics, Bureau of, 82, 90
Lag time, 7
Lamm, Richard
   managed care, 67
   nurses' future, 72
   workforce, 79, 81–82
Lathrop, Phil, 44
Lauer, Chuck, 3
Layoffs, 34–36, 43, 108
Leadership, *x*, 3, 138
   abilities, *x–xi*
   challenges, 30
   language, 18–19
   practices, 144
   role, 29

traits, 90–91
trends, 19–23
value-centered, 144, 147
Leadership Gap study, *x–xi*, 193
Learning organization, 10–11, 130, 195
Least effort principle, 146
Lee Hecht Harrison, 107
Legislation, 168
Licensed products, 54–55
Life Care Centers, 106
Lindblom, Charles, 129
Litigation, 97
Long-term care facilities, 112, 118
Lovelace Health System, 86
Lump-sum merit increases, 28
Lungren, Dan, 167
Lutz, Sandy, 189
Lynch, Robert Porter, *ix*

Maccoby, Michael, 92
Managed care, *xii*
    alternative therapies, 5
    automated transactions, 191
    benefits, 76–77
    challenges, 68–70
    consequences, 67
    economic pressures, 4
    enrollment, 66
    excess capacity issues, 165, 166
    health promotion emphasis, 100, 102
    hospital demand, 165
    integration, 60
    Medicare/Medicaid plans, 2, 182–83,
        186
    reform, 184–85
Managed competition, 186
Management
    attitudes/styles, 18–23
    global perspective, *xii*
    incentives, 77
    myths, 18
    open-book, 62, 149–50
    proactive approach, *xi*, 128
    reactive approach, *xi*

role, 29
team, 65, 69–71, 77
    tensions, 143
    training, 77
    value-based, 29, 143–45
Management services organization
    (MSO), 50, 51, 57–58
Managing the Whirlwind, 96, 157
Market
    concentration, 186–89
    consumer-driven, 195
    dominance, 61
    forecast, 134
    observations, 130–31
    redefinition, 4
    segmentation, 192
    share, 51, 54–55, 82
    strategy, 19–20
    tests, 136
    trend prediction, 6
*Marketing for Healthcare
    Organizations*, 130
Marriott Corporation, 98, 147
Massachusetts Business Roundtable,
    173
Massachusetts General Hospital, 100
Mass-customization
    competition, 2, 8
    integration, 53
    leadership trend, 20–21
    patient-centered focus, 84
Mastery, 92
Mayo Clinic, 100
Meaning, 92
MedCost, Inc., 60
Medicaid, 2, 76
Medical clinic, 112
Medical College of Wisconsin, 86
Medical Matrix, 8
Medical records
    electronic, 184–85, 191
    privacy proposals, 185
Medicare, 81
    fraud, 189
    HMO forecast, 182–83

managed care plans, 182–83, 186
market assumptions, 2
MEDPARS database, 100
MedPartners/Mullikin, 58
Mega-medical groups, 187–87
Mercer (William R.) & Co., 156
Mercer Management Consulting, 82
Mergers, 187, 188
Merit pay programs, 43
Merrick, Scott, 103
Metastrategy, 133
Methodist Hospital, 117
Microsoft, 195
Mid-Columbia Medical Center, *xii*, 108
capitation, 151–52
community projects, 157
customer service, 98, 106
Planetree program, 124
Middle class, 130
Middlesex Hospital, 41
Miller, Kurt, 54
Milliman & Robertson, 150
Mind/Body Medical Institute, 193
Mintzberg, Henry, 129–30
Mische, Michael, 1
Mission statement, 43–45
Modern Healthcare, 3, 114, 147, 167, 192
Modification, 6
Monitor Company, 136
Moore, Thomas, 142–43
Mortality rate, 100
Motorola, 182
MSO. *See* Management services organization
Mueller, Pat, *xii*
Multidimensional corporation, 157

Nail Clinic, 91
NASDAQ, 190
Natchez General Hospital, 174–75
National Center for Health Design, 120
National Civic League, 155
National Committee for Quality Assurance, 109, 191

National Health and Human Services Employees Union, 168
National Hockey League, 133
National Information Infrastructure, 59
National Library of Medicine, 123
National Opinion Research Center, 100
National Panel Survey, 55
National Symposium on Healthcare Design, 120
NCR, 133
Netscape Communications, 99
Network model HMO, 26, 49–50
New Century Healthcare Institute, 104, 116
Newsletter of Consumer Health Information and Online Health, 190
New York Times, 132, 181, 191, 192
Nordstrom, 120
North Bay Healthcare System, 142
North Carolina Baptist, 60
North Hawaii Community Hospital, 123
North Memorial Hospital, 102
Northwestern University, 52, 68
Notre Dame, 133
Nurse
case managers, 73
extenders, 67, 74
future, 71–73
manager, 74–75
opportunities, 73–74
roles, 71–77
supply, 74
demand, 75–77
managed care issues, 67
Nursing Management, 72

Oakwood Health System 173
O'Neal, Sandra, 28
Open-Book Management, 149
Operational effectiveness programs, 132
Opportunity horizon, 5–6
Organizational change
barriers, 12
implementation, 12

leaders, 11
Orr, Robin, 108, 123, 124
Orr Group, 124
Outcomes, 3
Outreach programs, 14
Oxford Health Plan
    alternative therapies, 192–93
    growth, 83
    stock, 181, 183
    strategies, 132

PacifiCare, 26, 104, 114
PacifiCare/FHP, 49
Package prices, 55
Packard (Lucille) Children's Hospital,
    124
Paracelsus Healthcare Corporation, 60
Paradigm shift, *ix*, 44, 145
Parker, Derek, 124
Parry Consulting Services, 27
Participation, 136
Patient
    bill of rights, 184
    high-risk, 75
    satisfaction, 52, 98
    universal medical records, 83
Patient-centered care
    corporate soul, 148–49
    criticisms, 108
    design trends, 112
    evolution, 46
    model, 98, 100
    projects, 44
Patient-Focused Care Association, 44
*Patients, Profits and Health System
    Change*, 175
Pattern reversals, 6, 19
PCFA, 50
PCP. *See* Primary care physician
Pennsylvania Hospital, 149
Performance assessment, 42
Performance monitoring, 77
Performance rewards, 47
Perot, Ross, 38
Peters, Tom, 129, 133

Peterson, Kristine, 44–45
Peterson (K.E.), Inc., 44
Pew Foundation, 67, 81, 86, 169
Pharmacists, 81
Philanthropy, 168
PHO. *See* Physician-hospital
    organization
PhyCor, 58, 91, 189
Physician
    acquisition, 61
    demand, 87
    groups, 187–89
    integration issues, 61–62
    management services organization,
        57–58
    market assumptions, 2–3
    oversupply, 81
    performance, 3
    practices, 51
    salaried, 87
    surplus, 86
Physician-hospital organization (PHO),
    xi, 50, 57
Physician management company
    (PMC), 58
Physician-population ratio, 131
Physicians Park, 113
Pioneer Valley Economic Development
    Council, 154
Planetree program, 106, 123–24
Play, 92
Pleasure, 92
Pollard, C. William, 21–22
Population, 96, 97
Porras, Jerry, 127
Porter, Michael, 132
Positive Medicine project, 149
Posner, Barry, 144
Postsurgical center, 174
Prahalad, C.K., 127
Preferred provider organization (PPO),
    182
Premier Hospitals Alliance, 46, 73
Presbyterian Hospital, 91
Price, 3, 7, 55, 95
Primary care network, 61

Primary care physician (PCP), 87, 131
Principle-Centered Leadership, 30, 138
Priorities, 148
Private Healthcare Systems, 182
Proactive strategies, *xi*
Product development, 7
Product elimination, 136
Profit motives, 156–57
Program managers, 112
ProMatura, 106
Provider networks, 61
Provider-sponsored organization (PSO), 180, 186, 187
Psycho-architecture, 123
Public hospital, 117
Public relations, 168
Purchaser demands, 135
Pure potentiality, 146
Purpose, 147

Quality, 83, 135
Quality improvement, 12
Quinlan, Karen Ann, 14

Rastallis, Jane, 90
Rationalization, 51
Ray, Michael, 145
Reactive strategies, xi
Recycling, 6, 14, 19
Redesigning Healthcare Delivery, 56
Reengineering, 6, 29–30
  corporate culture, 39–40
  criticisms, 8–9, 33–34
  excess capacity, 172–73
  human costs, 33
  implementation strategies, 46–47
  issues, 38–39
  limitations, 132
  middle management reductions, 25
  mission statement, 43–45
  priorities, 45–46
  reintroduction, 36, 38
  strategies, 36, 37, 40–43
  terms, 34–35
Reengineering the Corporation, 35
Regionalization, 51–52
Regulation, 135, 168, 184–85
Reinventing Leadership, 148
Relatedness, 92
Remaking Health Care in America, 49, 53–54
Report cards, 3
  health indicators, 151
  ratings, 92, 95
  strategy, 46
Reputational data, 100
Restructuring, 34, 40
Retail marketing strategies, 191–92
Revolution, 2, 11
Rifkin, Jeremy, 80–81
Rise and Fall of Strategic Planning, The, 129–30
Risk, 3
  management, 65–66, 68–69, 76–77
  reduction, 7
Roesch, Anthony, 115
Ruga, Wayne, 111, 120–21
Rule-breaking, 4
Rural hospital, 171

Sachs, Michael, 119, 162–65
Sachs Group
  demand predictions, 114, 119, 162–65
  seal of excellence, 191–92
Sacred Heart Community, 144
Sacred Heart Medical Center, 153
St. Elizabeth Hospital, 153
Salick, Bernard, 105
Salick Health Care, 99, 105–6
SalickNet, 105
San Jose Hospital, 123
Santa Monica Hospital, 104
Santa Monica Medical Center Medical Group, 104
Scott, Mark, *xii*, 106, 124, 152

Scott, Richard, 176, 193
Seamless care, 52
Securities and Exchange Commission, 150
Selbert, Roger, 96
Self-care, 104–5
Senge, Peter, 130
Sensitivity training, 27
Sentara Health Systems, 192
Servant leaders, 21–22
Service, 3, 4, 135
Service Employees International Union, 108
Service management, 6
ServiceMaster Corporation, 18, 21
Seven Habits of Highly Effective People, The, 30, 143
Shared governance, 58
Shared vision, 11, 195
Sharp Healthcare System, 120, 146, 167
Sherlock Company, 183
Shortell, Steve, 49, 52–54, 68
Sisters of Charity of Nazareth, 56
Slater, Philip, 81
SMG Marketing, 60
Smith, Douglas, 21
Smith, Ralph, 186
Social activism, 97
Social issues, 12–14, 96–97
Social responsibility, 144–45, 152
Sony, 5
Soul of a Business, The, 143
Southwest Airlines, 18
Specialists, 87
Specialty care, 61
Specialty carve-outs, 55
Speed, 7–8
Spiritual laws, of success, 146–47
Stabilization, 51
Staff model HMO, 131
Standardization, 9, 46, 56–57, 61
Stanford Shopping Center, 120
Stanford University, 145
Stanford University Medical Center, 103, 120

Stanley Cup, 133
STEEP framework, 134
Strange attractions, 6, 19
Strategic audit, 137
Strategic foresight, 4–5
Strategic planning, 41–42, 51, 127–39
Strategic positions, 132
Stretch goals, 41, 155
Sturm, Jr., Arthur, 147
Sturm Rosenberg Cafferata, 147
Sun Microsystems, 58
Survival, 92
Symbolic action, 148
System building, *xi*
Systems thinking, *xi*, 11, 130

Tax-exempt status, 153
Team-based pay, 28
Team learning, 11
Teamwork, 86, 195
Technology, 3
    future spending, 194
    hospital demand, 165
    shared, 2
    utilization, 105–6
Technology, Office of, 74
Telecommuters, 25, 83
Temporary Society, The, 81
Tenet, 189
Territory, 4
Therapy centers, 119
Thierot, Angele, 123
Think Customer, 98
Third Wave, 13
Third Wave, The, 81
Third-party administrator (TPA), 182
Thornton (Matthew) Health Plan, 4
3M, 5
Thriving in Chaos, 129
Time, 6–8
Time-and-motion studies, 6
Timelines, 134
Toffler, Alvin, 13, 81
Tom's of Maine, 13, 142, 143, 157

Total quality management (TQM), *xi*, 34, 86, 108–9
Towers Perrin, 28
Tradeoffs, 136
TriBook/AM&G, 187
Trinity University, 142
Trust, 42, 148
Tufts University, 154
Turned On: Eight Vital Insights to Energize Your People, Customers and Profits, 98
21st Century Organization, The, 1

UCLA Health Network, 104
UCLA Medical Center, 100, 104, 108
Uncompensated care, 153
Unemployment rates, 82, 91
Unihealth, 50
Uninsured population, 194
Unions, 80, 168
United HealthCare, 104, 182
United Physicians of Santa Monica, 104
U.S. Health Corporation, 141
U.S. News & World Report
  healing environment, 119
  hospital rankings, 99–100, 101, 130
  sociopolitical groups, 96, 97
University of California–San Francisco, 103
University of Chicago, 100
University of Southern California, 81, 148
University of Texas, 193
Upsizing, 45
USA Today, 130
Utilization predictions, 135

Value Oncology Services, 99
Value-added services, 83
Values, 43–45, 97, 134
Vandewater, David, 193
Vertical integration, 49–50, 182, 187
VHA, 46

Virtual organization, 26–27, 83, 130
Vision, 3
  interest, 155
  pathways, 147–48
  shared, 11, 195
Volunteerism, 14

Wall Street Journal, 19
Ward, Terry, 180–81
Ward Group, 180–81
Watson Wyatt Worldwide, 90
Weingarten, Scott, 56
Wellpoint, 183
Westrend, 96
Whitman Corporation, 182
Why Work: Motivating and Leading the New Generation, 92
Wienstien, David, 102
Williams (Roger) Medical Center, 168
Wisconsin Independent Physicians Group, 189
Wishard (William N.) Memorial Hospital, 191
Witt/Kieffer, Ford, Hadelman & Lloyd, 90
Women's centers, 118
Work force
  aging trend, 85–86
  concerns, 9–10
  demographics, 9
  diversity, 27, 85, 96
  employment changes, 12
  empowerment, 10
  ethical issues, 67
  expectations, 89–90
  future forecast, 80–82
  future requirements, 68
  hospital consolidation impact, 167
  independent contractors, 83
  issues, 9–10
  job insecurity, 89–90
  job satisfaction, 92
  knowledge, 26–27
  leadership traits, 90–91
  models, 87–88

morale, 80
motivation, 91–93
nonclinical personnel, 80
part-time, 84
productivity, 88
quality-of-life issues, 90
temporary, 84
training, 85
trends, 83–87
turnover, 98

value drivers, 92
wage issues, 67, 80
Work Force 2000 report, 90
Workplace
democracy, 25
future, 23–29

Yun, Lin, 121
Zaifert, Michael, 106
Zenaca Pharmaceuticals, 105

About the Author

Russell C. Coile, Jr., M.B.A., is a futurist specializing in the health industry. He is senior vice president of Chi Systems and is based in Dallas, Texas. He provides market forecasts and strategic advice to a wide range of U.S. hospitals, medical groups, managed care organizations, and suppliers.

He is the author of five books in the past ten years on the future of the health field. His monthly newsletter, *Russ Coile's Health Trends,* is now in its ninth year, and his predictions on last year's "Top Ten Trends" were 100 percent accurate.

In the past year he has participated in over 100 seminars for groups including the American Hospital Association, American College of Physician Executives, the Governance Institute, and Rand Healthcare Roundtable. He is a member of the editorial boards of *Managed Care Outlook, Healthcare Systems Strategy Report, Nurse Week,* and the *Medical Network Strategy Report.*

Mr. Coile holds a B.A. degree from Johns Hopkins University and an M.B.A. in Health Services Administration from George Washington University.

* Carl Wall

___

    * no insurance products

    * Mike Hulett - *
                               *
                               *